A NEW LOOK AT HISTORY

A New Look at History

A Collection of Essays by Frank Eyck

Edited and translated by

Rosemarie Eyck

DETSELIG
ENTERPRISES LTD

Calgary, Alberta, Canada

A New Look at History: A Collection of Essays by Frank Eyck
© 2011 Rosemarie Eyck

Library and Archives Canada Cataloguing in Publication

Eyck, Frank
      A new look at history : a collection of essays / by Frank Eyck ; edited and translated by Rosemarie Eyck.

Includes bibliographical references.
ISBN 978-1-55059-409-6

     1. Germany--History--20th century. 2. Eyck, Frank--Interviews. I. Eyck, Rosemarie II. Title.

DD232.E943 2011   943.087   C2011-900856-4

Detselig Enterprises, Ltd.
210-1220 Kensington Rd NW
Calgary, Alberta T2N 3P5
www.temerondetselig.com
temeron@telusplanet.net
Phone: 403-283-0900
Fax: 403-283-6947

Detselig Enterprises, Ltd., recognizes the financial support of the government of Canada through the Canada Books Program.

Also acknowledged is the financial assistance of the Government of Alberta, Alberta Multimedia Development fund.

SAN 113-0234
ISBN 978-1-55059-409-6
Printed in Canada.
Cover design by James Dangerous.

To Richard Chadborne

Professor Emeritus of the Faculty of Humanities at the University of Calgary, Romance Languages and Literature. Contributor and member of the board of editors: *Encyclopedia of the Essay*, ed. Tracy Chevalier (Chicago: Fitzroy Dearborn, 1997).

For my generation the past is still very present.
—Bernhard Schlink, *Guilt about the Past*

The past is never dead, it's not even past.
—William Faulkner, *Requiem of a Nun*

Contents

Foreword

FRANK EYCK'S LIFE SPANNED A CRUCIAL PERIOD of the twentieth century, which is reflected in his work as a historian. Born in 1921 to secular Jewish parents in Berlin, he was a schoolboy when the Nazis came to power. His father was a prominent lawyer and an outspoken critic of the National-Socialist idea of law. Frank was enrolled in an elite school at the time, the French lycée where he was valued and protected but also warned at a certain point to get out while it was still possible. In 1936, at age fifteen, he was sent to London, on his own and with barely a word of English. His parents were able to join him the following year via Italy, while in Germany their possessions were confiscated by the Nazis.

At the outbreak of the Second World War, German citizens in England were declared enemy aliens and, eventually, most of them were interned. Frank was teaching at a school outside London at the time and wanted to join the British army. He even wrote a letter to *The Times* to this effect. Finally enrolled as a non-combatant, he found himself loading railway cars and paving roads, but even at this time he was teaching modern British history, together with a Cambridge don, to his comrades and carrying a heavy kit bag stuffed with books from one job to the next. British civilians, in particular the widow of a Labour MP, caught on to the waste of talent, and he was made an army co-education instructor lecturing, ironically, on "The British Way and Purpose." From there Frank moved on to the Publicity and Psychological Warfare Branch where he monitored radio stations in occupied France; after the Normandy landing in 1944, when Frank was only twenty-three, he was ordered to interview German prisoners of war for material to be aired on an allied propaganda radio station aimed at German soldiers. The POWs must have been very surprised at meeting a German in British uniform. Typically, Frank managed to reconcile these two identities through his fundamental human decency, treating them as people, not as representatives of a hated regime. Prior to shipping out to Normandy, Frank converted to Methodism, again reconciling two apparent opposites as he came to see himself as a Jewish Christian, harking back to the very origins of Christianity.

When the war was over, Frank was sent to Northern Germany with the British Army of Occupation to assist in the denazification of German newspapers. He took no pleasure in the devastation he saw of Northern German and of Hamburg in particular, and despite his own experience, he had an appreciation of the extent to which the German people had been fed lies and propaganda (since part of his job had been to monitor the radio broadcasts of Joseph Goebbels) and of the ways people had chosen not to know about the atrocities that they had suspected. Frank worked on the Hamburg and Flensburg newspapers, getting them to eliminate propaganda, separate fact from opinion, and to reintroduce the notions of democracy and the rule of law. These papers were widely read and appreciated at the time and Frank's contribution to postwar German journalism was ultimately recognized and honoured by the Prime Minister of Schleswig-Holstein. In essence, Frank had turned a job that was really a type of censorship into a form of teaching objectivity as well as the fundamental practices of a liberal democratic state to which he was personally committed. On a weekend furlough to Berlin he reconnected with old friends and took particular notice of the sister of an old school friend, Rosemarie, whose own medical studies had been interrupted by the war. They ended up getting married in yet another, personal triumph over the inhumanity of war and the potential of permanent separation and alienation.

After demobilization, Frank went to study (not surprisingly) Modern History at Worcester College, Oxford, from 1946 to 1949, and he worked as a journalist for the BBC Foreign Service from 1949 to 1956. Following a research fellowship at St. Antony's College, Oxford, he taught history at Liverpool and Exeter Universities. In 1968 he was appointed Professor of History at the University of Calgary, where I had the privilege of getting to know him as a colleague and where I heard him present a number of the fascinating papers collected here, in particular "Spies and Spy Catchers," on the scandal involving Long, Burgess, and Maclean, some of whom he knew from his work for British Intelligence during the war, as well as a remarkably fair essay on Pope Pius XII and the accusations against him for having done little to save the Jews during the

Second World War. These unpublished writings and others on topics such as Germans and their history, German reunification (natural and desirable according to Frank), anti-Semitism, National Socialism, and Zionism and the State of Israel have been edited posthumously for this volume by his widow, Rosemarie Eyck.

Frank Eyck's monographs include a study of the Frankfurt Parliament of 1848/49, whose contemptuous characterization as a "professors' parliament" by Disraeli he disproved through a careful study of the backgrounds of the parliamentarians. A masterful and enormously time-consuming biography does justice to his mentor and benefactor, the Liberal politician, author and journalist, George Peabody Gooch. Frank's most ambitious work attempts to account for the relationship between religion and politics in German history in a broad sweep from earliest times to the French Revolution.

Frank's lived experience became a challenge for understanding its historical roots, a task he approached through meticulous research and unusually open-minded interpretation. This also made him an ideal teacher, who expounded the historical material with great clarity, often enriched by personal experience and insight, without imposing a bias on his students, always willing to (re)consider the arguments.

This biographical sketch could not possibly do justice to the complexity of Frank Eyck's life and the challenges of identity posed by the historical upheavals he experienced in his own life. For a more complete picture, see the recent publication *A Historian's Pilgrimage: Memoirs and Reflections*, ed. Rosemarie Eyck (Calgary, AB: Detselig Enterprises, 2009).

—Haijo Westra

Preface

THIS COLLECTION OF UNPUBLISHED TALKS on historical events by Frank Eyck, my late husband, is offered with little editing to serve as a companion volume to his autobiography, *A Historian's Pilgrimage*. Only the talk of "The Germans and their History" had to be translated. The other talks were given in English. For a less detailed but lively personal account of his life, the reader will find transcribed a Canadian Broadcasting Corporation (CBC) interview from the program *Mountaintop Classics*.

The essays reflect Frank's research and vast knowledge of European and contemporary world history, some of it based on his own experience. He was expert at asking salient questions, and would always weigh the available documents of the chosen theme and carefully argue the topic at hand, judging without being judgmental in order to elicit the essential historical truth. Sometimes the essays reflect the happenings within a narrow space of time, such as his talk "Munich: Appeasement, 1938," in which he gave practically an hour by hour report of the dramatic developments; whereas in talks like "Nationalism and Internationalism" and "Anti-Semitism," he covered the wide span of centuries. In the essay on George Peabody Gooch and Harold Temperley, "Clio and the State," and the Cambridge Five in "Spies and Spycatchers," Frank gives an insight into the British establishment. While G. P. Gooch used his personal wealth for the writing of history and current events as well as constructive help for his fellow men, Donald Maclean and his conspirators used their privileged positions to turn to treachery. In his talk on Pius XII, Frank tried to put light on the sheer incomprehensible political tension of the time. The editor remembers her father quoting from the Pope's speech at Fatima. Generally speaking, for his research into many topics, Frank naturally went back to his roots: German (you might even say European), Jewish, and Christian.

As the talks had to be pressed into a given time period of three quarters of an hour or so, always followed by a lively discussion, it was felt that some editing was advisable to clarify a given statement or situation. Most of the talks have notes or a bibliography, but the editor did not think it necessary to add them to those talks that do not. Much general information on these topics are readily found in any library or on the internet. There is an occasional short overlap with Frank Eyck's autobiography, but offering his talks here should lead to a greater depth of understanding.

The essays are meant to be *on* a given subject or event, so they are not meant to be a finite conclusion but are an invitation or a foundation to further research – more as an opening up to deeper thoughts. Although the essays stem from Frank's research over several decades, they are still topical and enjoyable to read and discuss.

Acknowledgements

I would like to mention that Richard Chadborne, Professor Emeritus, through his work on the *Encyclopedia of the Essay*, gave me the idea of publishing this collection and allowed me to dedicate it to him.

My thanks go to my sons, Andrew and George Eyck, and my friends, above all Irving Hexham, Professor of Religious Studies at the University of Calgary, for patiently listening to my many questions and who gave me advice and help – technical and otherwise.

With thanks I mention the archivists who helped me obtain the various pictures: Berit Walter of the Bundesarchiv Bild, Koblenz, Germany; Diana Reeve of the Art Resources, New York; David Batzner of Fotosearch, Wisconsin; Erica McDonald, librarian of Peterhouse, Cambridge, England. Barbara Howards had a thorough look at the translation of the originally German talk. She and Joan Dixon thankfully shared in the proofreading. I owe thanks to my grandson, Brandon Eyck, for his help in transcribing the CBC interview.

I also thank Haijo Westra, Professor of Greek and Latin Studies at the University of Calgary, who wrote the foreword, for his understanding of Frank's pilgrimage through life.

—Rosemarie Eyck

Chapter One

CLIO AND THE STATE: G. P. GOOCH AND THE FOREIGN OFFICE

This paper is largely based on my biography G. P. Gooch: A Study in History and Politics (London: Macmillan, 1982). It was originally presented June 1975 for the Canadian Historical Association in Edmonton, Alberta. Presented again in slightly altered form June 28th, 1993, at the School of Economics in London, England, for the Conference on Historians and Officials.

I N THE SUMMER OF 1924, the Foreign Secretary Ramsay MacDonald asked G. P. Gooch to edit an official British publication on the origins of the First World War. Gooch in turn suggested Harold Temperley as his collaborator, and so the project on the *British Documents on the Origin of the War 1898–1914* was conceived, to be delivered a few months later by Ronald MacDonald's conservative successor. Thus the tender embryo survived the change of government only to be faced with some stormy years during its slow but steady growth. Thanks to the reduction of the closed period for the British public archives by MacDonald's eventual successor as Labour Prime Minister, Harold Wilson, the story of the relations between the editors and the Foreign Office can now be told.[1] Various private papers supplemented the story and filled some gaps.[2] At times the relations between the historians and the government were strained to the breaking point. The editors emphasized the historian's duty to seek the truth fearlessly and to omit no essential document from publication. The government, represented above all by the responsible minister, the Foreign Secretary

Ramsay MacDonald (1866–1937)

© Fotosearch 2011

Austin Chamberlain, asserted that in certain circumstances the maintenance of good relations with friendly states, and sometimes even the preservation of peace, would have to be of paramount consideration. On occasion, the conflict assumed great bitterness and was aggravated by matters of personality.

When MacDonald approached Gooch, the latter was fifty years old. He was well established as an historian even then, though he was not yet half-way through his remarkable writing career, which continued almost right to his death in 1968 at the age of nearly ninety-five. In 1913 he produced *History and Historians in the Nineteenth Century*, perhaps his most outstanding work. His extensive knowledge and sympathy for both Germany and France found expression after the bitterness between the two peoples during the First World War in his study *Germany and the French Revolution*, published in 1920. In a unique way, Gooch managed to combine the expertise of the specialist with the appeal to the educated general reader, which helped to put popular history of the best kind on the map not only in Great Britain, but in the English-speaking world beyond the seas where he was widely read. The interest Gooch took in the non-specialist was part of his outlook on life. Born into the late Victorian affluence of a minor Forsyth dynasty owing its wealth to the financial opportunities of the city of London and the prudent investment in real estate, Gooch wished to give thanks for the favourable position into which he had been born by serving the community.[3] Although he was a man of independent means from an early age, he worked harder throughout his life than many of his contemporaries and continued to do so for decades beyond the age at which most people retire. After the disappointment of failing to receive a fellowship from Trinity, his own Cambridge College, in 1897, he went out into the world. He travelled widely, but particularly to Germany and France, where he carried on his historical studies and heard lectures from leading scholars. In Britain he worked in the East End settlements of London, participated in the activities of the Church Army, and took an active interest in the London City Mission. He had a tremendous interest in people and a great understanding for them, indeed a real love and compassion, and throughout his life was a good Samaritan to those who for some reason had fallen on evil days. He also engaged in adult education work.

Coming from a broad Anglican Church background, his Christian belief made him realistic as well as compassionate, rather than judgmental about man's failings. He felt deeply about victims of injustice, whether at home or abroad. He became an active politician through the South African War, arguing in *The Boar War and its Causes* in 1900 that the question could have been settled without resorting to military means. During the South African War, Gooch had to brave his share of public wrath as the member of an unpopular minority, accused of being unpatriotic, which was also to be his fate to some extent in the First World War. On both occasions, Gooch demonstrated his conviction that somebody who truly loved his country was obliged to voice his dissent over a war with which he did not agree, and which he felt was being prolonged unnecessarily to achieve the desirable objectives. But he did not press matters to the extreme. Even during the South African War, of which he objected, he was convinced that the soldiers at the front had to be supported. In his book *The Heart of the Empire*, he included an essay on imperialism published in 1901. He wrote:

What little progress has been made from international savagery's due to the effect of individuals to take an unprejudiced view of questions at issue, and to think not only of the supposed interests of one's own country, but of the larger interests and well-being of the world.[4]

As a young adult, Gooch abandoned the conservatism of his family and became a liberal – a radical one. He was adopted as one of the liberal candidates for the Bath two-member constituency and was elected to the House of Commons in the liberal landslide victory of 1906. He had a deep affection for Sir Henry Campbell-Bannerman, Prime Minister at the time, whose stand against the British concentration camps in South Africa Gooch had applauded. But he never really liked the second chief, Lord Asquith. Gooch was a member of the Balkan Committee and a member of the Persia Committee; he was critical of aspects of Sir Edward Grey's foreign policy. After a fascinating four years in the House of Commons, which enriched his historical understanding, he was, however, defeated in January 1910.

A year after losing his seat in the House of Parliament, Gooch became co-editor of the *Contemporary Review*, a leading monthly journal with which he remained associated until his death. He was a good and sympathetic editor, working efficiently, quickly, and simply. His wide contacts both in Britain and abroad secured many prestigious contributors for the journal. He helped to weather the storms any independent journal had to face during wartime. The outbreak of a war in which Britain and Germany, as well as France and Germany, fought each other bitterly for years was a great shock for Gooch. Without ever becoming an out-and-out pacifist, Gooch collaborated up to a point with the Union of Democratic Control and favoured bringing the war to an end at the earliest possible moment on any reasonable terms. In the postwar period, Gooch opposed simplistic war-guilt theories and in 1923 scored a considerable success with his *History of Modern Europe, 1878–1919* in which he examined the war and its origin with care and objectivity.

In 1924, Ramsay MacDonald was looking for a historian of established reputation whose name would carry weight in quarters which were critical and suspicious of earlier British governments. He knew Gooch well. Both had done social work in the settlement of the East End of London. They served for some years at the same time as members of the House of Commons and had met also in the more intimate atmosphere of the *Rainbow Circle*, a small dining and discussion club consisting mainly of Liberals, radicals, and socialists. They had also participated, MacDonald more than

Gooch, in the activities of the Union of Democratic Control during the First World War.

In January 1924, MacDonald formed the first Labour Government, in which he took the post of Foreign Secretary in addition to that of Prime Minister. There was mounting pressure for the publication of British documents relating to the war, in which E. D. Morel, one of the founders of the Democratic Control, took a prominent part from the Labour benches in the House of Commons. In February 1924, Morel of the official British archives finally agreed to publish the documents, due in no small part to the sympathy for the idea among professionals in the Foreign Office. Both the men most closely concerned, the Librarian and Keeper of the Papers Stephen Gaselee (himself a distinguished classical scholar), and the Historical Advisor James Headlam-Morley (an authority in the field of ancient as well as modern history), supported the project. In many cases, the story of negotiations in which Britain was involved had already been told from the point of view of other countries, such as Germany. MacDonald encouraged the two officials to work out the many details which had to be settled before the project could be approved.

During the early stages of consideration, no clear decision was taken concerning the degree of Foreign Office control over whoever edited the series, and, indeed, whether the responsible editor should be an official, for instance Headlam-Morley himself. Eventually, Gaselee formulated the principle which was to be adopted, namely to "find . . . men for the task . . . who will be trusted by those who believe in us least – people who really think we are trying, or have tried, to hide damaging documents." This implied removing the editorial direction from the control of the Foreign Office. For the critics would only trust the historians appointed to the task if they were allowed to remain independent, unfettered by instructions from the Foreign Office. Gaselee and Headlam-Morley were fortunate in receiving the backing of the Permanent Under-Secretary Sir Eyre Crowe, who had himself been one of Sir Edward Grey's principle advisers. MacDonald's preference for "histories" about the origins of the war was politely rejected by Headlam-

Morley and the debate brought back to the publication of documents.

Who was to edit the series? Once the decision was taken to remove the edition from the Foreign Office, various names in the historical world were canvassed. The first of them was that of B. Kingsley Martin, later to be editor of the left-wing *New Statesman*, who had just published a book The *Triumph of Palmerston* on the minister's interaction with public opinion during the Crimean War. Kingsley Martin was only 26 years old at the time. What commended him to Gaselee was that nobody of any political outlook would be able to accuse him of trying to find excuses for the British Government. The second suggestion of Gaselee's was R. B. Mowat, a Fellow of Corpus Christy College, Oxford, who had attended the Paris peace conference and had published some works on diplomatic history.

MacDonald attached so much importance to the proposed project that he undertook to make independent enquiries about the historian suggested as possible editors. At this stage Gooch entered into the story, for MacDonald consulted him in June. In his letter to MacDonald, Gooch at once expressed an interest in becoming the editor himself, but did not press the point. MacDonald presumed that Gooch did not wish to commit himself to a responsibility extending over many years. Like everyone else, MacDonald underrated the length of time publication would take, regarding five years as the maximum. In actual fact, the task begun in 1925 was only completed in 1938.

Gooch replied promptly, as was his wont. While complimentary about the two other fellow historians suggested, he regarded such men as Harold Temperley and Charles Webster as better qualified for the task. But in August, MacDonald asked Gooch to undertake the editorship himself:

> I would place at your disposal all the documents at the Foreign Office and of course you would work with the people we have there, especially those in charge of the archives . . . I am sure your name would carry the weight that is necessary.

The correspondence be-tween the two men reflected warm regard and mutual respect. Gooch wrote at once that he would do what he could. But he emphasized that MacDonald's "historical narra-tive" was not what was needed: "What students of war origin require is the essential docu-ments, not extracts worked into somebody's narrative." He asked for the appointment of more than one editor, as was the case with the German series *Die Grosse Politik der Europäischen Kabinette 1871–1914.*

George Peabody Gooch, circa 1938
(1873–1968)

In arranging for Gooch to visit the Foreign Office, MacDonald called him "by far and away our ablest historian." Gooch was not entirely a stranger to the world of departments, having given the Historical Section assistance in the complication of the series of handbooks for the peace conference in 1918/19, for which he was formally thanked by the then Permanent Under-Secretary Lord Harding of Pankhurst. Gooch had a discussion with Gaselee in the middle of August on the general principles to be followed in the publication, and there seemed to be broad agreement between them. Gooch incidentally stated his preference for working without payment and would not be moved by Gaselee's attempts to per-suade him to change his mind. Sir Eyre Crowe endorsed the results of the discussions and drew attention to difficulties which might arise in connection with the publication of minutes, some of the most famous ones which he had himself written.

In September, Gaselee offered the co-editorship to Harold Temperley, who accepted. Temperley, a Fellow of Peterhouse and university reader in modern history at Cambridge, had edited the six-volume edition of the *History of the Peace Conference of Paris*, of which the last instalment appeared in 1924. He was familiar with

Austin Chamberlain (1836–1937)

© Fotosearch 2011

the Foreign Office procedures. In view of what happened later, it is worth noting that Temperley himself called attention of the necessity of consulting friendly governments, such as the Belgium, as to the publication of dispatches which concerned them.

MacDonald's fears, which he had expressed to Gooch, that he would not remain in power for long proved justified. The Labour movement was defeated at the polls and a Conservative government with an overall majority in the House of Commons was formed in November 1924. Fortunately, the new Foreign Secretary, Austin Chamberlain, was keen to finalize the arrangements made by his predecessor. As parliament was not sitting, it was arranged that the distinguished historian R. M. Seton-Watson, who had pressed for an official British publication, should write to him calling his attention to the matter. Chamberlain replied to Seton-Watson on November 20th, and the correspondence was published in the press on December 3rd. The new Foreign Secretary handsomely acknowledged the preparations which had been made by his predecessor and that it merely remained for him to confirm them:

> As regards to publication of the official documents bearing on the general European situation out of which the war arose, a collection of documents will be edited for the Foreign Office by Mr. G. P. Gooch and Mr. M. M. V. Temperley, who will, I hope, be in a position to begin serious work at a very early date. The reputation of the editors offers the best guarantee of the historical accuracy and impartiality of their work.

Chamberlain's statement about the reputation of the editors is borne out by the warm welcome their appointment received from one of their opposite numbers in Germany, Professor Albrecht Mendelsohn Bartholdy.[5]

The British Documents on the Origin of the War, 1898–1914 were to be issued commercially by H. M. Stationary Office without being formally laid before parliament. The first volume in the series to be published, in fact, covered the final weeks preceding the outbreak of war. The reason for this was that Mendelsohn-Bartholdy had already done considerable work on putting together documents for that period. As editor of volume eleven, Headlam-Morley was responsible to Gooch and Temperley and not to the Foreign Office.

Headlam-Morley had the great advantage of knowing the office machine from the inside. Even he encountered some difficulties, but surmounted them with a mixture of firmness, skill, tact, and patience. The fundamental problem arose in connection with the internationally established procedure of clearing documents, including confidential information from friendly foreign governments with them. The French authorities made difficulties, but these were overcome with the help of Eric Phipps, Minister at the British Embassy in Paris. The introduction to the volume was used with great sensitivity to put into perspective passages in the documents about which the French had expressed concern. The volume eventually appeared in December 1926. Gooch and Temperley were well pleased with the standard set in it.

Perhaps it was not to be expected that the harmony between those producing the *British Documents* and the authorities would continue

Harold Temperley (1879–1939)
Photo courtesy of Peterhouse Library,
Cambridge, England

once the editing was done exclusively by independent outsiders with strong personality. This had already happened with Headlam-Morley's volume. The main problems were caused by delays and objections at the hands of foreign governments to which material was sent for clearance. Neither editor was happy with the effect the procedure was having, though Temperley was well aware of the custom of consultation at the time of his appointment. The editor wished to be relieved from the necessity of having to obtain the consent of friendly governments concerned and, indeed, argued that the procedure conflicted with their terms of appointment, particularly with the historical accuracy and impartiality to which Austin Chamberlain had referred in his letter to Seaton-Watson. When the Foreign Secretary adhered to the convention, they asked him in July 1926 for a formal assurance that no attempt would be made to compel them to accede to the demand of any government for the omission of documents which they considered vital. At the same time, perhaps alternatively, they asked for the imposition of a time limit of three months on foreign governments to give their consent. Gaselee replied that the Foreign Secretary would be only too happy to oblige, "but that he has to consider on what terms he can preserve the possibility of the confidential relations and that free intercourse with foreign governments on which peace may, or indeed must, depend."

The issue was finally solved about one year and a half after Gooch and Temperley had begun their work. Basically the editors were not prepared to accept any direction whatsoever regarding any class of documents clearly within their province, such as Foreign Office dispatches. The Foreign Secretary argued that while he wished the story to be told as fully as possible, there were situations in which he had to rate the maintenance of good relations with friendly powers and the preservation of peace higher than the satisfaction of historical truth. These matters were elaborated more fully in separate interviews the editors had with Sir Austin Chamberlain.

As Harold Temperley was abroad, Gooch alone saw the Secretary of State on July 30th, 1926. Chamberlain emphasized that he regarded himself as the colleague of the editors for the purposes

of the publication of the *British Documents*, with the same fundamental interests. The Foreign Office would not wish to give any
grounds for allegations that it was concealing essential facts. In
view of the identity of interests, Chamberlain resented the attitude
and tone the editors had recently adopted toward him. Although
the convention of clearing documents with friendly governments
concerned had been breached in some recent memoirs, the rule
was still necessary and justified:

> The Secretary of State had in the last few years had . . . long and
> intimate conversations on political subjects with reigning sov-
> ereigns, the publication of which in the lifetime of the speakers
> would not only be justly resented as a serious breach of cour-
> tesy, but would dry up for ever those and simpler valuable
> sources of information and means of political negotiation.

Although improbable, it was conceivable that the publication of
a specific document might imperil peace, and so the judgment of
the Secretary of State must be final. Chamberlain assured the editors the project on which they were working had his full support.
He himself would, if necessary, accept responsibility for the omission of a document. The editors could withdraw at any time.
However, about the last thing he wanted was to be placed in the
extremely disagreeable position of having to explain in parliament
the resignation of the editors because they had been forbidden to
publish a document they considered vital. As Gooch put in the
record of the interview he sent to the Foreign Office, Chamberlain
said to him: "you have me in a cleft stick." Gooch was strong in principles and gentle in the way he pressed them – *fortiter in re and
suaviter in modo*. Gooch himself reiterated at the interview that
according to the announcement of the appointment, the editors
were to have absolute free hand in publishing all they found.

Temperley saw Chamberlain on November 18th, 1926. He stated
bluntly that the editors had to resign if documents they regarded as
vital had to be suppressed because the Foreign Secretary believed
its publication might damage the prospect of maintenance of
peace. In reply to a query, Chamberlain made it clear that any res-

ignation on the part of the editors would involve their complete severance from the project. Temperley strongly reiterated the various demands of the editors but failed to obtain any definite undertaking concerning a time limit to be put to foreign governments.

Following Temperley's interview with Chamberlain, the editors seemed to have pondered their position at some length, but on February 10th, 1927, they set another time limit to the Foreign Office. For volumes I and II, they allowed a period of eighteen months for publication, starting from the time documents they wished to include had been officially received by the Foreign Office. In their view this was ample time for negotiations with foreign governments and for the necessary publication arrangements: "Our resignation would therefore take effect from 20th June 1928 if the first volumes are not given to the public by that date."

During the absence of the librarian, the Historical Adviser was asked to comment on the letter. Headlam-Morley believed the editors had now implicitly withdrawn the demand for a formal assurance that they would not be compelled to omit what they considered vital. The Foreign Secretary had made it clear that they were free to resign if they could not have their way. The greater part of the letter from the editors was concerned with the less important of the two points they had raised, that of delay. In Headlam-Morley's judgment it was mainly Temperley who was interested in this question as he had pressed it at this interview with Chamberlain. With the threat of resignation of the editors, "they have therefore reversed to the procedures by 'ultimatum' in which they are unfortunately so prone. The position which they hereby adopted seems to me very absurd and in effect discourteous." The editors seemed to suspect that either foreign governments or the Foreign Office were trying to sabotage their services. There was not the slightest evidence for their belief. In its own interest, the British Foreign Office could not tolerate any attempt on the part of the foreign government to impede the project. Indeed, an assurance had already been given that the Foreign Office would do everything in its power to prevent undue delay. A general time limit and the resignation of the editors were not the proper way to deal with the difficulties. So far as the actual time limit was concerned, hopefully this was quite adequate. Headlam-Morley suggested a curt answer signed by the Private Secretary. The senior Foreign Office official Sir Hubert Montgomery minuted:

> Dr. Temperley is a very tiresome man. I think it is time we made it clear the foreign governments are not the only black sheep. I have discussed the question with Dr. Headlam-Morley and we have modified this draft to bring out this point.

Sir William Tyrrell, the Permanent Under Secretary added, "Dr. Temperley is not only tiresome but impertinent." The Foreign Secretary contented himself with initialling the minutes to show approval of the procedure.

In the letter signed by the Private Secretary, it was pointed out that if the editors resigned because of delays in the publication, the Foreign Secretary would have to explain that only a portion of these were due to causes outside their control. Confidence was expressed that the two volumes would come out before the expiry of the time limit.

As anticipated, Temperley – who replied in the absence of Gooch who was on a lecture tour in the United States – was deeply offended by what he called the Foreign Secretary's "indirect reply." Under cover of resentment over this slight, he did, however, retreat somewhat and admitted that possibly misunderstandings had arisen about circumstances in which he and his colleague might feel compelled to resign. They would only do so if asked to suppress a vital document, or in the case of serious or needless delay in the clearing of documents by foreign governments. Dr. William Terrell minuted, "Dr. Temperley continues to displays all the sensitiveness and impertinence of his race." It is not clear whether this refers to Temperley's ethnic background which was English North country, or in general to the breed of historians. Sir Austin Chamberlain commented, "Dr. Temperley is as difficult than [*sic*] a Prima Donna, and as argumentative, disputatious and litigious as the occasional terrors of the Law Courts." He amended the draft of the letter to Temperley for his own signature by considerably stiffening the final paragraph: "I am sorry that you insist on treating me as if I was a hostile power, but I shall continue my efforts to forward your work."

In some comparatively minor matters, the editors were prepared to compromise, but neither Gooch nor Temperley were prepared to compromise over essentials. In April 1927, Gaslee asked for the alteration of a dispatch from Lord Lansdowne to the British Ambassador in Paris of October 1902, in which he reported a conversation with the French Ambassador, Paul Cambon. Gaselee did so at the request of the French government which was unhappy about the way the dispatch might reflect the memory of one of their great French ambassadors of the period. The French authorities suggested a rewording. Gaselee regarded the matter as a small affair and supposed the editors would not object to a trivial change. Temperley firmly refused ever to alter a written word of a dispatch. He, however, offered to strike out the offending sections with asterisks, though he did not consider them trivial. Temperley might have stopped here. But he continued by raising the question of the preface: "We shall not now insert in our preface an indication that starts and gaps do not necessarily mean that a trivial matter is omitted." He also stated that if the editors were ever again asked to alter a dispatch, all his own letters relating to this matter would be sent to the press immediately. Gooch expressed his general agreement with Temperley's stand in a letter to Gaselee on his return from America. Gaselee minuted, "Heavy weather again. These historians' consciences are very tender." Headlam-Morley agreed with the determination of the editors to resist all modification of the text, but added, "Dr. Temperley's attitude has as usual spoiled what seems to me as an unanswerable case by violence of statement." In view of Temperley's attitude, Gaselee decided to mark his communications to him, "private" in future.

The military staff talks between the British military authorities and their Belgian and French counterparts approved by Sir Edward Grey in January 1906 at the time of the first Moroccan crisis were among the most sensitive matters with which the editors had to deal. Even after the First World War, the Belgian government was reluctant to agree to the publication of any document relating to the pre-war period which might be construed as evidence of a breach of neutrality. Thanks to the understanding attitude of Gooch and Temperley in this matter, an editorial solution was found which was satisfactory to all concerned. Matters did not go so easily in the case of the documents concerning the military talks with France.

Gooch and Temperley wished to publish a communication from the French to the British General Staff sent February 13th, 1906, dealing in detail with the arrangements to be made for British troops coming to the aid of the French in case of a German attack. The French government refused to agree to publication, which severely upset the editors. Unfortunately, the French attitude at once increased the friction between the editors and the British Foreign Office. Gooch and Temperley proposed to indicate the refusal of the French authorities, though also to add that they did not consider the omission a vital one. They intended to include the following passage in their preface after referring to the action of the French authorities in relation to the document: "The editors take the opportunity of stating that they would feel compelled to resign if any attempts were made to insist on the omission of any document which is in their view vital or essential." All attempts by the British Foreign Office to get the editors to leave out the reference to the refusal of the French authority and to their resignations in certain circumstances proved unavailing. This stalemate delayed the publication of volume three. Sir Austin Chamberlain intervened personally. On his instructions, Sir Eric Phipps approached M. Berthelot, the Secretary-General of the Quai d'Orsay, and persuaded him to consider the matter. Berthelot neutralized the opposition of the French General Staff by offering to accept personal responsibility for publication.

As a footnote to this web of negotiation it might be mentioned that part of the opposition to the publication of the document about the British landing in France came from the British government. In July 1928, Chamberlain's colleague in the cabinet, the Secretary of War Sir L. Worthington Evans, asked the Foreign Secretary for proof of the forthcoming volume of the *British Documents* insofar as they concerned the activity of his department, although they had already been cleared by his department.

Sir Austin Chamberlain rejected this attempt at last-minute inter-ference. Gaselee believed that the British War Office might well put up the French military authorities to try and prevent publication of the document.

Although Chamberlain's help with the French improved rela-tions between the editors and the Foreign Office, the question of the passage in the preface concerning their possible resignation was still unresolved. On July 3rd, the editors found themselves clos-eted with the Foreign Secretary in response to an appeal from Chamberlain to drop the passage in view of the French concessions. Gooch said that the statement was directed at the crisis of the his-torical independence and integrity of the editors, rather that at the Foreign Secretary. Chamberlain was also not happy at the intention of the editors to mention the omission of nonessential documents, but Gooch replied that these references only strengthened the posi-tion of the others. Chamberlain withdrew this objection to the pref-ace, thus clearing the way for publication of volume three, which appeared the following month. The preface contained a passage about the possible resignation of the editors which was in sub-stance as drafted and as quoted earlier.

There was also a general discussion at the interview of problems which had arisen with the department, such as the India Office, and procedures for detailing with various classes of documents. Sir Austin Chamberlain promised to help with the India Office. Sir Hubert Montgomery, one of the officials in attendance, minuted:

> The impression I carried away from the interview was that if Mr. Temperley would only let Dr. Gooch conduct the written correspondence with the Office, instead of doing it himself, our lives would be less of a burden to us!

In accordance with his assurances, Sir Austin Chamberlain soon afterwards wrote to the Earl of Birkenhead, the Secretary of State for India. Chamberlain fundamentally accepted the position adopt-ed by the India Office and indeed by the Eastern Department of the Foreign Office, that conditions in the East had not undergone the same change as in the West and that therefore, for instance, the publication of documents twenty years old about Persia or Afghanistan might still do harm diplomatically. But there were practical difficulties preventing the editors from publishing India Office papers which they had seen in the Foreign Office:

> You will understand what would be my position and incidentally that of the Government, if, having announced this publication to the world and having begun it, the editors threw up their task on the ground that they were prevented from presenting a true picture of British policy.

Chamberlain added that from the British point of view full publication was the best policy and asked for Lord Birkenhead's help to make this possible. Lord Birkenhead replied:

> I have read with much sympathy your letter . . . about Messrs. Temperley and Gooch. I am afraid Ramsay MacDonald left you a very uncomfortable legacy, and I will gladly do what I can to prevent trouble arising for you in respect of my sphere, though I am little disposed to be dictated to by a couple of dons who (from what you tell me) seem to think more of their professional reputation than the public interest.

Stanley Baldwin
(1867–1968)
© Fotosearch 2011

Lord Birkenhead suggested certain methods of limiting the questions with which the editors were allowed to deal in the *British Documents*, but these were regarded as too sweeping by the Foreign Office. In order to formulate a general policy framework that would allow the various government departments to adopt a consistent attitude to the editors, Chamberlain obtained the consent of the Prime Minister, Stanley Baldwin, to the setting up of a committee of officials to review the progress made with the publication. The officials were to make recommendations to the Prime Minister, the Foreign Secretary, and the Secretary of State for India. The Committee consisted of Sir Maurice Hankey, Secretary of the Committee of Imperial Defence – of which some papers were being made available for publication – as well as Gaselee and Headlam-Morley from the Foreign Office.

The officials made a full report which was read in September 1928.[6] The editors were blamed for seriously underestimating the work and time required for the project. They thought in terms of two or three years, although neither of them was able to give his whole time to the series. By August 1928, about three and a half years after they had begun their work, four volumes had been published and a further three were in print, but not yet published because of difficulties in obtaining clearance. A good deal of work had been done on the later volumes. The committee expected the whole series to be completed within another three years, thus adding another considerable underestimate.

The report was highly complimentary of the work done so far. The editors had justified the confidence placed in them. In their general scope and form the volumes already prepared met the requirement both of the Foreign Office and of historians. The selection of documents had been judicious and there had not been any sign of bias or partisanship:

> The suggestion that the British Government did not dare to imitate the action of Germany and disclose the secrets contained in its own archives, have been silenced. . . . The Government and the [Foreign] Office have been placed in a much stronger position by this publication.

It was important to bring the work to a successful conclusion. Any serious difference which led to a termination of the arrangement between the editors and the Foreign Office "would undoubtedly be very detrimental."

The editors were criticized for several times beginning the discussion by presenting to the Foreign Office something in the nature of an ultimatum, and for again and again resorting to the threat of resignation:

> While they rightly rate very highly the responsibility which they have to "historians" and the general public, they do not seem to have the existence of an equal responsibility to the Foreign Secretary, who has invited them to undertake the work.

They had been slow to recognize the exceptional effort made on their behalf by the Foreign Secretary himself, who had taken a keen personal interest in the project, as well as by the Foreign Office staff generally and indeed by the British government departments and the foreign governments. Gooch and Temperley were "unduly sensitive to adverse criticism and doubts as to their integrity."

The memorandum dealt with the question of the definition of the different categories of documents with which the editors had to deal and the extent to which they were to publish them. The Foreign Office reserved the right to refuse permission for the publication of minutes by permanent officials. However in volumes one, two, and three, all the important political minutes written in the Foreign Office had in fact been included. The committee recommended that in the very exceptional circumstances permission to publish these minutes and memoranda should be continued for the rest of the series, but the Foreign Office should reserve the right to refuse permission in particular cases.

Although the arrangements made by Ramsay MacDonald were made in his capacity as Foreign Secretary in 1924 and therefore related to the documents of the Foreign Office, the committee supported the wish of the editors to draw on the papers of other departments in appropriate cases. The War Office had indeed made available to the editors material which had never been communicated to the Foreign Office. Also, the publication, in accordance with the definition of the project, had to confine itself to whatever was "direct or indirectly connected with the origin of the war." Particularly with regard to the affairs of the East, the editors had recently shown a tendency to include matters outside this

scope. However, unofficial representation to the editors had resulted in some excisions. In general the committee concluded:

> Hitherto a solution for each point of controversy had been
> reached by dealing with it on the merit of the particular case.
> Experience shows that it is not desirable to embark on a dis-
> cussion of general principles with the editors.

The recommendation of the committee helped to clear the air.
Still, their threats of resigning did not cease and as late as July 1937
the editors beat off an attempt by the Colonial Secretary, W.
Ormsby-Gore, to suppress documents concerned with Zanzibar.[7]

The work on the *British Documents* took much more time than
anticipated. The last volume, number eleven, was published just
before the beginning of the Second World War. During this time of
co-operation, Headlam-Morley, while admitting to some sympathy
with the editors, felt the editors had often spoiled a good case by
the crude and ungracious manner in which they expressed themselves. For the latter, Temperley's irascibility is to blame. Anybody
who knew Gooch, as I did during the last thirty or so years of his
life, found him a harmonious personality, at peace with himself and
God. It was a matter of personal preference whether one regards
losing one's temper as the best way of making one's point. The natural authority Gooch carried may well have been sufficient.

Each of the editors contributed valuable qualities to the work.
Gooch had considerable writing and editorial experience. He had
co-edited the *Contemporary Review* since 1911. As a member of the
pre-war House of Commons he had participated in active politics
and had taken a great interest in foreign policy, particularly Balkan
affairs. He was personally acquainted with many leading personalities in the Liberal governments before 1914, among them Morley
and Haldane. He had published a biography of Lord Courtney, a not
unimportant figure among the critics of Joseph Chamberlain's
South African policy. He also had an extensive knowledge of
Germany and of France.

Temperley at that time had an almost unrivalled experience in
the handling of the type of historical documents with which the

editors of the British series were concerned. In 1926 his *Foreign Policy of Canning* was published, which with C. K. Webster's work on Castlereagh broke new ground in the handling of diplomatic history. Temperley had a wide knowledge of the Balkans, and unlike Gooch, he had served as a soldier during the war.

Both editors were men used to independent judgment. Neither of them owed his livelihood to the editorship of the *British Documents*. In Temperley's case, the salary as editor was a supplement to the income derived from his teaching posts in Cambridge. His colleague, though, worked free of charge.

Gooch may have played the major part in settling the format and general layout of the series. He was very much to the point, slightly austere, did not encourage frills, and believed in economy of words. He contributed general commonsense and a tidy mind. Temperley, an outstanding intellectual, had a personality of great strength. Initially he had more extensive experience in the handling of diplomatic documents than Gooch, though the latter quickly caught up with him. On the whole their team-work was good. Occasionally there appears to have been some friction between them, mainly due to Temperley's quick temper. Gooch's equanimity must have helped to keep their relationship on an even keel. All in all, they possessed a good mixture of characteristics, and it is fair to say that Gooch's choice of Temperley as a collaborator seems to have been judicious.

The work produced by the editors was undoubtedly of a high standard. In the circumstances prevailing in the inter-war period, it is hardly conceivable that a more extensive publication of confidential material than Gooch and Temperley achieved would have been feasible. In all essentials the fear that the procedure of consulting foreign governments would prove a stumbling block proved unjustified. Generous facilities were granted by the British authorities for the publication of material which might have been excluded, such as the minutes of the Foreign Office officials and of King Edward VII, as well as certain papers of the Committee of Imperial Defence.

The stand of principles the editors took to safeguard their independence and to mark their refusal to alter documents was fully justified and entitles them to the gratitude of later generations of historians.

That leaves the complex issue as to whether ultimata and threats of resignation were necessary to ensure that their principles would be respected. One wonders whether it would have been sufficient if the editors had taken a strong stand on fewer occasions. Some friction was due more to Temperley's temperament than to anything else. Gaselee noted in 1932 that Gooch was "quite a mild man." Still we cannot know for certain whether the authorities would have done so much for the editors as they did if they had not been afraid of trouble.

The tension between Clio and the State, between the historian's wish for full revelation and the authorities' desire for protection of confidentiality, continues. The relationship between Gooch and Temperley and the Foreign Office illustrates, not unfairly to both sides, some of the difficulties which are bound to arise between these two legitimate shares of interest.

In the acknowledgements to his *Harold Temperley: A Scholar and Romantic in the Public Realm*, John D. Fair[8] states that there are "numerous scholars and friends who gave me special assistance, advice, and insight over the years. I shall be grateful to U. F. J. Eyck." However, in the text of his book, Fair on several occasions criticizes the manner in which I handle the story of the editors' relation with the authorities, asserting that, using many of the same documents as myself, there was "a quite different and more complex rational behind the editors' conduct." Unfortunately, his argument is based on the wrong premise that the decision to publish the *British Documents* was taken in a spirit of national self-righteousness. Actually, Ramsey MacDonald, who played a vital part in initiating the British documentary publication, and G. P. Gooch, just to mention two personalities who helped the project forward, were motivated by anything but a spirit of national self-righteousness. As is amply documented in my biography, Gooch strongly supported the principle of accountability of the government to parliament and to public opinion, particularly in the field of foreign policy. Deeply patriotic in his critical concern for the honour of the country during two wars, far from being motivated by a spirit of self-righteousness, he was on the contrary convinced that any deviation from high standards had to be admitted and examined. In connection with what Professor Fair calls Temperley's "many intemperate outbursts over editorial independence" make it clear that while Gooch broadly agreed with his colleague on matters of editorial policy, he was always civil in his dealings with the Foreign Office and was clearly unhappy with any discourtesy, whereas Temperley's prickly temper caused considerable difficulties. Professor Fair confused Temperley's personality problem with deep-rooted policy difference between the two editors of the *British Documents*. It does not make any sense for Professor Fair to assert "that Temperley was acting on a hidden agenda [of] actively promoting his country's interest against the somewhat nearsighted policies of the Foreign Office." Professor Fair presents Gooch both as pliable towards the Foreign Office and as exercising a pro-German influence, an alleged "hidden agenda," which the co-editor had to counter. Surely none of the parties involved in the publication of the *British Documents* wished to make the publication of documents dependent on importance and relevance. Otherwise the *British Documents* would have never achieved an international reputation for high standards of selection and editing. The editors and the authorities had, after all, agreed on attempting to achieve maximum disclosure and objectivity. The major disputes concerned the exercise of editorial diplomatic judgment and independence related mainly to not merely historical but current diplomatic problem as to how objections of governments of friendly countries to publication should be handled.

Professor Fair's argument leads into a veritable maze. Gooch is in some way represented as a fool and Temperley as a knave. Gooch was no fool. Temperley was an outstanding historian, as well as a highly conscientious and very able co-editor of the *British Documents*, even though he could not control his temper. These two aspects are on two entirely different levels.

The trial of strength with the Foreign Office left no ill feeling in Gooch, who fully recognized Austin Chamberlain's calmness, fairness, and helpfulness. He was "a thorough good fellow." As to Harold Temperley, he was a difficult partner not only for the Foreign Office, but also for his fellow editor. Gooch carried no rancour. With his usual selflessness and generosity he stated in the British academy obituary that Temperley's "unflagging energy was in large measure responsible for the successful accomplishment of the formidable task." To this outcome not only the editors, but also Austin Chamberlain and the Foreign Office officials, all of them patriots, contributed their part.

Notes

1 From the Foreign Office 370 series in the Public Record Office in London. The author wishes to thank its officials for their help. Transcripts of Crown-copyright records in the Public Record Office appear by permission of the Controller of H. M. Stationary Office.

2 The author is grateful to Mr. Bernhard Gooch for the loan of his father's papers, and to other owners of papers and to institutions for allowing him access. He hopes to acknowledge obligations more fully in a larger work, on proposed parts of which this paper is based. Inevitably, during the part of his career with which this paper deals, Gooch's work is closely interlinked with that of Harold Temperley. The author is indebted to the Canada Council for a generous research grant.

3 G. P. Gooch, *Under Six Reigns* (London: Longmans, 1958). See also Frank Eyck, "G. P. Gooch," in *Historians in Politics*, ed. Walter Laqueur and George L. Mosse (London: Sage Publications, 1974), 1:169–90.

4 "Essay on Imperialism," in *The Heart of the Empire* (London: T. Fisher Unwin, 1901), 359ff.

5 Gooch papers are kept in the Special Collection at the library of the University of Calgary.

6 By courtesy of Mr. C. L. J. Child of the Historical Sections of the Cabinet Office, L 5138/5/402.

7 The author is indebted to Professor M. N. V. Temperley, Harold Temperley's son, for evidence of this.

8 John Douglas Fair, *Harold Temperley: A Scholar and Romantic in the Public Realm, 1879–1939* (Newark: University of Delaware Press, 1992).

Chapter Two

SPIES AND SPYCATCHERS: MID-TWENTIETH-CENTURY SOVIET PENETRATION OF BRITISH SECURITY

Presented April 7th, 1988, at the History Department of the University of Calgary

O N JUNE 7TH, 1951, the London press broke the story of the disappearance of two British government employees. They were believed to have left London with the intention of getting to Moscow. The British government tried to stall, but in view of the persistence of the media, the following statement was eventually issued:

> Two members of the Foreign Office have been missing from their homes since May 25th [1951]. One is Mr. D. D. Maclean, the other, Mr. G. F. de M. Burgess. All possible enquiries are being made. It is known that they went to France a few days ago. Mr. Maclean had a breakdown a year ago owing to over-work but was believed to have fully recovered. Owing to their being absent without leave, both have been suspended with effect from June.[1]

The official British statement had been rightly called a classic example of Whitehall damage control.

I was at that time a news sub-editor at the BBC in London and still vividly remember both the pathetic attempt by the government to play down the whole matter and the consternation felt in our newsroom. It gradually became clear that the two British Foreign Office officials had defected to the Soviet Union, and it did not take much imagination to realize that their sudden departure had taken place because they had been relaying British government secrets to the Soviets and had come to the conclusion that their cover was about to be blown. The latter certainly applied to Donald Maclean.

To deflate the defection, the government stated (correctly) that Guy Burgess was of junior status in the Foreign Office, though this did not tell the whole story. For many years, various British governments attempted, with far less justification, to downgrade the importance of Donald Maclean in the Foreign Office hierarchy. Maclean served in the British Embassy in Washington from April 1944 to October 1948, rising from the rank of First Secretary to acting Head of Chancery. During this time he had access to important secret information, including atomic energy matters, and a non-escort pass to the Atomic Energy Commission in Washington D.C. According to the U.S. authorities:

> In October 1947, Maclean attended a three-day declassification conference at which time discussions were limited to atomic energy information held in common. . . . This conference included a discussion on atomic weapons.[2]

Maclean was also a participant in secret meetings held in Washington that led to the formation of The North Atlantic Treaty Organisation (NATO). He was thus able to pass on to the Soviets vital information on atomic and Western defence matters.

Important secrets had obviously been leaked to the Soviets from inside the British embassy in Washington for some years, and by the middle of May 1951, the trail clearly led to Maclean, now Head of the American Department at the British Foreign Office in London.[3] The British authorities decided to interrogate him, but by the time Maclean was due to be questioned, he had fled, in company with Guy Burgess. Burgess was under Soviet orders to assist Maclean in his departure, but his simultaneous flight was not part of the plan. Maclean rather than Burgess was the one who was clearly under suspicion. All this left the worrying question about a possible inside tip to Maclean that his espionage activities had been finally uncovered.

Why did Maclean's defection to the Soviet Union cause such a stir? After all, other unpleasant espionage activities had come to light earlier. The British physicist Dr. Alan Nunn May had been sentenced to ten years' imprisonment for passing atomic secrets to the Soviet Union. May, incidentally, had been a friend of Maclean's at Trinity Hall, Cambridge. A non-Jewish refugee from Nazi Germany, Dr. Klaus Fuchs, a mathematical physicist engaged in atomic weapons research, had been sentenced to fourteen years' imprisonment for passing secrets to the Soviet Union. However, neither Nunn May nor Fuchs were in government employment or employed at such a senior level as Maclean, which was so worrying a feature when his disappearance was discovered because Donald Maclean was of British descent and a member of the establishment, the trusted British elite.

In the first half of the century, what one might call the British establishment was still comparatively centralized, probably to a greater extent than was the case in other large countries, such as the USA, Canada, or Germany. Integrating factors for the establishment – besides the preponderance of London's old families – were particularly the "public schools" and some universities, especially Oxford and Cambridge. While I shall comment on certain negative aspects of these institutions in the context of the agents, at their best, Oxford, Cambridge, and the "public schools" were superb institutions in this period.[4]

"Public schools," in English terminology, are not run by the state authorities like the so-called "grammar schools" that cater to the vast majority. The British "public schools" are administered by a board of governors independent of the state and are thus entirely private. Of the five Soviet agents in question, four were educated at public schools in the sense I have described: Guy Burgess went to Eton, the art historian Anthony Blunt to Marlborough, Kim Philby to Westminster – all well-known leading public schools – and Donald Maclean went to Gresham's School in Norfolk. Leo Long did not go to any of this kind of public school, but was educated in the state system. The higher strata of society – in other words the "old families," the professions, and money – set the tone in the public schools. But scholarships allowed a proportion of other social groups to participate in public school education. All the four – Burgess, Blunt, Maclean, and Philby – went on to Cambridge, as did Leo Long.

The public schools were single sex, as all schools at that time, they catered generally to students of age 13 to 18 or 19, and consisted mainly of boarders, meaning they lived in school houses during term-time and only went home during the school holidays. These schools devoted a great deal of attention to training young men for leadership positions in Britain and the Empire and Commonwealth, both on the civil and the military side. The "right" spirit was inculcated in public school boys by isolating them from "ordinary people" and by promoting a strong corporate spirit in each school. At least in term-time, the influence of parents and home was considerably reduced, particularly for boarders more so than for day boys (boys who either lived at home or were boarded privately). The emphasis was on endurance, rules, and team spirit, practiced endlessly in all sorts of sports and games; on a sound general education, on social polish and self-assurance, on loyalty to King and Country, and on a kind of muscular Christianity. There was a strict hierarchical system in force, with masters delegating authority to senior boys, who were usually called prefects. Junior boys had to "fag" for the elder boys (i.e., run personal services and often unwelcome errands for them). The prefects enforced rigorous punctuality and numerous rules, usually enforced by ritual beatings, sometimes in circumstances which can only be called obscene.

Concerning the four Soviet agents who were educated at public schools, perhaps certain features of this system are worth noting. One learned the hard way how to fit in: one had to develop self-reliance and to keep one's counsel. One would never give away any member of one's group, even the bullies who made life a misery.[5] Homosexuality was rampant in the boys' public schools. Of the five agents we are examining, Kim Philby (who went to a public school) and Leo Long (who did not) seemed to have been exclusively heterosexual. Guy Burgess and Anthony Blunt practiced homosexuality, certainly from their time at the university onwards. Donald Maclean, a married man and a father, appeared to have indulged his homosexual inclination on occasion. In dealing with this rather emotional subject, I should like to take my cue from the interrogator of Anthony Blunt in describing their conversation: "We didn't sit down and discuss sex. I was pretty careful not to make moral judgments about it, but we discussed it in the context of spying."[6]

Homosexuality, though not the main cause, does appear to have played a part in our story in the hold that Guy Burgess, a promiscuous homosexual, had over Anthony Blunt and Donald Maclean. Many public school boys may have found the behaviours of their homosexual contemporaries odd, but they would not normally have given them away, then or later. There was a certain conspiratorial or "secret society" atmosphere about all this, particularly in view of the fact that homosexual acts were still subject to the criminal law at the time. All this carried over into Oxford and Cambridge, whose student and faculty body was dominated by the people coming from public schools. Naturally an entirely different spirit prevailed in the "red brick universities" such as Manchester or Liverpool.

We now follow our group to Cambridge, where they began to study at the age of eighteen or nineteen. In Oxford and Cambridge, the Colleges to which one belongs are of considerable importance, and the atmosphere surely helped the undergraduate member. All – Blunt, Burgess, Philby, and Long – jointed Trinity College, while Donald Maclean went to Trinity Hall. Trinity College is one of the outstanding institutions in that University. The one to get there first was Anthony Blunt in 1926, where he stayed until 1937, rising to a faculty position as a "fellow of Trinity." The latest to enter was Leo Long in 1935, when he won a university scholarship. He went down in 1938. The presence of these men in Cambridge thus covers a period of slightly longer than a decade: from the years of the British general strike to just before Munich. Several of them, Burgess, Leo Long – including the much older Blunt – also joined a prestigious Cambridge secret debating society, the Apostles.

How was it that these five men embarked on a course of action which by various stages led them to being sympathetic to the communist cause and to allowing themselves to be put under a Soviet controller whose orders superseded their loyalty to their country and to the government they were supposed to be serving? We have to start from the premise that all five men became Communists from conviction. This was due to a combination of circumstances: the presence of some active left-wingers and communists among the students and faculty members at Cambridge, as well as a belief that the old world of the West (including democracy and capitalism) was doomed. The First World War had not created a world fit for heroes to live in. The improvements in Europe which followed the Locarno treaties in 1925 proved to be short-lived, especially under the shadow of the world economic crisis which began with the Wall Street crash of 1929. Europe had already had one major Fascist regime, in Italy, during the 1920s. Democracy made very little progress in southeastern Europe. There was widespread doubt as to whether traditional democratic parliamentary regimes would be able to deal with the critical challenges which were constantly being presented to society, such as mass unemployment and severe economic distress. These worries affected the group with which we are concerned.

All except for Long came from well-established families. Anthony Blunt was the son of an Anglican clergyman and grandson of a bishop. His family had close social ties with royalty, including Queen Mary. Guy Burgess was the son of a British naval officer, himself serving for a time as a trainee-cadet at the Royal Naval College, Dartmouth, between spells at Eton. Donald Maclean was the son of a Liberal cabinet minister and Presbyterian lay preacher, Sir Donald Maclean, who died in June 1932. The historian G. P. Gooch, the elder MacLean's fellow Member of Parliament for Bath before the First World War, recalled the pride with which the father told him that his son Donald had been sponsored for the Foreign Office by Stanley Baldwin, a former and future Prime Minister.[7] Harold Adrian Russell Philby, called Kim Philby after the hero in Rudyard Kipling's novel, also came from a comfortable, if somewhat less orthodox background. Kim's father started off his career in the

Indian civil service, but resigned because of disagreements with superiors and turned his attentions to the Middle East, acquiring fame as an explorer, archaeologist, cartographer, and naturalist. He became a convert to Islam. The elder Philby was interned by the British government for some months in 1940/41 because of his unbridled hostility to Britain's fight against Hitler. Only Leo Long came from a different background, being the son of a frequently unemployed carpenter. He appears to have felt bitter about a system which often condemned the bottom end of society to mere subsistence, if that, while at the upper end of the social scale, the better-off people lived in the lap of luxury, as he himself witnessed in Cambridge. The other four, who had always enjoyed a good standard of living, felt guilty in a way about their privileged place in the social and economic order, while being comfortable about continuing to enjoy the benefits of their position.

In 1933, Hitler came to power in Germany. Obviously Europe was facing a deep crisis. What was the answer? The Soviet Union! In 1932, Sidney and Beatrice Webb, the famous Fabian couple, had made a study of Russia. They published their mainly positive findings in 1935 under the title *Soviet Communism: A new civilisation?* The following year the Spanish Civil War, in which there was outside intervention, broke out. To many observers, all these developments – and particularly the Spanish Civil War – pointed to an all-out struggle between the Left and the Right, requiring the solidarity of the Left against Hitler, Mussolini, and Franco. Under this scenario, it was essential for the socialists and Liberals to cooperate with the Communists and to enlist the support of the Soviet Union. The international Communist organisation, the Comintern, had a key part to play in support of a "popular front" against Fascism.

But how was a coalition of all these disparate groups to be managed? Who was to call the tune? Many Communists believed the only way forward lay in Communist leadership, provided on an international basis by the Comintern, inspired by the Soviet experiment, and backed by the might of the Russian state. Several of the group visited the Soviet Union: Burgess in 1934 and Blunt in 1935. The experience of the Soviet Union certainly did not discourage them; indeed it appears to have confirmed them in their view of the

world along Communist lines. Their political development coincid-
ed with a determined effort by the Soviet government to secure as
potential agents a number of British intellectuals among the high-
flyers likely to move into positions of political and military importance. The tactics used by the talent spotters in Cambridge were
quite subtle. The initial approach was: "Will you work with us for
peace?" Then later, if thing went well, the question of help for the
Comintern came up. The Communist International was supposed
to be independent of the Soviet government, though its headquarters were in Moscow. Only gradually did the five begin to work
directly for the Soviet government, or realized that they did so.
Actually one had to be rather naïve to believe that a distinction
could be made between the Comintern and the Soviet government,
especially during the period of Stalin, which began during the 1920s
and carried on into the 1950s. The aim of the Soviet authorities was
to put the recruit under the instruction of a Soviet controller. From
that time onwards any agent was under increasing pressure to do
what he was told, to carry out the assignment laid down and to
attempt to secure secrets. There was no turning back, and the agent
undoubtedly laid himself open to blackmail from the Soviet authorities if his enthusiasm waned. In Cambridge, Guy Burgess was
recruited early. He was an almost brilliant maverick, a promiscuous
homosexual, and an alcoholic, but should not be underrated. He in
turn enlisted others, including Blunt, and probably Maclean. Blunt
then became a talent spotter and secured eventually – when is not
clear – the service of Leo Long. Philby was also recruited while
studying at Cambridge.

The next task was to try and manoeuvre the five members into
key positions in the diplomatic, military, and political sphere.
Above all, one obstacle had to be removed: Communist affiliation
was not precisely a recommendation for government service in
Britain in the middle of the 1930s, when these men began to hit the
job market. As we saw, Sir Donald Maclean had already paved the
way for his son to enter the Foreign Office; obviously the initiative
for younger Donald's diplomatic career did not come from the
Soviets. When the younger Donald Maclean was interviewed for
admission to the Foreign Office after taking his degree in 1934, he

was asked about his attitude to Communism, but managed to give an answer of "disarming honesty" that satisfied the committee. In this closed circle of the establishment centring around the public schools and Oxbridge, Maclean's Communist sympathies during his studies in Cambridge were known to Whitehall.

In Philby's case, matters were carried to inordinate lengths. Kim Philby, perhaps their most intelligent and determined, and also most ruthless of the five, and had his left-wing baptism in Vienna in 1934 when he associated with the Communist opposition to the right-wing regime in power in Austria at the time. He displayed considerable courage, as well as a capacity for enduring hardship. Soon afterwards, while in fact a Soviet agent, Philby pretended that he had given up Communism and now professed sympathy with a right-wing point of view. He was even decorated by General Franco when he covered the Fascist campaign in Spain as a newspaper correspondent. In 1935, Guy Burgess served as secretary to a right-wing conservative member of parliament, who was a member of the Anglo-German Fellowship (at the time of the Nazi regime). Actually, it is strange that all this did not boomerang when Britain declared war on Nazi Germany in September 1939. Burgess usually managed to be in the centre of things, in or as well as out of government service, and during a spells with the BBC. As the five advanced in their careers, they could help each other get into key positions, just as later on they could at times warn each other and come to each other's rescue.

In August 1939, Stalin concluded his pact with Hitler, which was soon followed by the outbreak of the Second World War and by the partition of Poland between the two dictators. The five agents were not swayed from their pro-Soviet conviction by this supreme act of cynicism. They were able to persuade themselves that the anti-Soviet prejudices of Western governments left Stalin with no alternative but to settle with Hitler. Throughout, the five men applied entirely different criteria to their own country than to the Soviet Union. They were over critical of the West; some – for instance Maclean – developed a strong anti-Americanism. At the same time they were gullible about the Soviet Union, ignoring the forced collectivization in the Ukraine, Stalin's purge trials, and even the ruthless treatment of European Communists who did not fit into the current Soviet line. The group refused to face the main issue of principle, namely that the chief struggle was between democracy and dictatorship. They were totally blind to all points of similarity between totalitarian Nazism and totalitarian Stalinism.

In spite of much political miscalculation, however, the five agents had succeeded to a remarkable extent in getting into key political and military positions by 1939. Maclean was progressing up the bureaucratic ladder in the diplomatic service and was at the British embassy in Paris when war broke out. His earlier reports to the Soviet Union may well have contributed to Stalin's decision to settle with Hitler. Philby accompanied the British Expeditionary Force to France in 1939 as a *London Times* correspondent. In 1940, with some help from Burgess, Philby joined the British Military Intelligence. Burgess himself had a spell with the War Office after 1938. Blunt joint the British Army in 1939 and got into Military Intelligence in 1940, as did Long. This was not a bad score.

The five agents thus made considerable headway during the period of Soviet collaboration with Nazi Germany between August 1939 and June 1941, which ended with the German invasion of the Soviet Union. In this time, Maclean as a Foreign Office official, and War Office military intelligence personnel Philby, Blunt, and Long passed sensitive information to the Soviets. When Britain and the Soviet Union became allies in the summer of 1941, they continued to supply the Soviets with material the Russians demanded or in which the agents thought Moscow might be interested. They did so in the – probably mistaken – belief that the British government was withholding from the Russians information essential for their fight against the Germans on the soil of their country. Here Leo Long did his bit.

After going down from Trinity College in 1939, Long had a spell in Germany doing some language coaching. He joined the Army after the outbreak of war and was transferred to military intelligence about December 1940, though he claims this was not on his initiative. His service in this section was mainly concerned with assessing the strength and organization of the German Army, and he was intimately familiar with the highly secret decrypts of the "ultra" organization analyzing intercepts. We do not know the full implication of Long's leaks, which *may* have begun before the German invasion of Russia, but they are not likely to have been unimportant. At the very least, the waters were muddied and the smoothness of wartime cooperation between the Soviet Union and Britain is not likely to have been enhanced by the use of this unofficial channel. Some time before the Allied invasion of Normandy in June 1944, Long was transferred to the Headquarters of the British Army Group under Field-marshal Montgomery's command. Long later claimed that he had had enough as a Soviet spy and that he arranged this move to get away from Soviet control.

I met Leo Long soon after the beginning of the Normandy invasion when I was posted to Public and Psychological Warfare (P&PW) Branch at British Army Group headquarters in which Long was serving as major. I still remember reporting to him the results of my monitoring of enemy radio stations in Normandy: he used to sit at a table in a tent with another Intelligence Corps Major. Naturally, I have checked the literature particularly carefully where I have personal experience or knowledge to see how accurate descriptions are. Long is mentioned by Peter Wright in his book *Spycatchers: The Candid Autobiography of a Senior Intelligence Officer*. Wright interrogated Long after he had been given away by Blunt in 1964. Wright recalls, "I met Long several times . . . and disliked him intensely. Unlike the other members of the Cambridge Ring, he lacked class, and I often wondered how on earth he was accepted into the Apostles. He was an officious, fussy man with a face like a motor mechanic's."[8]

I remember a different Leo Long: highly intelligent and alert. In fact, in a piece finalized before the news of Leo Long's espionage was revealed I stated that "from what I saw and heard, the standard reached by intelligence officers at various levels was very high."[9] Recently I phoned a former intelligence officer who was several rungs on the ladder above Major Long at British Army Group Headquarters. He confirmed my impression of Major Long, calling him "agreeable, clever, disillusioned, amusing, and cynical." The reasons for this cynicism and disillusionment – features that I did not notice in 1944 – have only since become clear. This disillusion-

ment and cynicism should be taken into account in evaluating the
statements made by Leo Long after his confession was made public. He spoke to interviewers, for instance, about the psychological
warfare section in which we served together. Penrose and Freeman
recall his remarks on this unit: "Long was in what he called a 'real
bullshit section,' working on various hare-brained schemes to try
and demoralise the German troops once the Allies had landed in
France. Long was in the rearguard of the first wave of troops but
soon tired of his job – dropping leaflets on the Germans."[10] Actually
dropping leaflets was only one of the tasks the section fulfilled.
There were also amplifier units which attempted with the use of
loudspeakers to secure the surrender of German troops if the circumstances appeared propitious. The short answer to Long's
downgrading of this kind of psychological warfare – as I pointed
out in my piece – is that it would have been unthinkable to have left
the propaganda field entirely to the Nazis. In any case, the section
in which Long was a major also monitored enemy radio stations,
including those from French collaborators. The reports of our monitoring were passed on to the intelligence branch at headquarters
for analysis, and I believe every piece of information that could be
secured was potentially useful. The senior intelligence officer to
whom I referred, E.T. Williams, wrote to me recently about the
experience of his "anxieties of out-thinking the German."[11]

Apparently Long told his interrogators that while he was in military intelligence in London during the war, he was asked by Blunt
to get him details of personalities within the British War Office to
pass to the Soviets. Long reminisced to Penrose and Freeman: "I
just ignored him [Blunt]. All intelligence services, British, Soviet, it
doesn't matter, have this obsession about getting the other side's
order of battle. I don't know why the Soviets were interested."[12] Well,
we have only Long's word for it that he did not supply the information Blunt demanded. However, there may be a postscript to this
story about names supplied to the Soviet authorities by agents. In
the summer of 1970, I attended the International Historical
Congress in Moscow and much to my surprise was allocated an
interpreter for the period of my stay, a young lady student from
Moscow University. I was very happy about this, because I get easi-

ly lost. I realized that I did not owe this favour – and naturally the extra supervision – to my status as a historian at the time, because many professors far senior to me in the profession did not have interpreters. I assumed it had something to do with my service either in the British Army or with the BBC. I am just wondering now whether I owed this interpreter to the former Major Long.

The *London Times* on November 2nd, 1981 published a photograph of Leo Long with a report of a press conference he gave. I do not think the difference between the Leo Long of the summer of 1944 in Normandy and his picture in the *Times* can be explained simply in terms of aging. Every one of the group paid a heavy – if different – price for his treachery. Several took to heavy drinking. Leo Long, bright and alert in his undergraduate days in Cambridge and of the Normandy campaign, lost his zest and spark.

Blunt, after the end of the Second World War, returned to his art history professorship and also became Surveyor of the King's and Queen's Pictures. I must admit that – having myself carried out research in the Royal Archives in Windsor Castle and knowing something of the care that is taken to scrutinize people – I was *very* surprised when I saw the news of Blunt's espionage activities. Obviously something went badly wrong, because everything possible is done by the royal staff to shield the King or Queen from controversy. Blunt was well placed for the appointment as Surveyor of the King's Pictures through professional qualifications and the links of his family to Queen Mary. Also, he appeared to have undertaken a confidential mission to Germany for King George VI just after the war ended – a sign of royal confidence in him. Furthermore, his service with Military Intelligence must have appeared in 1945 as evidence of his political reliability, minimizing the importance of earlier left-wing associations. Blunt's personality illustrates particularly well the difficulties the spy catchers must have had in finding their quarry. Blunt was genuinely attached to the royal family and undoubtedly valued his position as a member of the establishment, appointed to a knighthood in 1956 to become "Sir" Anthony Blunt. And yet he had engaged in subversion. Also he was prepared to endanger his position in society by indulging in homosexual activities illegal at the time and by exposing himself to the possibility of blackmail. He was, in a way, an unlikely spy, such as was perhaps only possible in this particular way in England, and therefore a difficult spy to catch. He played several parts, but he was playing himself: he was not an actor who impersonated others. Peter Wright in *Spycatcher* makes some acute observations regarding his interrogation of Blunt: "Blunt was capable of slipping from art and scholar one minute, to intelligence bureaucrat the next, to spy, to waspish homosexual, to languid establishmentarian."[13]

Of the group of five, all, with the possible exception of Blunt, continued their spying for the Soviet Union after the end of the Second World War. Maclean's activities were mentioned earlier. Burgess did his bit and acted as a link between the agents. Leo Long after the Second World War served in a senior intelligence position in the British Control Commission in Germany and probably abused the trust placed in him. Philby played a key role, frustrating British policy and betraying opponents of Communism in the interest of his Soviet master. In September 1945, Konstantin Volkov, a Soviet secret police officer working as a diplomat in the Soviet Embassy in Istanbul, offered to supply the British with valuable intelligence. Volkov insisted on special precautions because of the presence of Soviet agents among the British authorities. Unfortunately, Philby was entrusted by the British military intelligence with the task of negotiating asylum with Volkov. On various pretexts, Philby was allowed to procrastinate so that he was able to secretly warn the Soviet authorities and to give them time to take preventive measures. Presumably, Volkov's life must have been on Philby's conscience, like the fate of anti-Communist Albanians who landed in their homeland in 1950 under Anglo-American auspices to attempt the overthrow of Communist regime. And when they reached Albanian soil instead of the expected welcome, they found a more than unpleasant reception committee awaiting the guerrillas. These are just a few examples of the harm done to British and Western interests – and to Anglo-American cooperation – by some of these men, culminating in Philby's tip-off to Maclean leading to the Foreign Office officials' flight and in Philby's help in the escape.

So far the story has dealt more with spies than spycatchers, except insofar as some of the Soviet spies – like Philby – were supposed to be spycatchers themselves. One may well ask what the other spycatchers – the loyal ones – were doing and why it took so long to identify, capture, and neutralize these Soviet agents. It was only in May 1951, when Donald Maclean was clearly found out as a Soviet agent by the British authorities, that the plot began to be uncovered, gradually and slowly. British security was helped by Burgess's unplanned defection, which led them to Philby and Blunt. Philby was only completely unmasked in 1963, Blunt and Long following in 1964. However, it took until 1979 – another fifteen years – for official public confirmation of Blunt's spying and until 1981 – seventeen years – for Long's. None of the five was brought to justice, partly due to lack of evidence which could be used in a court of law to convict, partly due to bungling.[14] Blunt gave information to the security authorities in return for a pardon. Long was told that prosecution was unlikely in his case.

Philby, after being strongly suspected of Soviet espionage by the British authorities, operated in Beirut from 1956 to 1963 in circumstances which have still not been entirely cleared up, and then left for the Soviet Union to claim his rightful rank as a general in the Soviet Secret Police. With the serialization of interviews in the *London Times*, he is once more in the limelight. While the *Sunday Times* material is worth reading, some caution is in order. Philby is not a free agent and must toe the Soviet line. He is not giving interviews to help historians.[15]

СОВЕТСКИЙ РАЗВЕДЧИК

КИМ ФИЛБИ
1912—1988
5 к ПОЧТА СССР 1990

1990 Russian commemorative postage stamp picturing Kim Philby

There are lessons to be learned from the story of these Soviet agents, though we may not all come to the same one conclusion. Certainly the whole issue of State security, of its successes and failures, of the degree of desirable or permissible supervision by the state, is very topical, not only in Canada and the USA, but also in many other countries, including Western Germany. There is a whole multitude of questions that might be asked, of problems that might be discussed.

One of these is: To whom do we owe our primary duty and loyalty? The famous novelist E. M. Forster, who belongs to the society of the Cambridge Apostles, wrote that if he had to choose between betraying his country and betraying his friends, he hoped he would have the guts to betray his country. This sounds clever, but it does not make sense. Blunt apparently quoted Forster's aphorism – with his approval – in a conversation in 1951.[16] Surely, in some situations, members of the ring acted in certain ways, at least partly because they felt a strong loyalty to each other. But in the end even Blunt had to see that E. M. Forster's view did not get one very far. By betraying his country, Blunt betrayed friends who were aghast at his treachery. These had assumed that the country of their birth, of their families, of their homes, its history, and its literature, "this England," was a common bond between them. Even Blunt had regrets, but only when his spying became public knowledge and when his friends would never again see him in quite the same light as before.

Spies have always been bought and blackmailed and will be bought and blackmailed in future. Any security is only as strong as its weakest link, its weakest brethren of sisters. Spying for convictions to the detriment of one's country is a matter of a different order and was something new for Britain. Obviously, the British authorities in the 1930s were unprepared for the degree of deception and betrayal from senior officialdom and some of their key security officers practiced by these five men. British people, even at the highest levels, had great difficulty in understanding totalitarian regimes both of Stalin and Hitler. It took the British authorities several years after the end of the Second World War to realize that the loyalty even of the British-born senior officials could be subverted and could no longer be taken for granted. Many key officials knew each other from public school and Oxbridge. Yet early Communist association of this tiny minority of Soviet agents, for instance at the university, was passed off as youthful indiscretion, long since overcome. Other countries have their spies, too, to be explained in the historical context. Why did men like Blunt, Maclean, and even Philby escape detection for so long? It was at least partly because the British system of building up members of the establishment by a whole mystique of titles and mannerism, and of creating a leadership caste which shared common values and behaviour, and above all, their absolute trustworthiness was taken for granted, which had made the idea of this kind of betrayal almost unthinkable.

Notes

1   Barrie Penrose and Simon Freeman, *Conspiracy of Silence: The Secret Life of Anthony Blunt* (London: Grafton Books, 1987), 387.
2   Ibid., 357.
3   Robert Cecil, "The Cambridge Comintern," in *The Missing Dimension: Governments and Intelligence Communities in the Twentieth Century*, ed. Christopher Andrew and David Dilk (London: Longmans, 1966), 185–95.
4   I have to disclose that the last four years of my school education took place at St Paul's, a leading London "public school," and that I spent several years at Oxford as an undergraduate belonging to Worcester College and the as a research fellow of St. Antony's College.
5   I personally had a difficult year at St. Paul's School as a boarder, but was afterwards very happy at the school as a day-boy.
6   Penrose and Freeman, 450.
7   G. P. Gooch on Sir Donald Maclean in *History Survey and Portraits* (London: Longmans, 1966), 240–43; For the reference to the younger Maclean's preparations for entry into the Foreign Office see p. 243; See also Frank Eyck, *G. P. Gooch: A Study in History and Politics* (London: Macmillan Press, 1982).
8   Peter Wright, *Spycatcher: The Candid Autobiography of a Senior Intelligence Officer* (Toronto: Soddart Publishing Company, 1987), 221.
9   Frank Eyck, "Psychological Warfare and Newspaper Control in the British-Occupied Germany: A Personal Account," in *Men at War: Politics Technology and Innovation in the Twentieth Century*, ed. Timothy Travers and Chris Archer (Chicago: Precedent, 1982), 138–39.
10 Penrose and Freeman, 321.
11 Frank (U.F.J.) Eyck, *A Historian's Pilgrimage: Memoirs and Reflections* (Calgary, AB: Detselig Enterprises, 2009), 224.
12 Ibid, 301.
13 Peter Wright, 225.
14 The Conservative Home Secretary Henry Brooke authorized the offer of immunity from prosecution to Blunt. I knew Brooke and agree with his judgment in Penrose and Freeman, 440–41, that this upright and

responsible minister would never have been swayed in his judgment but for the fact that he had been Blunt's prefect at Marlborough College.

15 Since the piece was finalized in April 1988, Philby died in Moscow in May 1988. Maclean had already died in Moscow on March 6th, 1983, and Blunt twenty days later in London. Burgess had died in the Soviet Union in August 1963.

16 Penrose and Freeman, 381.

Chapter Three

MARTIN LUTHER

Presented November 21st, 1983, as one of a series of talks on Luther sponsored by the Lutheran Campus Ministry of the University of Calgary.

M ARTIN LUTHER WAS BY COMMON CONSENT one of the greatest Germans to have lived in the last five hundred years. Thus it may be desirable to look at the impact Luther made on the religion and politics of his native Germany, both during his own time and ever since. I'm speaking tonight as a historian of Germany with an interest in the relationship between religion and politics. I'm not here to judge any of the theologies to which, however, I shall refer. I'm not concerned with whether this angle of looking at Luther in the German context will show him to particular advantage or not. Indeed, to my mind, much more harm has been done to Luther by those who gave excessive praise than by his detractors. That so many of you turned out this evening under inclement weather conditions – to put it mildly – is a tribute to the continuing importance of the reformer half a millennium after his birth. I would say that Luther's greatness speaks for itself.

What were the conditions in the country into which Luther was born, the country on which he was to have so very strong an impact, in his own time as well on subsequent centuries? In Luther's times, when we visualize Germany, there was not yet a national German state. Any reference to Germany or Italy was used in a geographical sense. We must not think in terms of a unified country such as that founded by Bismarck in 1871. There were a large number of different and not only German territories loosely held together in what was called the Empire, or the Holy Roman Empire of German Nation (*das Heilige Römische Reich deutscher*

Nation). These territories were of many different types, e.g. electoral domains, duchies, earldoms, bishoprics and archbishoprics, free imperial cities, and so on. Seven dignitaries were electors *ex officio*, that is to say they elected a German King who would become Holy Roman Emperor. These seven consisted of four secular rulers, including Luther's ruler, the Elector of Saxony, and of three arch-bishops. Since the year 800, when Charlemagne was crowned emperor by the pope in Rome, the precise balance of power vacil-lated between the emperor and the rulers of the different territo-ries. Emperor and rulers were linked in an originally feudal system which was gradually being modified. There were some very power-ful emperors and some who had comparatively little influence over the territories. Frederick III of the Habsburg Dynasty, who was Emperor at the time of Luther's birth in 1483, only had very limited power and authority in the Empire outside his dynastic territories. Traditionally, at least in theory, the Holy Roman Emperor was the leading secular ruler in Western Christendom, that is to say, in that part of Europe that belonged in religion to the church of the Western or Roman, as opposed to the Eastern or Orthodox, rite. In this respect, the Holy Roman Emperor had a special relationship with the pope, the spiritual head of the church of the Roman rite who also ruled over the Patrimony of St Peter, the Papal State. Indeed, Frederick III, who died in 1493, was one of a whole series of German kings who were crowned emperor by the pope in Rome. His son and successor, Maximilian I, who also appears in the Luther story, due to circumstances discontinued the practice; his corona-tion at the Cathedral of Trent was a few days later confirmed by the pope. In turn, the successor of Maximilian I, Charles V, who was of great importance to Luther, established the procedure of adopting the title of Roman Emperor–elect immediately after being elected German King by the Electors. Only Charles V followed up after-wards with his coronation in Rome by the pope. At many levels the links between church and secular authority were complex and close, frequently leading to bitter disputes and even to war. In gen-eral, the Emperor took for granted the necessity of the mainte-nance of religious orthodoxy and uniformity represented by the church of the Roman rite. Any challenge to religious orthodoxy and uniformity in Western Christendom and in the Empire constituted a threat to the very existence of the Holy Roman Empire, and such a challenge was represented by Luther. What I would like to do tonight is to mention some of the developments and events that are essential to the Luther story.

Martin Luther was born 1483 in the general region of Thuringian Saxony in Northern Germany, in Eisleben, which at that time came under the Count of Mansfield, one of the many petty rulers in the Empire. Martin Luther's father, Hans, was a peasant-miner, certainly not at the top of society, but not by any means at the bottom of the social ladder. He was successful enough to enable his son Martin to study at the University of Erfurt. The father's choice suggested the study of law. But, when the young student experienced what to him appeared to be a life-threatening violent electric storm, he vowed to become a monk, and joined the strict Augustian monastic order in Erfurt. There he studied philosophy and theology that traditionally included the languages of Latin, Hebrew, and Greek. His questioning mind often led him to suffer from severe "scruples;" to overcome these he was greatly helped by his confessor Johann von Staupitz. Luther was ordained priest in 1507 and soon after became professor of biblical studies at the recently founded university in Wittenberg, the capital of the Elector of Saxony, Frederick the Wise, who was proud of his university and his brilliant theologian.

In his studies Luther went back to the biblical sources and the Church fathers. He published his first discussion paper, the ninety-eight theses, in 1517, which caused public unrest. That they were nailed on the door of the castle church at Wittenberg is pure popular tale, but they were certainly printed and widely known among scholars and lay people. Luther had come to the conclusion that the orthodox interpretation of his time failed to provide the explanation or proper interpretation to guide the way to salvation, and for that he blamed the scholastic theology developed during the Middle Ages with its emphasis on salvation through work. One of the questions he raised was about indulgences: "An indulgence is the remission of the temporal punishment due to sin, never of the guilt itself. The remission is worked out either on earth or in purgatory."[1]

Gradually this interpretation had lost the finer point and had become instead a major source of revenue for the Holy See. Luther also questioned the supremacy of the pope and the church councils which, at times, had been known to err. He mainly meant to use an academic way to revise practices that were in his understanding not fully supported by his theological studies. In this criticism, he was not alone. There were the reformers, Calvin in Geneva after being evicted from Paris, Reuchlin in Cologne, and Zwingli in Einsiedeln, Switzerland. It was the age of the famous humanist Erasmus of Rotterdam. Luther certainly was not aware of, or even intended, any political implication in his endeavour. Unfortunately, controversy and tension between the different points of view and practice increased. Several attempts of finding a way out did not bring any agreement, solution, or compromise. Among others, there was in March 1518, the theological discussion at Ingoldstadt with Eck, a famous theologian and initially a friend of Luther and at Augsburg in October of the same year with the papal Legate, Cardinal Cajetan. Any suggestion of calling a church council did not succeed either. But all this led to the growing suspicion, and the later accusation, of heresy by the church. Luther's temperament brought only increasing resistance on his part and failed to bring about any idea of softening his stand.

It so happened that during the early stages of Luther's controversy with his church and the Papacy, the Holy Roman Empire was going through a period of uncertainty which in turn affected Luther's fate. The royal and imperial crown of the Empire was elected, but, the dynasty in power usually tried to secure the imperial succession. The Habsburg family had produced a number of emperors since the thirteenth century, but Maximilian I was only the third one in uninterrupted succession. The heir of Maximilian was not his son, who died in 1506, but his grandson. It was easier to get a son elected king or emperor than a more distant relative like a grandson to succeed him as emperor after his death. The procedure Maximilian followed was to try and have him elected "Roman King" during Maximilian's lifetime. This election as Roman King was not guaranteed, but as close as one could get to secure the eventual succession to the imperial crown. There was an additional complication. Maximilian's grandson Charles, though he would eventually inherit the German territories of the Habsburgs, i.e., Austria and territories elsewhere, had even greater interests outside of what was considered strictly German lands. Charles, through his mother Joan, who was excluded from the succession because of insanity, had in 1516 inherited the Kingdom of Spain with its vast overseas colonies. He was also heir to Burgundy and the bulk of the Low Countries, as well as the kingdom of the two Naples that included Sicily. However, in part and possibly because of this, in 1518 Maximilian failed to secure the election of his grandson Charles as Roman King.

The electors always had the final say after the death of the German King and Holy Roman Emperor, but when Maximilian I died in January 1519, just before his sixtieth birthday, the question of the succession was more widely open than when Maximilian himself had succeeded his father Frederick III. Even before Maximilian I's death, the electors who carried out the various elections for Roman King and German King had become very important, one of them was the Elector of Saxony, Frederick the Wise, at whose university Luther taught. The Elector Frederick was not somebody it was prudent to antagonize. Frederick was proud of his university and its leading light Martin Luther. Frederick remained attached to the old and universal Western church and certainly did not agree with all of Luther's theology, but neither did he want Luther to come to any harm. Not only those who aspired to the imperial crown, but also the pope, treated the Elector Frederick of Saxony, Luther's protector, with particular care during the final months of Maximilian's reign and in the run-up to the election of the new Emperor. The Papal Curia was very interested in the choice of emperor, not only because of the general concern of the Church, but because of the Papal State. The pope, particularly, as ruler of the Papal State, could not be indifferent to what happened to the ruler of the neighbouring Kingdom of the two Naples. Charles had succeeded to the Kingdom of the two Naples to the south of the Papal State in his capacity as King of Spain, and it did not suit the pope that this King of the two Naples, Charles, as Emperor might have an even greater influence in Italy as he would then be in a better position to put pressure on the Curia. Therefore, Pope Leo X, a Medici, at first supported Charles's main rival for the imperial crown, King Francis I of France. When Francis's cause appeared hopeless, the pope and France attempted to persuade the Elector Frederick of Saxony to become a candidate, but they were unsuccessful. Even if the votes of the Electors were not for sale, the Electors were not unhappy to accept favours. All of them saw their influence increase for a time, particularly the Elector Frederick of Saxony, and Luther benefited from this. In the end, on the 28th of June, 1519, Charles, at twenty years of age, was unanimously elected and became Emperor Charles V. Before his election, however, Charles had to accept restrictions drafted by the Elector Frederick, designed to prevent him from misusing the German lands and the Empire in the interest of the Habsburg dynasty. These stipulations or agreements were embodied in the election capitulation (*Wahlkapitulation*), the electoral re-enlistment.

One article of this treaty is of special relevance to us in the context of Luther: No German was to be punished unheard by having the ban of the Empire inflicted on him. Any person under the ban of the Empire faced immediate arrest by anybody who found him and had to be delivered to the Emperor as a prisoner. The Elector Frederick insisted that Luther should be heard by an impartial body before he was condemned. This request became particularly urgent as the conflict between Luther and the Church authorities escalated.

I do not want to duplicate the theological explanation already given in the series of talks. It suffices to say that there were theological differences between Luther and the Church, the old traditional Church, that could not so easily be bridged. There was much in Luther's doctrine of salvation by faith through grace that could not simply be reconciled with the emphasis of the old Church on work. The fundamental stumbling block to any agreement between Luther and the Church was Luther's questioning of Church tradition and Church authority: not only of the popes, but also of that of the Church councils. Luther pointed out, unfortunately correctly, that both popes and councils had erred in the past.

Now, each one of us has to revise or make up his own mind about the respective merits of the theologies at the time and since. Without taking sides, we have to appreciate that for the Church authorities, or indeed for any organization, Luther was not an easy man to deal with. Every further disputation drove Luther into greater opposition to the teachings of the Church. While the methods used to deal with heresy are abhorrent to us today, we must try and understand the wish of the Church to keep doctrine pure and accepted; therefore Luther had a special responsibility, not as a monk, but as a teacher and professor of theology. From a practical point of view, the pursuit of Luther as a disobedient son of the Church achieved exactly the opposite of what was intended. The best weapon against Luther would have been to ignore him. It was the seriousness with which the church authorities followed up his case which gave Luther the publicity that helped to make him famous. In June of 1520, the papal bull *exsurge Domine* condemned as heretical certain statements by Luther and gave him sixty days to recant. Canon law decreed that unless Luther did so within this period, he would fall under the papal ban. At least in theory, the papal ban meant a quarantine of the condemned person, in the case of Luther, from the body of the faithful by excommunicating him. Pope Leo X issued the ban formally in January 1521 in the bull *Decet Romanum pontificem*. The cooperation between the secular and the ecclesiastical authorities was generally close in late medieval and early modern Europe. The secular ban had to follow the ecclesiastical ban in the Empire within a certain time and the Emperor Charles V wanted to act accordingly. But the German princes, even those who did not support Luther theologically, would not accept that and insisted on a hearing. In spite of the opposition by the Pope, the hearing was scheduled for the imperial Diet (*Reichstag*), the representation of the estates or the territories of the Empire, which included many ecclesiastical dignitaries. The Emperor Charles V issued "a safe conduct" for Luther to appear at the Diet which met in Worms in April 1521.[2]

Luther showed great courage in obeying the summons to the Diet. After all, the Czech reformer Johannes Huss, who was the Rector of the Prague University and the renowned leader of the fifteenth-century religious reform movement opposing the worldliness of the church, had received "a safe conduct" from the Emperor Sigismund for the Council of Constance; however, this had not prevented Huss from being burned at the stake. In Worms, during dramatic scenes at the Diet, Luther refused to recant, but was allowed to depart in accordance with the "safe conduct" issued by the Emperor Charles. In May 1521, the Diet approved an imperial edict putting Luther under the ban of the Empire (*Acht und Bann*) which made him an outlaw, and is usually followed by excommunication. But in the meantime, the Elector Frederick of Saxony had Luther spirited away to the Wartburg castle in Thuringia for his own protection. In Luther's case, Emperor and Pope attempted to collaborate but had been unable to stifle Luther. The reformer had proved stronger than the combination of an Emperor who was also ruler of a European (indeed a world) empire, and of the pope with his vast international organization and spiritual influence.

The emperor Charles was a sincere and faithful son of the Church; he was sure of the need for orthodoxy and abhorred heresy. He also bore in mind the support of dynastic interests of the Habsburgs, but wished to use these in support of the spiritual unity of Western Christendom. Charles realized that the Holy Roman Empire would be fatally weakened by a religious schism. Sometimes the Emperor had difficulties in reconciling the spiritual and dynastic objectives, such as in his relations to the pope, with whom he often found himself in conflict. The pope, in turn, believed that the interest of the Western Church required the spiritual supremacy and the political independence of the Papacy. In pursuit of the spiritual supremacy, the Papacy in this period resisted the conciliar movement which might have contributed to a timely reform of the Church. The Pope, in trying to preserve his political independence, was very much concerned with his secular power-base in Italy, which was liable to entangle him in conflict with the Emperor, thus weakening the coherence and unity of the Old Church, as seen in the struggle against Luther. Unlike Luther, both pope and emperor always weighed the political implications and consequences of their policies.

The reformer was primarily a theologian, an interpreter of the "Word of God," and as such he saw himself mainly in this light. In his intense and sincere spiritual struggle, Luther gradually discovered answers to the questions that had troubled him, and he pro-

Portrait of Martin Luther as "Junker Joerg," 1521, by Lukas Cranach the Elder.

bpk, Berlin / Museum der Bildenden Kuenste, Leipzig, Germany / Ursula Gerstenberger / Art Resource, NY

claimed these answers to the world. He was absolutely sincere and deeply religious. He said and wrote what he felt, which certainly in the early years of his conflict with the Church required great courage. Luther, in the proclamation of his faith, did not consider the effect this would have on the Church to which he owed obedience. He regarded being true to himself spiritually as more impor-

Portrait of Martin Luther, ca. 1532.

bpk, Berlin / Stadtmuseum, Regensburg, Germany / Lutz Braun / Art Resource, NY

tant than to keeping the vows that he had taken, including those of obedience. While Luther as a theologian was intimately versed in his subject, he was not well acquainted with the affairs of the world, from which he had been sheltered to some extent through life in a monastery. While he developed a theology which is regarded as consistent by many, its application to the existing society in Germany is not always so clear.

To pick out a few developments where we can see the consequences of Luther's teaching: There is the rejection of the Papacy, which involved a breach with the Church of the Roman rite and was bound to mean the rupture of many international links. In the initial stages, and indeed for quite some time, the precise geographical area to which the Lutheran reformation would apply was not settled; much of this took until the seventeenth century to sort out. Then there is on the positive side the Bible translation which is a tremendous achievement, and he had done so in a rather short time, even if it is now no longer permissible to say that Luther founded the modern German language. Luther is recognized as one of the greatest interpreters of the Bible. He had considerable influence on Bible translation in general, and there are some cases where even Catholics at times copied Luther's Bible. There is no doubt that Luther enhanced the importance of the German language, as he brought some uniformity among the many dialects. But this also initiated a declining importance of Latin, and contained a weakening of the international links. Thus Latin in a certain sense became a Catholic symbol, and German a Protestant one, which in the long run made any unification more difficult. Then here are his wonderful hymns in German about those you heard in the previous talk. The influence of the Bible translation was particularly strong because the printing press had come into its own. In all these developments, there is inherent in some respect a strengthening of German national feeling, weakened at the same time by the division into the Protestant and Catholic populations. Luther appealed to many sentiments that existed before – antipapal, anti-Roman – which really shows there was already a rudimentary, indeed very rudimentary, German national feeling. These sentiments may have existed before, though rather spurious, but he strengthened the trend and speeded up the process of their development.

What is not clear is Luther's attitude to the social and political order. For the historian, one of the difficulties in interpreting Luther is to find out at what level Luther was speaking when he made his pronouncements. Did his statements have actual application to current problems, or were they on the level of other-worldly theology – of pure theory? Luther's contemporaries were just as confused as some of us are still, and the extreme language Luther used on many occasions aroused false expectations, for instance in the minds of the peasants, as is seen in the revolt of 1525. Luther tried to mediate before the revolt by asking the rulers to grant just demands and by warning the peasants against precipitating a civil war. However, when the uprising took place, Luther, in May 1525, published his tract *Against the Robbing and Murdering Horde of Peasants.* He urged the princes of fierce retaliation as a Christian act of mercy! In June 1525, Luther replied to critics of his harshness in his *Open Letter about the Harsh Booklet against the Peasants*, and a brief quote from him reads:

> If people think my answer was too harsh, I answer: that is right! For an insurrectionist does not deserve to be answered with reason since he does not accept it. . . . The peasants will not listen, they will not let anyone say anything at all, so one must unplug their ears with buck-shots, to that their heads jump in the air.

This shows Luther with all his faults, and I hope that will be permitted. Of interest theologically, there is another passage from the same tract:

> There are two kingdoms, one is God's kingdom, and the other is the kingdom of the world. I have written this so often that it amazes me that there is anyone who had not yet learned it or become aware of it. For anyone who knows how to distinguish correctly between these two kingdoms will certainly not be annoyed by my little book, and will easily understand the pas-

sages about mercy. God's kingdom is a kingdom of grace and mercy, and not a kingdom of wrath or punishment, for in it there is sheer forgiving, caring, loving and serving, doing good, possessing peace and joy, and so on. But, the worldly kingdom is a kingdom of wrath and severity, for in it there is sheer punishing, restraining, judging and condemning, crushing the evil and protecting the upright, for this reason it both possesses and wields the sword, and in Scripture a prince or lord is called God's wrath, or rod.[3]

There are obviously a number of difficulties here we won't solve tonight, like the interpretation of St. Augustine's doctrine of the two kingdoms.[4] What moral restrictions are there on the earthly kingdom? What is the power of the state? Luther is often accused of selling out to the princes and to the state, perhaps unjustly so, but he does lay himself open to misunderstanding.

If I may just get a few critical things out of the way, there is Luther's attitude to the Jews. Here the comparatively favourable attitude to the Jews expressed in 1523 *Jesus was born a Jew* has been contrasted with his book on *The Jews and their Lies* of 1543. The comparative progressiveness of the young Luther has been set against the harshness of the old, but this has now been disputed. In the later work, Luther advised the burning of the synagogues and of Jewish homes.[5] In view of the importance of this theme for the history of Germany in the twentieth century, I quote from a moving statement made in 1930 by the non-Zionist organization of German Jews (*Centraslverein deutscher Staatsbürger jüdischen Glaubens*) a few years before the beginning of the Nazi persecution and before the actual burning of synagogues in 1938:

> As a child of his age Luther shared the prejudice of his time during certain periods of his life. His whole striving was devoted to spreading his teaching and to get the Jews, too, to accept Christianity. His endeavour did not have any success. He therefore turned very sharply against the Jews in his old age. But his motive only had to do with religious difference. Luther was no anti-Semite [in the racial sense].[6]

What can be said about the effect that Luther had particularly on Germany and the Empire by the time of his death in February 1546? First of all, the general point is that Luther had intended to reform the Church of the Roman rite, not to split from it. Alas, his call for reform was not sufficiently heeded. This was partly because the task of reforming the church was a very considerable one, and it was beyond the capacity of the Church of Rome when Luther first made his call. When the Council of Trent attempted the momentous task from 1545 onwards, beginning its work just at the very end of Luther's life, the schism could no longer be undone. Also, we must say in fairness that Luther was not always particular tactful in his way of proceeding. The result was a schism, not only between the Roman Catholics and Protestants, but also between various Protestants. For Luther was not able to carry with him all those who separated from Rome, for instance, neither Zwingly and Calvin, the Swiss reformers, nor the more radical reformation, or indeed the English reformation. In the Protestant territories some new organization had to be put in the place of the international institution of the Roman Church, and the answer of different Protestant groups to this varied. Luther opted for entrusting the rulers of the territories with the supervision of the church, preferring this, for instance, to the development of congregational participation which was inherent in the ministry of all believers, according to the Protestant theory. It is true that the secular authorities had for some time been making visitations of religious institutions, and perhaps Luther effectively had no other choice. Still, through Luther, the Elector of Saxony and other Lutheran rulers in Germany acquired greater and more exclusive direction over spiritual matters than their Roman Catholic counterparts, the Catholic rulers. For those who were subject to the Protestant rulers, the authority of the princes with the combination of secular and ecclesiastical power became crushing. There was an exact territorial coincidence of secular state and religious authority without any appeal or reference to Rome to balance the ruler in spiritual matters. It is a matter of some irony that Luther, who had attacked the weight given to worldly and political matters in the Roman Church and who used such scathing terms for the princes, did more than anybody else on the European continent in the sixteenth century to strengthen the power of the secular rulers.

There is one more critical thing: I am also not satisfied with the explanations given for Luther's secret consent around 1539 to the bigamy of the Landgraf Philip of Hessen, a leading Lutheran ruler. The specifics were that Philip was allowed to contract an extra marriage (in the German, *Nebenehe*) a marriage contract "alongside," whatever this may be, during the life-time of his wife to whom he remained legally married. He, in other words, had two legal wives. This is a fact, though I wonder whether any of us want to emulate it. Luther was in this case more subservient to political interests than the Roman Church had ever been. I don't think Luther's approval was even particularly clever. Matters came to light, as they were bound to do sooner or later, although he had given his permission secretly. Obviously, all this did great harm to Luther and the others involved, such as Melanchthon, a master of classical languages and friend at Wittenberg University. Incidentally, from a political point of view, the parallel marriage allowed the Emperor Charles V to put pressure on Philip as bigamy was a crime under the law of the Empire.

What was the effect of Luther on the Empire and on Germany in particular? The Empire was certainly weakened, or weakened further, by religious division. Luther did not create all religious divisions; you can't make Luther entirely responsible for this weakening and this disunity, perhaps it was coming anyway, and the actual day-to-day practice of the Holy Roman Empire was very much removed from the theory of some kind of unity. But one can and may be able to say that at least Luther helped in the process of disintegration, which was perhaps inevitable.

We may now ask what happened after Luther's death and which events were a result of his reforms. There is the religious peace of Augsburg in 1555 that established the principle of *cuius regio eius religio* and thereby acknowledged the division between Roman Catholics and Lutherans; both were recognized and declared legitimate churches. In the Peace Treaty of Westphalia 1648 at Osanbrück at the end of the Thirty Years' War, the Calvinists were added to the recognized Confessions. The efforts of two

Emperors – Charles V in Luther's life-time and Ferdinand II in the following century – to restore the authority of the emperorship failed. These rulers adhered to the Old Church. They believed that to achieve the aim of strengthening the integrity and unity of the Empire and also their power in their own territories they had to re-Catholicize, which at the same time would reduce the power of the other princes. The dual task proved beyond anybody's ability. One might have been able to do one, but not both. Also, by 1635 it was clear that the Roman Catholics could not crush the Protestants and that the Protestants could not triumph over the Roman Catholics in Germany and the Empire. The Protestants were not united; in fact there were deep divisions between the Lutherans and the Calvinists which showed up during the Thirty Years' War. These combined events led to the delay of German unification so that Germany became the "belated nation," only being united in 1871.

A few matters about the long effects of Luther are worth discussing. There was the foundation in Germany of a Protestant, mainly Lutheran but also Calvinist, culture alongside that of the Roman Catholic Church. Luther's translation of the Bible into German was very much at the centre, only being sometimes displaced in church services in our own days. Religious music, to which Luther contributed so much by way of hymns, reached new heights, for instance through the compositions of Heinrich Schütz, Johann Sebastian Bach, and others. The Lutheran rectory became a cultural centre, often the home of highly educated families nurtured on the Word and the music of worship, counting among their numbers not only a succession of clergymen and church organists, but also members of the professional classes, including some of the leading lights of scholarship. Doubtless the beautiful, profound, spiritual text of Luther's Bible translation was a factor in the literacy which led to the great German literary revival of the eighteenth century being mainly in the hands of Protestants. The spiritual strength of the eighteenth- and nineteenth-century Protestantism is to be seen in the Pietistic movement which combined deep inward religion with a strong emphasis on social tasks.

Unfortunately, certain long-term problems were also a part of Luther's religious achievement. In his time, Luther did what he regarded as necessary for that period, but he was not able to foresee future developments, about which in any case he often did not trouble himself because of the influence of apocalyptic and eschatological ideas. The Lutheran reformation in Germany was far more connected with one person than for instance the English Reformation. That left a number of unanswered questions: What were the authoritative pronouncements relevant to the Lutheran Churches in each of the German states besides the Augsburg Confession of 1530? This detailed document that analyzed the Christian faith was written by Philip Melanchthon and defended by Luther at the Reichstag of Augsburg in front of Emperor Charles V, with the main controversy arising over the interpretation of faith versus work. Or was it also the whole body of Luther's writings, or perhaps only some of them? How was agreement to be reached on changes to be made or re-interpretations in theology or alterations in church organization? Had Luther's reformation done all that was required, or was a further reformation necessary? In all this Luther became a key factor, now to be posthumously analyzed. Obviously, it was important for the various groups seeking influence over the Protestant church to have Luther on their side. The interesting thing about the reformer is that he indeed inspired people of many different viewpoints who quite sincerely all quoted him in support while coming to diametrically opposite conclusions. While this continuing interest and relevance of Luther is further evidence of his greatness, the difficulty of interpreting his text faithfully is compounded by the subjectivity of the reader. So far every theological movement within Lutheranism has claimed the authority of the founder, from the Orthodox to the Pietisits to the Enlightened. One can say that Luther provided some stimulation or inspiration for every season. Naturally, all claims of support from Luther have to be carefully analyzed.

I think one should be aware of oversimplification about Luther's effect on German history. Luther at times has been pictured as both an extreme German nationalist and a lackey of the princes. But when the hour of trial came at the time of the Nazi regime, many German Protestants went along with the Nazis, certainly enough of them; however, people such as Dietrich Bonhöffer, Otto Dibelius,

Martin Niemöller, and many, many others showed that there were limits to what the state and nation could demand. There was something higher which demanded the duty of resistance to authority which Luther had already preached in certain circumstances.

P.S. At the beginning of the 1980s, Frank Eyck started his work *Religion and Politics in German History: From the Beginning to the French Revolution*, published in 1998. It includes a chapter on Martin Luther and the Reformation. His talk of November 21st, 1983, was intended as an introduction to the general course on Luther and therefore covered only limited aspects of this vast topic. The editor has taken the liberty of including some explanations which could not be given in his talk partly because the topics on Luther were shared between several speakers and the talk itself had a time limit.

Notes

1   Joseph Adam Lortz, *The Reformation in Germany*, trans. R. Walls (London: Darton, Longman & Todd,), 86ff, 225ff.
2   Bruno Gephardt, *Handbuch der Deutschen Gescchichte* (Deutsche: Verlagsgesellschaft, 1955), 2:42ff.
3   The quote is taken from Ian D. Kingston Siggins (ed.), *Luther* (Edinburgh: Oliver & Boyed, 1972), 99–100. For a German biography, see Rudolf Thicl, *Luther* (Wein, Bohn: Paul Neff Verlag, 1952).
4   For the complexity of this problem, see Bernard Lohse, *Martin Luther: Einführung in sein Leben und sein Werk* (München: Max Hüber, 1981), 190–96.
5   Johannes Brosseder, *Luthers Stellung zu den Juden im Spiegel seiner Interpreten* (München: Max Hüber,1972), 579.
6   Brosseder, 153, my translation.

Chapter Four

THE GERMANS AND
THEIR HISTORY

Originally presented in German, March 29th, 1995, at Bildungwissenschaftliche Hochschule-Universitä-Flensburg.

FTER A SHORT INTRODUCTION, I would first like to dispassionately describe the problems of the German Unification. Before the outbreak of the 1848 revolution, there still existed the German Confederation of 1815, *der Deutsche Bund*, a loose confederation of not only German states; Prussia as well as Austria belonged to it. When thinking and debating about the possible ways to establish a national state, a decision had to be made whether to constitute it with or without Austria, i.e., a greater (*großdeutsches*) or a smaller (*kleindeutsches*) Germany. A further question was how the German national movement might be able to justify unification historically. What was this German historical picture? In a sweeping way I will try to describe this, and then follow it up by comparing this picture with what, in my opinion, really took place in earlier centuries, mainly during the thousand years of the Holy Roman Empire of the German Nation that lasted from the coronation of Charlemagne in AD 800 to the abdication of Emperor Franz II in 1806. Finally, I will attempt, hopefully without prejudice, to shed new, or at least a different, light on the history of the German national movement, and will try to see what consequences might be drawn from the development of the now bygone German nationalism.

Perhaps I ought to quite simply begin by talking about how, slowly over the years, my own historical picture changed. I was born in Berlin in the year 1921. During my childhood I did not doubt that the then existing German Reich reflected the natural development of German history. This Second Reich, known as "the small German solution," was constituted roughly within the borders drawn by Bismarck, which were based on the borders of the German Confederation that had been constituted at the Congress of Vienna in 1815, but was consequently eliminated by the Frankfurt Assembly in 1848/49. Certainly, among the German-Jewish educated bourgeoisie (belonging to the *Bildungsbürgertum*), among whom I grew up, people would have preferred that things had transpired differently. We would have preferred, for example, that in 1888, the Three-Kaiser Year, Emperor Fredric III would have lived long enough to succeed in adjusting the German government more in line with the customs of the English parliament. But, without question, the general and popular opinion was that the German Confederation was simply outdated, and the "small-German Unification" was without a doubt the only solution.

In my Berlin school, the French Gymnasium, which I had attended since 1931, I had to give a talk to my class about Alsace-Loraine, the territories west of the Rhine, which were taken over by Bismarck after the war of 1870/71 and which were returned to France in 1919. The question for my talk was: were these lands German or French? To my satisfaction I proved that Germany had the legal claim to them, as in the Middle Ages they had belonged to the Empire. To me the Holy Roman Empire of the German Nation was "obviously" a German Reich and thus the historical and legal predecessor of Bismarck's Germany. I had only some vague idea about the Holy Roman Empire, and looked at it in the same light as the German country in which I lived.

Portrait of Otto von Bismarck, 1873.
Bundesarchiv Bild, Koblenz.

But during the Nazi regime people started to doubt whether there was something uncanny in the way the German Unification of 1870/71 had come to pass. However, it is certainly not correct to say that the Nazi regime was a necessary consequence of the German unification, or to blame that later development for the way it was constituted. Other explanations are feasible. While studying the Bismarck period I was intrigued when I discovered that the so-called *Kulturkampf*, Bismarck's struggle with the Catholic Church, had started shortly after the unification of the new German country. I could not understand why directly after the establishment of the German National State measures had to be taken that discriminated against a considerable religious minority; Catholics amounted to a third of the population.

Many years later, stronger doubts emerged about the small-German solution during my work on the Frankfurt Parliament, the elected German National Assembly in Frankfurt/Main of 1848/49. There I realized that those who supported German unification and entered into the discussion were completely unprepared for the one decisive question. To sum up, in 1848, during the *Vormärz* (i.e., the assembly prior to the actual parliamentary assembly) of the somewhat diffusely so-called German national movement, people did not sufficiently analyze and discuss the problem: How, in a political and geographical sense, should this to-be-created German state be defined? Ought this Germany to include all Germans wherever in Europe they lived? What role should the questions of language, culture, or blood play? How should one define a German? Are the questions of language, culture, or descent sufficient? What about the position of the states within the German Confederation? The German Confederation, established at the Congress of Vienna in 1815, enclosed only the western half of the Habsburg Empire; as to the Kingdom of Prussia, West and East Prussia and Schleswig did not belong to the Confederation, but the Duchy of Holstein did; also there were territories further afield like Alsace-Loraine, which was part of France, and after 1871 belonged to the Bismarck Empire. If one were to proceed from the premise that all states belonging to the German Confederation were to be included, should for instance all territories of the Kingdom of Prussia belong to the German

State? Ought the Poles with their different culture and language living in West Prussia to be automatically considered German citizens? Should the northern border of the intended National State correspond to the one of the German Confederation (i.e., the Eider River), or did the Duchy of Holstein also belong to it?

Much more complicated was the question of how much of the Habsburg Monarchy might belong to Germany? Should the ethnically German speaking and culturally German subjects of the emperor of Austria become part of the evolving Germany? And what should happen to the parts with a mixed population like Bohemia? Without too great a problem, the western parts of the Habsburg Monarchy might be considered to belong as it was part of the German Confederation. But could such a constellation still continue to exist when the German Confederation was replaced by a federal or even a centralized state, an *Einheitsstaat*? How would the emperor of Austria/Hungary react to a situation like this?

Besides, there were also German speaking peoples outside the borders of the German Confederation in parts of the Habsburg Monarchy that did not belong to the Confederation, for example in the Kingdom of Hungary, the Saxons in *Siebenbürgen*, as well as the Baltic Germans in Czarist Russia. In fact, none of these groups outside the German Confederation could be found on the agenda of the Frankfurt assembly of 1848.

No matter how far flung, if the plan to build a German National State was based on the German Confederation and the states therein, there still remained the question whether the Habsburg Monarchy should be excluded or if, at least, a part should be included. Expressing this differently: should the assembly aspire to the small-German (i.e., without Austria) or the greater-German solution (i.e., with Austria)? History decided upon the small-German solution despite the disadvantages it might bring. Around 1848, however, it is important to bear in mind how painful it was in the eyes of at least some of the people in the German national movement to exclude the culturally German part of Austria. But its inclusion would, as already described, also bring with it great difficulties. To find a way around these hurdles, the aim had to be staked back, and the assembly had to be content considering and deciding on the smaller Germany.

In this situation it is not altogether surprising that the two monarchs who would have been affected by the decision for either the small Germany or the greater Germany, the emperor of Austria and the king of Prussia, demonstrated little enthusiasm for German unification. The historians did not always do justice to King Fredric IV of Prussia particularly. It is not feasible to simply describe him as old fashioned and behind the times because he was reserved towards the Frankfurt Constitution of the Reich. He was very conscious of the danger it would produce with Austria if he accepted the Imperial Crown from the hands of the Frankfurt National Assembly. He knew that a small-German solution would in all likelihood lead to war, as indeed happened under Bismarck in 1866. As for Franz Joseph, the Austrian emperor, it was not in his interests to give up his twin position as Emperor of Austria and President of the German Confederation. On the one hand, from his seat in Vienna he was able to reign over the whole of the Habsburg Monarchy, especially after he broke the resistance of Hungary and Northern Italy in 1849. On the other hand, through the western parts of his Monarchy, the presidency of German Confederation enabled him to considerably limit the influence of the other member states of the Confederation. For a Monarch ruling over people of many nationalities, there was no advantage in identifying with one of them. Independent of the emperor's personal attitude there was, for instance, the question of how in a national state to handle Bohemia with her mixed population. If Bohemia, a part of the German Confederation, were to be integrated into a national state, would this not mean bringing millions of Czechs into – what would be for them – a culturally foreign state? How could the cultural Germans be separated from the cultural Czechs? Barring force and economic destruction, it was impossible. Considering the small-German versus the greater-German solution there would be either an ethnically mixed population in the German national state with a strong non-German population, or, by excluding the Habsburg Monarchy, a great part of the culturally German heritage would find itself outside the German State.

In the end, after the war with France, the small-German solution became a fact in 1871. The new state had a strong non-German majority of Poles in West Prussia, Frenchmen in Alsace–Loraine, and Danes in the Northern part of Schleswig. By all means the preservation of Northern Schleswig and the annexation of Alsace-Loraine were necessary consequences of the decision for a smaller Germany. However, one cannot reject the small-German solution out of hand. At the same time and in the prevailing political mood there was no morally justifiable argument against the wish of the Germans to form their National State as the French and Italians had between 1859 and 1870. All of this is primarily a practical question. But were the arguments of the German national movement during the first three quarters of the nineteenth century convincing? What about their historical foundation? Or expressed differently: did the small German solution emanate from the German history, and how did people look at that history? What was the German historical concept of the national movement in the nineteenth century? As in other nations, there is the tendency to present the past as gloriously as possible. So the Germans praised their virtues and contrasted them with the vices of their neighbours. In this the German National movement did not differ from, for instance, the Italians. It is said that a nation without a history has to invent it. The Germans did not have to invent their earlier history. The decisive question is whether the German national movement interpreted that history correctly, and right away there is a confrontation with religion. For the Poles, the Catholic Church was a symbol of their nation that they used particularly against their Orthodox Russian neighbours, but also to some degree against Prussia with her mainly Protestant denominations. As for Italy in 1848 and the following years, there seemed to appear even a unifying role for the pope, although in the end it did not turn out as practicable. In contrast to the Poles and Italians, religion was a disturbing factor for the German unification. Reformation and Counter-Reformation had left several churches fighting with each other, but none had been strong enough to displace the other. Whereas religion and its institutions presented an obstacle, it was the historian who gained in importance. It now depended on which historian would face up to the challenge. Also, as religion could not act as a unifying factor, a secular basis had to be found. Therefore the cultural inheritance offered a necessary component – German literature being key, particularly since the enlightenment. In this respect, the Protestant duchy of Weimar, with Johann Gottlieb Herder, Johann Wolfgang von Goethe, and Friedrich Schiller, played key roles. Both Catholicism and Protestantism traditionally tended to support cultural and spiritual values, though the emphasis was placed in different spheres. One only had to think about the church and residence architecture in the Catholic centres to see this. But after the French Revolution of 1789, the Catholic influence in German public life tended to decline. Because of the monumental changes of the following decades, Catholicism was at a disadvantage. Due to the secularization in the time of the French Revolution and Napoleon's reign, the worldly power of bishops was abolished, which weakened the strongholds of Catholicism in the Rhineland, Westphalia, and Franconia. The cultural centers of bishop-universities and many monasteries were lost, too. This development contributed to the so-called catholic educational deficit. Additionally, the redistribution of territories under Napoleon had a negative affect for Catholicism. Finally, the German Confederation contained only two Catholic states, even if their size were considerable, namely Austria and Bavaria, in comparison to roughly three dozen Protestant, often dwarf-sized states. Still, the two Protestant territories of Baden and Wuertemberg had a predominantly Catholic population. Their disadvantage was not balanced by the fact that the King of Saxony was a Catholic monarch in a Protestant state. In the small-German State a third of its people were Catholic, and the pushing back of Catholicism was detrimental to its influence. Additionally, it is worthwhile mentioning that the Catholic Church hierarchy was unsupportive of political agitation. All this left the field to the non-Catholics: the Lutherans, the Calvinist, and the liberally inclined Protestants including the free congregations, the non-religious, and anti-religious forces.

In its initial stage, and for quite some time, the national movement was in the hands of the Protestant Germans and Protestant students' unions like the *Burschenschaften*, founded in 1817. Clearly, and it cannot be explained otherwise why the *Burschenschaften* selected especially the Wartburg, a strong Luther symbol, to celebrate the German contribution to the 1813 defeat of Napoleon in the *Völkerschlacht* of Leipzig with the aim to bring the various German tribes closer to each other. Was there so little interest in the Catholic Germans? Even among the historians it was mainly the Protestants who interested themselves in German unification and its related history. If one looks at the chief representatives, particularly those of the so called Prussian school, in favour of a small-German solution – Johann Gustav Droysen, Heinrich Sybel, and Heinrich von Treitschke – all three were Protestant. Droysen, a son of a protestant pastor, became Professor of History in Kiel in 1840 and pledged for the empire's historical rights to the duchies of Schleswig and Holstein against the Danish Crown. In 1848 he was elected to the Frankfurt Parliament where he became Secretary of the constitutional committee. Droysen wrote important works about German and particularly Prussian history. The decidedly anti-Catholic Sybel taught at the universities of Bonn and Munich. In some contrast stood Leopold von Ranke, who established the historical maxim "history must be written as it actually happened" (*"wie es eigentlich gewesen is"*); but even he was still somewhat open to politicizing his historical research. Finally there was Heinrich Gotthard von Treitschke, whose historical writing I will analyze in more detail.

Treitschke was born 1834 in Dresden as the son of a Saxon army officer who eventually became a General. Treitschke's son later adopted Prussia as his home state, which brought him into intense controversy with his father. Initially a liberal opponent to Bismarck, however, he moved closer to the Prussian statesman when the latter showed a more national leaning and desisted from his battles against the Liberals. From 1871–84, Treitschke was a member of the *Reichstag*, the German Parliament, as a national-liberal until 1878 and then as an independent member with increasingly conservative views. He held a series of chairs. In 1866 he spent a short time at Kiel, in the following years at Heidelberg, and later at the Berlin University. His most important work was *German History in the Nineteenth Century*. Treitschke was a master of style. He often wrote with great passion. Even today his writing is fascinating to read, whatever one might think about his perspective. I analyzed two of his essays, "The Territory of the Teutonic Order of Prussia" *(Das Deutsche Ordensland Preussen)* and "Federal or Unitary State," *(Bundesstaat oder Einheitsstaat)*, a sort of manifest. Both of them first appeared with a preface in October 1864 in the month of the peace treaty of Vienna with Denmark, after the victory of Austrian and Prussian troops over the Danes. In some sense one can say that Treitschke was a his-

Heinrich von Treitschke (1834–1898)
Photo courtesy of Bundesarchiv,
Bestand Bild 183.

torian who also made history through his writing and through his influence on Bismarck. His academic colleagues criticized his way of mixing history and politics. But for the lay public, who admired his learning and practically devoured his brilliantly written work, this appeared to be more of an advantage. More than any other historian, Treitschke has coloured the interpretation of German history.

Quite openly Treitschke pursued political aims in his historical writing. By describing the, for him, glorious chapters of German history, he aimed to awaken the belief in the German people of their mission and to affect in their own lifetime a renewed position of importance. He maintained that the "correctly" interpreted history, namely the one from his point of view, offered a lesson for the present time; therefore he portrayed a German history that, in his interpretation, explained what had gone wrong. In his lessons he invited his readers the opportunity to learn from the past and how to steer the future development in certain directions so it would lead the Germans to unification under the leadership of Prussia. In order to achieve this aim, the present particularism of the individual state was an obstacle. He considered the small-state system to be a betrayal of the German mission and a disloyalty towards the greater German past.

For Treitschke, the Holy Roman Empire was the German Empire, although it had included the kingdoms of Italy and Arles (Burgundy). In the light of this equation he was able to research the thousand years of the Holy Roman Empire to examine whether German interests had sufficiently been secured. His answer turned out negative. Interestingly, in his essay he accused particularly the Staufen Emperor Fredric II of neglecting German interests, although it had been this prince who played a leading role in founding the Teutonic Order in the east of Europe that was to develop the interest of the Empire. Treitschke considered Emperor Fredric II to be more a Mediterranean personality than a German sovereign. But the main culprits for the breakdown of the Holy Roman Empire, according to Treitschke, were the Habsburgs, because they allegedly had put the interest of the dynasty before that of the Empire. In the sixteenth century, Emperor Maximilian I allegedly sacrificed the Teutonic Order to the Poles to secure an inheritance for his family. After the Reformation the Habsburgs carried a doubled guilt, because now, after the confessional division, they had returned to and consolidated the Catholic side in the conflict. Besides, according to Treitschke, from the fifteenth century onwards, the Habsburgs did not grant the Hohenzollern, the Prussian reigning family, enough influence in the Empire.

In a second essay that I would like to analyze, "Federal or Unitary State," Treitschke immediately starts to attack the Habsburgs. The Seven Years' War (1756–63) – the European part of the conflict between the Empress Maria Theresa of the Habsburg Empire and the King Fredric II of Prussia – brought victory to Prussia and the cession of Silesia, to which it had dynastic claims. Treitscheke sees here the Habsburger not giving the Reich sufficient support – in fact betraying it – but at the same time he views the Hohenzollern's victory and acquisition of Silesia as patriotic German. Amazingly, Treitschke shows strong dislike for the country squires (the *Junker*) which is difficult to combine with his admiration for Fürst Otto von Bismarck and Prussia. But he insinuates that the country squires would oppose the German national idea as he did not see a possibility to convince them otherwise. He hoped the influence of the *Junker* class could be excluded from the united Germany. But why could they not be won over? How can national unity work unless all the main groups feel content with the political structure? Or is it sufficient to merely issue orders from on high? Similarly, as a Protestant, he is critical of the Catholics in Germany, and with their strong affiliation to Rome he writes them off as Ultramontane (beyond the mountains [Alps]), meaning they were too attached to Rome. His antipathy towards the Habsburgs is only partly religious and is somewhat strange when he describes the forced union of Lutherans and Calvinists in Prussia by Fredrick William III as an achievement of German policy, along with the Customs Union, the *Zollverein*.

Even if he is not in every way a typical historian serving the German unification movement, Treitschke's essays threw a glaring light on some of the movement's basic concepts, and by predating the growing national sentiment of the nineteenth century, he prepared the ground for the popularized view of German history, which contributed to the excess of the later German nationalism. In any case, any attempt of the social sciences, incliding the historical science, to put itself into the service of the politics of the day bears with it great dangers. It almost sounds trite, that the historian must try to reconstruct the past as it was, not as he would like it to have been, and he should do this as well as he possibly can, even if such undertaking does obviously carry with it the background in which he lives. But by no means should he perceive the past mainly as a prelude to influence the future.

This begs the question: what really happened in the Holy Roman Empire? The assessment of it was ill conceived by many of the historians connected with the national movement as it predated a German National movement. In the Middle Ages there were surely at times altercations in Italy between the armies of the emperor when the soldiers, considering themselves as Teutonic or German, engaged in battles with the *Welschen* or Italians. But this sentiment was a far cry from the modern national consciousness. For troops from north of the Alps, any intervention in Italy was not so much a national war but primarily a service rendered for a higher cause, namely to support the emperor, the main pillar of the world order. The German king, or more precisely the *rex teutonicum*, was of a different order than kings of England or France. For, since the coronation of Otto the Great of the Saxon Dynasty in AD 962, the German king embodied the Roman Crown and therefore was in a certain sense the successor of the Roman emperors of antiquity. This played a role when the Pope needed the help of Otto I, like his predecessor did of Charlemagne who had been crowned on Christmas Day of the year 800. This explains why the Teutonic East-Frankish realm, and not the West-Frankish one (i.e., France) became the successor to the imperial tradition of Carolingians.

That the papacy entrusted the Teutonic kings with the task of governance was certainly often a burden for the latter. Unlike the kings of France or England, every German king had to undertake far-reaching and often risky steps to secure his rights. After being elected and crowned German king, or as he eventually was called, King of the Romans, he had to establish contact with the pope in order to ask him to be crowned emperor. On these Italian expeditions, the crowning in his Lombard kingdom presented the first stage on his way to Rome, as this mainly North Italian territory belonged to the Empire. The circumstances in Italy and particularly in Rome were often intricate and confusing. Independent from armed intervention, the Italian climate, with her mosquito-infested marshes, presented a constant danger to the health of the transalpine army, to which even monarchs succumbed. There were, however, circumstances when the pope's right to decide on whom to crown could present a complication, as this put him in the position to decide about the legitimacy of the titles of a specific king. But on the positive side it was a great honour that it was to the Teutonic kings the papacy directed its requests for help. Thereby the king-crowned-emperor embodied a particular sacred role in western Christendom which put him high above the other kings. It goes without saying that the other kings did not want to be seen as minor kings, *Kleinkönige*, as they were sometimes called in the time of Barbarossa. That the kings of France were aware of the special status of the emperor is demonstrated by the attempt of several French monarchs to be elected German king after the reign of the Staufen Dynasty. Although the popes, even in battling the Staufen, sometimes pondered the ideas of placing the dignity of the emperorship on one of the other nations, it never happened. The Teutonic Crown remained the stepping stone to the Imperial Crown.

The Teutonic kings took their mission to guard over the church and the papacy very seriously. If one looks at things as they were looked at in the particular time, then the objection of the small-German historians falls by the way, namely that the kings and emperors dedicated too much time and energy in Italy and thus neglected German interests. Similarly, the nationalistic outlook bars, for example, the understanding of an important medieval Monarch like Henry III (AD 1039–1056). The papacy and the church were in deep distress when Henry III, a very pious monarch, intervened and selected several candidates for the papacy, who initiated serious reforms of the church, one of them being the very able Leo IX. It was an inevitable consequence of this development that the Holy See then no longer proved itself as submissive towards the Teutonic kings as in its times of distress. Under the successor of Henry III, his son Henry IV, a bitter conflict developed with Pope Gregory VII that led to Henry's path of penance to Canossa in 1077, that weakened his kingdom. Some historians have expressed the view that Henry III, by giving support to the papacy, disregarded his German interests. This view misinterprets the situation of that historic period. Henry III was not a German Monarch in any modern sense. The alleged national interests did not have priority for him. As a Christian and as the leading Monarch he considered it his duty to provide the church with the best possible head. To insinuate that he, by choosing a certain pope, should have considered future, possibly adverse consequences leads to doubting his deep faith and his integrity.

Additionally, the decline of the Teutonic kingdom and the Empire, with the ensuing fall of the Staufen, is often traced back to the hostile attitude of Pope Gregory IX and Innocence IV towards Emperor Fredric II. Gregory was indeed a passionate adversary of the Staufen, but he was an honest one. It was, howev-

er, Innocence IV – a very wise but hard, assessing, and calculating
man – who stood on the threshold of a papacy declining, if sporad-
ically, from its intellectual and spiritual heights. But two remarks
are worthwhile to add here. The first is that the position of the
emperor was no longer so overpowering as before because the
French monarchy had gained in strength. From time to time the
French monarchy had given asylum to the anti-popes who stood in
opposition to the emperor, which in turn provided a counterweight
to the Holy See. Secondly, Fredric II had also made great mistakes
in his relationship with the popes. Slightly more neutrally
expressed, the relationship between emperor and pope suffered
from far too many points of friction, particularly in Italy. On both
sides, the task should have been to find a *modus vivendi*, as striving
for a balance in their actions would have been better than the fight
to the bitter end that took place. It was obvious that the affairs of
the Staufen Dynasty went badly. The Teutonic Empire suffered from
the conflict and the resulting loss of a once strong dynasty. But, in
the end, even the victor, the papacy, lost out. Whatever separated
one side from the other, they agreed and believed in their faith of a
common universal mission, even if they could not agree on the division of power and the relationship to each other. The positive
aspect of their co-operation is evident in the fact that popes in a
variety of situations called on the emperors as the natural leader for
the crusades. Somehow they needed each other. Any weaknesses in
one institution also put the other at risk, while both demanded universality and stood above the nations. The bitter fight against the
Staufen that was probably misguided and was carried on by the
popes after the death of Emperor Fredric II in AD 1250, and it
destroyed the Staufen Dynasty. The result was that the papacy fell
under the influence of the French monarchy, which indeed brought
with it devastating consequences.

The papal court had made use of the French Dynasty – the
house of Anjou – to drive the Staufen out of Sicily. The Anjou kings
reigned at first over the whole of the Norman Kingdom of
Sicily – the realm Fredric II had had before them – but soon they
lost the Isle of Sicily and only kept the south Italian mainland,
including Naples. France and Anjou-Naples now gained decisive

influence in Italy, including in Rome, and in this way formed the predominance in Italy that the popes, during their opposition to the Staufen, had tried to avoid. Thus the curie had exchanged an international partner for a national opponent, and not always an easy one. Philippe IV, named the Beautiful, acted ruthlessly against the papacy, which he subordinated to the interests of his country to a degree the Teutonic kings had never done. The German Kings in their battles with certain popes had sometimes used hard measures; but never had they resorted to crime as the French Chancellor did by effecting the assassination of Pope Boniface VIII in Anagni in 1303. After this, everything changed. The Salier and the Staufen had battled against some popes, but not against the institution of the papacy.

If there was ever such a thing as German greatness in the Middle Ages, it was not due to pure national considerations but to the relationship between the imperial dignity and the papacy that was so close that, nearly by necessity, it was bound to lead to intense frictions. It was the Christian and supra-national mission of the Teutonic kings that the Imperial Crown represented or at least required a certain abeyance to. The contrast to France is apparent. The French were far more interested in a far-reaching independence from Rome for their Gallic church than to play a supra-national role. For them the Imperial Crown would only have been a means towards an extension of French power. The Teutonic kings saw it as much more than a national venture. This was very difficult to comprehend for the people of the national movement.

How did this un-historic view come to be accepted in the time of the national movement? In a national movement like the German one there straight away appears a paradox. For the purpose of the national movement, everything depended on the "correct" historical interpretation. On the one hand, in order to achieve unification, a new, un-historical criterion of the German nation was needed that seemed somehow to have always been there although not quite visible. On the other hand, the understanding of history was barred, as in some ways, and certainly quite selectively, the past was completely out of date. The Holy Roman Empire was ridiculed as neither Holy nor Roman, although earlier on in the high Middle Ages, in their historical connection, both terms held their meaning. As stated above, the system of the many small states and very small states, which certainly sometimes went too far, were condemned, although this did not always have negative consequences. That it was possible to avoid political or religious persecution through a comparatively quick and short move to another state was of great advantage. The radical rejection of existing institutions might in fact have disadvantaged the realization of a unified German. After the Carlsbad Decrees of 1819, the Federal assembly of the German Confederation exercised strong measures against some university students' unions (the *Burschenschaften*) and limited the freedom of expression for several university teachers; it is not surprising that this measure was extremely unpopular, and the reaction, to put it mildly, amounted to extreme dislike among Liberals and radicals. But the abolition of the Confederation by the Frankfurt National Assembly impeded the work of unification. This negative attitude towards the Confederation was not a necessary aspect of the national assembly, but a consequence of a certain tendency in favour of a united states versus a federated one.

It is quite feasible to say that, generally, the national assembly pursued its own political program concerning unification. This becomes evident through closer research of their meetings. Any unification, certainly when considering the fairly recent accession of the East German territories to the German Federal Republic in 1989, carries with it fundamental changes for all sides involved; it proved favourable for most people but would be unfavourable for others. One is not always able to predict the outcome of such basic changes, which often do not become obvious until subsequent years. In the nineteenth century, the predominant circles of the national assembly intended to loosen the conservative structure of the territories, also in respect of religion. There existed some alliances or associations between the political and religious liberals and the conservatives. But logically, from the point of view of the conservative faction, they rejected many ideas of 1848. Again, they and the advocates of the greater-Germany might be looked at more fairly. Most of the time and partly out of necessity the historian finds himself on the side of the victor. It ought, however, also to be equally valuable to look at the perspective of the loser, who is not always wrong.

Unfortunately, German nationalism based itself on the highly politicized interpretation of German history, which gave it a weak foundation, which in turn explains many of its excesses. In spite of its great achievements, the German national state founded by Bismarck did not succeed in securing a feeling of stability in its citizens, neither internally nor in its external policy. An undeniable anticipation neurosis was left even in the leading circles; there remained a not quite understandable fear about internal unrest and a fear directed externally against Germany's alleged enemies who were presumed to be envious of her great success. Compared to other nations, there was also the disadvantage that the Germans could not rely on the common moral basis of a unifying religion. Thus the small-German solution produced an actual predominance of Protestantism and discrimination against Catholicism. The Protestant prejudices inhibited an unbiased view of the Middle Ages, including a more positive view of the important services that the German ancestors had given to the papacy. German nationalism slid all too easily into a way of a pseudo-religion, to some degree already before 1933, but excessively so under the national socialist regime.

As the present time offers a more detached perspective, it is possible to see the national state, and not only the German one, in new and different light. The European Community, and now the European Union, has put limits on nationalism. Perhaps the time is ripe to have another look at the German Confederation and to ask whether it really was as anachronistic as the German national movement of the nineteenth century maintained. However, it is a saddening thought that in the age of an excessive nationalism, European states engaged in horrifying wars before Europe was ready to form a community and union.

In Germany today, an impartial attitude towards history is of grave importance. Perhaps it is possible to revive in the German youth an interest in history, as understandably the young people often appear to be a-, or even anti-, historical. I would like to maintain that a careful assessment of history does matter.

Bibliography

Boedecker, Ehrhardt. *Preussen eine humane Bilanz.* Olsog Verlag: Muenche, 2010.

Bußmann, W. "Treitschke als Politiker." *Historische Zeitschrift* 177 (1954): 294ff.

Dorpalen, A. *Heinrich von Treitschke.* New York: Port Washington, 1973.

Droysen, Johann Gustav. *Aktenstücke und Aufzeichnungen zur Geschichte der Frankfurter Nationalversammlung.* Osnabruck: Biblio-Verlag, 1967.

Eichstätten, Thomas, trans. *The Frankfurt Parliament, 1948–49.* London: Macmillan, 1968.

Eyck, Erich. *Bismarck.* 3 vols. Erlenbach-Zürich: Eugen Rentsch Verlag, 1943, 1944.

———. *Das Persönliche Regiment Wilhelm II: Politische Geschichte des Deutschen Kaiserreiches von 1890–1914.* Erlenbach-Zürich: Eugen Rensch Verlag, 1948.

Eyck, Frank. *G. P. Gooch, A Study in History and Politics.* London: Macmillan, 1982.

———. *Religion and Politics in German History From the Beginnings to the French Revolution.* London: Macmillan, 1989.

Iggers, Georg G. *The German Concept of History.* Middletown, CT: Wesleyan University Press, 1983.

Lill, Rudolf, ed. *Die Revolution von 1848/49 in Deutschland und Europa: Beiträge zu einem Karlsruher Symposium im Rahmen der 14; Europäischen Kulturtage.* Karlsruhe, 1998.

Mommsen, Wolfgang J. *1848: Die ungewollte Revolution.* Frankfurt/Main: Fischer Taschenbuch, 2000.

Peterford, Hermann von. *Allgemeine Deutsche Biography.*

Raumer, Friedrich von. *Lebenserinnerungen und Briefwechsel.* 2 vols. Leipzig: Brockhaus, 1861.

Sybel, Heinrich von. *Die Begründung des Deutschen Reiches durch Wilhelm I.* Translated by Marchal Livingston Perrin and Gamael Bradford. New York: Thomas Cornwell & Co., 1890.

Treitschke, Heinrich von. "Bundesstaat und Einheitsstaat." In *Historische und Politische Aufsatze.* Originally published in the first edition of the essays, expanded in 1865, and reprinted verbatim in the third edition in 1867.

⸺. "Das Deutsche Ordensland Preussen." Published in 1862. Revised for the first edition of *Historische und Politische Aufsätze* in 1964, but not for the third Edition in 1867.

Valentin, Veit. *Geschichte der Deutschen Revolution von 1848–1849.* 2 vols. Berlin: Ullstein, 1930.

Chapter Five

MUNICH:
APPEASEMENT, 1938

Originally presented September 29th, 1988, at the University of Calgary.

P RECISELY FIFTY YEARS AGO, on September 29th, 1938, the British Prime Minister, Neville Chamberlain, and the French Prime Minister, Eduard Daladier, flew to Munich to join Hitler and Mussolini in a final effort to avert a German invasion into Czechoslovakia, which might have led to a general European war. The Munich treaty, which was dated the same day, provided for a cession of the Sudeten German territories to Germany by Czechoslovakia, and peace was preserved.

How did Europe find itself on the brink of war in September 1938, less than twenty years after the end of the First World War? Why did the fate of the German minority in Czechoslovakia – called the Sudeten Germans, named after the mountain range in the territory – cause so severe a crisis?

At the end of the First World War, Czechoslovakia was one of the states carved out of the Habsburg Empire, the Dual Monarchy of Austria-Hungary (i.e., mainly German Austria and the Magyar Hungary). Czechoslovakia was largely based on the historical kingdom of Bohemia, whose crown of St. Wenceslas had been in the possession of the Austrian-Habsburgs for centuries. The historical territory was, however, peopled by a number of ethnic groups with different cultures and languages. The republic of Czechoslovakia created in the peace settlement after the First World War was ruled by the Czechs, with some influence given to the Slovaks. Even the Czechs and the Slovaks were different from each other in their history, their religious development, their culture, and to some extent in their language. There were also a number of minorities. In broad figures, the population of Czechoslovakia was somewhere between thirteen and a half and fourteen million. Less than half the population was Czech, and less than a quarter Slovak. Ethnic Germans, who had never belonged to Germany proper, counted for rather more than the Slovaks, about three and a quarter million, or rather less than a quarter of the population of the republic. There were also substantial numbers of Hungarians and Ruthenes, as well as some Poles and Jews. As the ethnic minorities were not properly consulted after the state was founded, everything depended on the ability of the republican regime to integrate them fully in the country and to make them content, and they certainly were not. The Czechoslovakian state had been in full existence for not even a decade and a half before a cold political wind began to blow from Germany – with the advent of the National Socialism regime in January 1933.

The Nazi regime quickly abolished parliamentary government and the rule of law in Germany. The internal order was characterised by brutal repression of all groups regarded by the Nazis as hostile or objectionable, including former political opponents such as the Communists, the Jews, and Christian critics of the regime. Some minorities were entirely without protection from the mercilessness of the regime. Two main planks of the Nazi programme appeared to be the hatred of Communism and their determination to free Germany from the perceived disadvantages and discrimination of the postwar peace settlement. Hitler, in order to be able to assert Germany's position internationally, put into effect an intensive and speedy rearmament programme in contravention of the military clauses of the Treaty of Versailles of June 28th, 1919. The whole question of continuity in German history, and of the degree of difference between the Nazis and their predecessors of the Weimar Republic, has occupied the attention of scholars a great deal, without agreement being reached. In any case, for the sake of objectivity, it must be mentioned that the Nazis did not begin the breaches of the military clauses of the peace settlement, and that the ground had been well prepared by their predecessors. However, the Nazis went much further in rearming than the republican ministers, who attached considerable importance to the maintenance of good relations with the victors of the First World War.

In March 1936, Hitler remilitarized the German Rhineland in contravention of the treaty of Locarno (*Sicherheitsvertrag*) of 1925, which the previous German government had freely accepted. France and Britain, which were parties to the Locarno treaty, did not seriously oppose this move, although they were fully entitled to do so. Fundamentally, whatever the views of individual ministers and politicians of the participating countries, the public was not sufficiently concerned to make military operations against the Nazi regime viable, certainly not without a strong lead from these governments. Hitler developed a technique of lightning-quick military actions, often during the weekend, which found slow-moving democratic governments off guard. In many quarters, the failure of the French government to undertake immediate military retaliation against the movement of German troops into the demilitarized zone in the German Rhineland was later seen as a tragic error. As German rearmament was still in its early stages, and as France had remained armed, it is believed that Hitler could then have been stopped without the outbreak of a major war. In another lightning-quick move, Hitler annexed Austria to Germany in March 1938 to the openly displayed wild enthusiasm of the population. But, by order of Hitler, behind the scenes, his Storm Troopers (*Sturmstafel*) levelled the village of his family origin, close to the Czech border; and vandalized the property of Jews and people in opposition; behind the scenes, atrocities were carried out.[1]

This incorporation of Austria into Nazi Germany had severe consequences for Czechoslovakia, and again, part of the peace settlement of Versailles was demolished. But while French military action against Germany might well have been feasible over the militarisation of the Rhineland, it was hard to see what the Western powers could do over Austria. It did not take Hitler long after the annexation of Austria to mount a propaganda campaign against Czechoslovakia and its democratically elected president, Eduard Benes. Czechoslovakia, which had alliances with France and the Soviet Union, was a thorn in Hitler's side. Hitler was determined to extend German territory and his influence in Eastern Europe in connection with the policy of securing more living space for the Germans (*Lebensraum*) and to either enslave or exterminate races like the Slavs that he considered inferior and harmful. Even outside Germany, enough was known or could have been known of Hitler's attitude before he got into power.

The strong card Hitler played in the case of Czechoslovakia was that of self-determination. He claimed that the ethnic Germans in Czechoslovakia had the right to secede from Czechoslovakia and to join the German state. By early 1938, the Sudeten German party had become an important factor in Czechoslovakia. Following the establishment of the Nazi regime in Germany, considerable support was given to this party by the Berlin authorities. In the elections for the Czechoslovakian parliament in 1935, the Sudeten German party, led by Konrad Henlein, garnered over sixty percent of the German vote and emerged as the strongest party in the Czechoslovakian parliament. Even critics of the Sudeten German party among the Sudeten Germans confirmed that, particularly after the annexation of Austria, the proportion of German opponents of Henlein in Czechoslovakia shrank, probably to about ten percent by September 1938. Henlein's party was a coalition in which the National Socialists played the leading role. Henlein eventually emerged as a loyal follower of Hitler publicly, but for some time his exact relationship with the National Socialist regime had been a matter of mystery. There was pretence that Henlein was independent of Hitler. For a while he appeared to be conciliatory, for instance on his visits to England in 1937 and May 1938. Even Churchill, then out of office, who received Henlein, was impressed by the Sudeten German leader. But we now know that Henlein was in close touch with Hitler. They had agreed that Henlein should constantly be adding to his demands or improve the terms in his favour whenever any agreement on the Sudeten German question with the government of Czechoslovakia was in sight. Before the union of Austria with Germany, perhaps some autonomy within Czechoslovakia might have been acceptable to the Sudeten Germans. After the *Anschluß*, the movement for incorporation into Germany gained the upper hand among the Sudeten Germans. A minority remained opposed, such as the Social Democrats and Jews; they knew all too well what to expect from the Nazi regime.

The president of Czechoslovakia, Eduard Benes, was an experienced diplomat steeped in the ideas of Western democracy and the rule of law. Even if he and his predecessor, the founder of the state, Tomas Masaryk, had not moved quickly enough to conciliate national minorities while there was time, Benes fully realized the seriousness of the situation, particularly after March 1938. He attempted to come to terms with the Sudeten German party, but found it a slippery eel. The government of Czechoslovakia was handicapped in its dealings with the Sudeten Germans by the knowledge that other minorities, such as the Hungarians and the Poles, were also getting restive and would be using any concession made to the Germans as a precedent for themselves. Hitler had very cleverly concluded a treaty with Poland soon after coming into power. Regrettably, the Polish government was not averse to profiting from the discomfiture of its neighbour to solve the border dispute over the Upper Silesia town of Teschen in its favour. The fact that France was the ally of both Poland and Czechoslovakia made no difference to the Polish attitude.

From at least May 1938 onwards, a sudden German invasion of Czechoslovakia could not be excluded from the realms of possibility. In that eventuality, France might be called on to fulfill her obligations to Czechoslovakia, involving both in a war with Germany that might also pull in Britain. It was feared that even an incident in the Sudeten German area of Czechoslovakia might lead to war. The example of the Sarajevo assassination and the origin of the First World War were very much on people's minds. France and Britain might be drawn into hostilities because of third parties over whom they did not exercise control. From April 1939 onwards, France and Britain certainly tried hard to find a solution to the crisis. Threatening declarations by Hitler on several occasions made it appear that he was working to a certain deadline, probably of September or October 1938, if not sooner, by which time he would invade Czechoslovakia unless his demands were met. These demands were not firmly laid down, certainly not in the form in which diplomatic relations are normally conducted, and Hitler, like

Henlein, always kept some room to manoeuvre so that he could raise his terms, as was his wont, at the appropriate time.

The government of Czechoslovakia found itself in a quandary in deciding how to react to the German demands. The grant of autonomy to the Sudeten Germans might easily encourage other minorities to obtain similar concessions. While it might in theory be advantageous to the government of Czechoslovakia to insist on a plebiscite in the Sudeten territories, this too might set a bad example. Whichever way, there was a great danger of Czechoslovakia finding itself on a slippery slope leading to a complete dissolution of the country. Trying to resist the German demands single-handedly hardly offered a serious policy choice. Naturally, the Czechoslovakian government put out soundings in Paris, London, and Moscow to try and discover what help they might receive from other countries.

Eduard Daladier, a left-of-centre politician, became Prime Minister of France in April 1938, and appointed Georges Bonnet, who was further to the right, as his Foreign Minister. France was deeply divided ideologically, and these differences were bound to have an important effect on foreign policy. Great nervousness was created in France by the Spanish Civil War, which had begun in 1936 and was still raging in 1938. While the French Right was sympathetic to General Franco and regarded Fascist and Nazi movements as a bulwark against the spread of Communism, the French Left was to some extent prepared to work with the Soviet Union and the Communist International against the Nazis and Fascists. However, in many parts of the Left there were considerable reservations about increasing armaments and a traditional military approach. There was strong antimilitarism and a preference for working through the League of Nations and collective security. Daladier judged rightly that the French people were not sufficiently united for action against Germany over Czechoslovakia. He was not keen on collaborating with the Soviet Union against Germany, fearing an extension of Communist influence, and Benes was strongly opposed to working together with the Soviets, though he put out feelers to find out their attitude in case of German military action against Czechoslovakia. The Soviets replied quite correctly that their policy would depend on what the French did, in accordance with the terms of their treaty with Czechoslovakia. In other words, the French government had to make up its own mind, which it found difficult to do. The buck was therefore passed to London. Here was somebody prepared, for better for worse, to face the question of what should happen over Czechoslovakia. The Prime Minister, Neville Chamberlain, did have clear ideas on the subject.

Hitler and Chamberlain turned out to be the main players in the crisis over Czechoslovakia in 1938, and we should therefore look carefully at the British Prime Minister. Neville Chamberlain was born in 1869 as the younger son of Joseph Chamberlain, the important radical and the later Unionist politician and minister of the period before the First World War. Like his elder half-brother Austin, Neville became a Conservative Member of Parliament and minister. While Austin was Foreign Minister and one of the architects of the Locarno treaties of 1925, Neville served in various domestic portfolios. After several years as Chancellor of the Exchequer in the so-called "National Government," he succeeded Stanley Baldwin as Prime Minister in 1937. It is incorrect to say that the son of Joseph Chamberlain and the brother of Austin knew little about foreign affairs. The new Prime Minister applied himself diligently to his post, where his predecessor had often slumbered, apart from the occasional burst of energy and brilliance. Chamberlain ran the government machine efficiently and was determined to try and solve outstanding problems. He applied a business-like approach to government, including foreign policy, and this is perhaps where some of the trouble started. Although he had a good knowledge of foreign affairs, Neville Chamberlain did not

Neville Chamberlain (1869–1940)
Photo courtesy of Bundesarchiv,
Bestand Bild 183

have the necessary flair for foreign policy which, I believe, his brother Austin had to a far greater extent. Soon Neville Chamberlain became a man with a mission: he wanted to spare Europe and the world the untold suffering of another war. This in itself was a praiseworthy objective for which he can hardly be faulted, but he gradually developed a belief that only he could do it and became impatient of any criticism of or opposition to his policies. The White House believed it could take over from the State Department; or rather 10 Downing Street took over from the neighbouring Foreign Office in Whitehall. This brought Chamberlain into conflict with the Foreign Secretary who had taken over from Stanley Baldwin, namely Anthony Eden.

Eden had succeeded to the Foreign Office on the rejection of the Hoare-Laval Plan regarding Abyssinia in December 1935. He had been minister for League of Nations affairs and had been closely associated with the policy of collective security against aggression. Eden was British Foreign Secretary at the time of the German remilitarization of the Rhineland in March 1936 and did not advocate action against Hitler. In this period he devoted his attention more to Italy than to Germany, trying to stop Mussolini in Abyssinia and to prevent Italian intervention in the Spanish Civil War. In many ways Chamberlain wanted to be his own Foreign Secretary. There were also disagreements on policy, particularly regarding Italy. Chamberlain wished to go ahead with coming to terms with Mussolini, whatever misdemeanours the Fascist leader might have committed. In February 1938, Eden resigned from the Chamberlain government and was succeeded as Foreign Secretary by Lord Halifax, a former Viceroy of India, and, like Eden, a Conservative. As soon as the Czechoslovakia question became acute after German annexation of Austria in March 1938, Chamberlain became determined to have the whole problem solved without war. His basic policy was to prevent German military action that might precipitate into an international conflagration and to use the breathing space obtained to bring the parties to the dispute together and to ask them to be reasonable. The Prime Minister, on his reading of history, was resolved to avoid all empty threats. Together with the French, Chamberlain attempted to apply pressure to whichever side appeared to be particularly troublesome. This meant he would at times send signals to Hitler that he, Chamberlain, might find himself opposed by the Western Powers if he moved more quickly in making concessions to the Sudeten Germans.

The crisis intensified in May when the government of Czechoslovakia feared a sudden German invasion or a Sudeten German coup, or a combination of both, and took some emergency measures. When the first reports suggesting an imminent German invasion were received in London and Paris, the two Western governments issued warnings to the Germans. In some quarters, the absence of a German invasion was ascribed to the efficacy of Western warnings to Hitler. We cannot be so sure that this was in fact so. We now know from the German records that after what the Nazis regarded as a Czech provocation in this crisis, Hitler, in an internal military directive, committed himself more definitely than before to "smashing Czechoslovakia by military force in the near future." The British and French governments were less than pleased with the way Prague had handled the situation. They increasingly tended to regard Benes and his colleagues as recalcitrant, as obstacles to a settlement of the Sudeten German question. Thus Anglo-French pressure on the government of Czechoslovakia increased. When little progress was being made in finding a solution, Neville Chamberlain hit on the expediency of the appointment of a mediator to try and find an acceptable basis for a settlement. The government of Czechoslovakia was prevailed upon to bring in a mediator. Chamberlain chose Lord Runciman, an elderly ship-building millionaire who had been a minister in the Liberal government and more recently in the National Government. Runciman arrived in Prague at the beginning of August, and his team continued to work on the Sudeten question in Czechoslovakia until the middle of September. The mission was a failure because the will to compromise was not there, certainly not on the Sudeten German or German side. President Benes realized that concessions to the Sudeten Germans might make the future existence of Czechoslovakia impossible. Whatever may be argued by historians about the precise details of Hitler's actions and plans, it was clear that Nazi Germany was allowing the crisis not only over the

Sudetenland but over the whole of Czechoslovakia to escalate. On September 12th, the Sudeten Party rose in several places and took over some towns illegally. In response, the Czechoslovakian government authorities declared a sort of a martial law and recaptured towns taken over by the Sudeten Party. The Sudeten Party then issued an ultimatum to the government of Czechoslovakia demanding a repeal of the measures affecting the Sudetenland, with a six-hour limit. The Prime Minister of Czechoslovakia, Hodza, a Slovak, accepted the conditions providing the Sudeten Party sent an authorized representative to discuss the maintenance of order, which it failed to do. The Czechoslovakian authorities had clearly won the round, as they were able to restore order. On September 14th, Henlein fled to Germany. Up to that point, Henlein's position as leader of the Sudeten Party in relation to Hitler had not been quite clear. He consulted with Hitler on many occasions, but it may well have been compatible with Hitler's plans to permit Henlein a measure of independence. This would have fitted in with Hitler's scheme of letting the Czechoslovakian crisis develop further. In a sense, now that Henlein was in Germany he was less valuable to Hitler than previously as leader of the Sudeten Party in Czechoslovakia.

However, all these considerations were no longer so important. Chamberlain had come to the conclusion that unless he moved quickly, a German invasion of Czechoslovakia, with its threat of an involvement of France and Britain, might be imminent. A German invasion date towards the end of September was mooted. On September 15th, Chamberlain visited Hitler in Berchtesgaden – Hitler's mountain retreat – which was one of the three trips to Germany that month. The French Prime Minister, who desperately sought escape from French commitments to Czechoslovakia by direct negotiations with Hitler, agreed with the move, but would have preferred to have been present at the table. At Berchtesgaden, Chamberlain went beyond any scheme for mere autonomy for the Sudeten Germans within Czechoslovakia. Their discussion was based on the cession of areas of Czechoslovakia with German majorities. Chamberlain emphasised that he was merely expressing a personal view, and would have to consult with his colleagues in the government. The British Prime Minister tried to warn Hitler against the use of force, but he took away from the often heated discussion the impression that Hitler was determined to invade Czechoslovakia unless he obtained the incorporation of the Sudetenland into Germany. After Chamberlain returned to London, discussions in the British Cabinet and with the French government resulted in the Anglo-French plan for the cession of the mainly German areas from Czechoslovakia to Germany. Interestingly enough, the idea of a plebiscite was rejected, partly because the Czechoslovakian government did not like it – as it constituted a precedent for other dissatisfied minorities – and partly because Daladier realized that a plebiscite seemed a weapon with which the German government could keep Central Europe in a constant state of alarm and suspense. At the request of the French Prime Minister, Chamberlain reluctantly agreed to have Britain participate with France in an international guarantee of the remaining Czechoslovakia. The Czechoslovakian government agreed to cede those mainly Sudeten German areas to Germany.

On September 22nd, Chamberlain flew to Germany for a second time to meet Hitler at Bad Godesberg, close to Bonn. As the main decision of principle had already been taken, namely that the Sudeten German territories would be transferred to Germany, the British Minister anticipated a working session, to sort out details. Instead he was told by Hitler that the concessions he was bringing were no longer enough; the problem of Czechoslovakia was not just the problem of the Sudeten Germans. Now the Poles, the Hungarians, and the Slovaks were also protesting, stating that their situation was intolerable. Hitler's deliberate raising of the whole question of Czechoslovakia and its future at this stage, which went far beyond the settlement of the Sudeten German problem previously debated, endangered weeks of patient work and brought Europe to the brink of war. Hitler now demanded that the German army must at once occupy the Sudetenland, without any formalities. Later on in the talks, a deadline of September 28th was set by Hitler for the handing over of the Sudetenland to Germany. The exchange between Chamberlain and Hitler became very heated at times. In London, the Foreign Secretary Lord Halifax and the

British Cabinet were reaching the end of their patience. Lord Halifax telephoned Bad Godesberg to say the British Cabinet proposed to cancel the advice previously given to the Czechoslovakian government not to mobilize. Naturally, the atmosphere at the talks did not improve when news of the Czech mobilization was received at Bad Godesberg. Chamberlain, on his return to London, engaged in intensive discussion with his ministers. Fundamentally, he advocated acceptance of the Bad Godesberg terms, however unpalatable these might be, on the grounds that procedure was involved to a greater extent than substance, that it would be tragic to have a war when the main German demand – the cession of the Sudetenland – had already been conceded. However, even Lord Halifax, after first agreeing with Chamberlain, deserted the Prime Minister, much to Chamberlain's chagrin. Both the British and the French governments now took a firmer line, the British fleet was mobilized for September 28th, and the Czechs pressed ahead with their mobilization, though the majority of the Sudeten German reservists failed to respond. It was believed in London that unless the government of Czechoslovakia accepted the German Bad Godesberg terms by 2 p.m. on September 28th, German forces would invade Czechoslovakia. It was clear to observers that at that point even a reluctant France and Britain might become involved in hostilities. Once more it was Neville Chamberlain who took the initiative. He made proposals for a timetable for the handing over of Sudeten territories to Germany, which he hoped would be acceptable to both parties. He also appealed to Mussolini to join in an international conference to settle the Czechoslovakia crisis. Chamberlain, unlike Eden, had cultivated the Fascist regime of Italy, preferring to draw a veil over Mussolini's actions in Abyssinia and during the Spanish Civil War. These tactics now paid off in bringing about the Munich conference. In any case, Mussolini was more than reluctant to be dragged into a general war on Hitler's coattails. When Chamberlain was in the middle of making a statement to the House of Commons on September 28th on the dangerous international situation, a message was brought to him that Hitler had accepted the proposal for a conference. Except for a few dissident members, the House of Commons rose to cheer. Not only in Britain but elsewhere, there was tremendous relief that war might be averted after all.

The Munich conference opened precisely fifty years ago. Only four countries were represented in the deliberations: Germany, Italy, Britain, and France. Neither Czechoslovakia nor the Soviet Union was present. Hitler was not prepared to have the Czechoslovakians sitting at the negotiating table, and his veto was accepted. The Soviet Union was not invited partly because Hitler's opposition to Communism was taken for granted, and partly because the Western governments did not desire an extension of Soviet influence in Central and Eastern Europe.

The Munich agreement, dated September 29th, 1938, and signed in the early hours of the following day, regulated the cession of the Sudetenland to Germany by Czechoslovakia, which had already been agreed to earlier in principle. It was supposed to bring "peace in our time,"[2] as Chamberlain exclaimed on arriving back in Britain.

The agreement stated that the evacuation by the Czechoslovakian authorities was to begin on the first of October, in other words, on the day following the signing. The government of Czechoslovakia was prohibited from destroying any installation from the ceded territory. Conditions governing the evacuation were to be laid down in detail by an international commission composed of representatives of Germany, Great Britain, Italy, and Czechoslovakia. The German occupation of predominantly culturally German territory was to take place by stages in defined zones, beginning on October 1st and to be completed on October 5th. In addition, an international commission was to ascertain the remaining territories of preponderantly German character, which were destined to be occupied by October 10th. The international commission was also to determine in which territories a plebiscite was to be held by the end of November. There was to be a right of opting in and out of the transferred territories for six months. The Czechoslovakian government was to release from military and police forces any Sudeten German who wished to be so released. All Sudeten German prisoners serving terms for political offences were to be freed by the Czechoslovakian authorities. Britain and France reaffirmed their earlier participation in an international guarantee of the new boundaries of the Czechoslovakian state against further change or aggression. Germany and Italy undertook to give a guarantee to Czechoslovakia to abstain from further territorial requests once the question of the Polish and Hungarian minorities had been settled. Finally, Chamberlain and Hitler signed an agreement to settle any differences between them by consultation and to continue their efforts to assure the peace of Europe.

The government of Czechoslovakia had no choice but to accept the terms of the treaty of Munich. President Benes's fears that concessions to the Sudeten Germans would trigger a gradual dissolution of the country now proved amply justified. The Poles demanded their pound of flesh in the Teschen area of Czechoslovakia, without giving much thought to the prospect that they might be devoured next. Slovakia ought to receive its own cabinet. The Czechs and Hungarians asked the Germans and Italians to arbitrate their frontiers. Hungary was enlarged, but not as much as the Hungarians had hoped. In the meantime, President Benes had resigned, to be replaced by a successor readier to collaborate with the Germans.

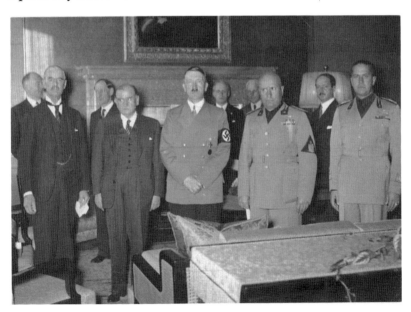

From left to right, Chamberlain, Daladier, Hitler, Mussolini, and Italian Foreigni Minister Count Ciano as they prepare to sign the Munich Agreement.
Photo courtesy of Bundesarchiv, Bestand Bild 183

In spite of some criticism, the Munich agreement was on the whole well received in both Britain and France. But gradually judgment became less favourable, particularly after the final dissolution of Czechoslovakia in March 1939. Hitler was quite open to Neville Chamberlain about his intention of destroying Czechoslovakia. He frequently talked about smashing Czechoslovakia, but this did not necessarily have to be done by war. The Munich agreements, including their reference to the question of the Polish and Hungarian minorities, marked an important stage in the destruction of Czechoslovakia. It was only too likely that the territorial losses for Czechoslovakia would not be confined to the Sudetenland and would lead to the breakup of the whole country.

And what would then be the fate of the Czechs, as opposed to the Slovaks and other peoples? Chamberlain took up the question with Hitler at their meeting in Berchtesgaden. Hitler then specifically stated that he did not want any Czechs, although in fact his demands for transfer to Germany of mixed areas with a German majority implied the inclusion of a Czech minority. British public opinion rightly hardened against Nazi Germany when Hitler established the so-called protectorate of Bohemia and Moravia. So, he was prepared to incorporate predominantly Czech territories, after having had his way by basing himself on the principle of self-determination. Thus self-determination was claimed for Germany against other states, but denied to other peoples. Could this have not been foreseen? Did any foreign statesman ever tell Hitler that he would have to delay any claim to the Sudeten Germans until he had shown that he was prepared to re-establish within Germany human rights for minorities and other groups persecuted by the regime? And how much attention was paid by Lord Halifax and Neville Chamberlain to the considerable number of Sudeten Germans whose fate was deportation to concentration camps: Jews, Communists, and all the others who had not done Hitler's and Heinlein's will?

War came eleven months later. The historian cannot fault the British Prime Minister for doing everything to try and prevent the outbreak of a European war in 1938. He rightly believed that a postponement could work, and war might never take place. But we also have to recognize that the aversion of war in 1938 constituted a major triumph for Hitler and weakened the forces for peace in Germany.

The doubting generals and diplomats had told Hitler that he would never get away with his plans regarding Czechoslovakia; the Western Powers would not permit it. But Hitler had the better judgment, at least from the short-term point of view. The historian is not able to decide whether some of the German generals would have overthrown Hitler, if it had come to war in 1938. However, after Munich, any internal rising against the Nazi regime was less likely than before Munich. This was one of the many vicious circles that made the conduct of foreign policy difficult for Britain and, in many ways, also for France. On the one hand, Chamberlain was right to ignore Mussolini's aggression, so that he could concentrate on Nazi Germany – potentially a far greater threat to Britain than Italy. But on the other hand, Hitler was more likely to think he could get away with breaches of treaties, if Mussolini had got off scot-free in Libya and Abyssinia. Also, in judging what options Chamberlain had, we have to remember that Japan presented a great potential threat to the British Empire. Whatever was foremost in the Prime Minister's mind – Britain's military weakness, combined with lack of French determination – is the chief justification for his policy. Naturally, the combination of Conservatives with National Liberals and National Labour in the so-called "National Government" must bear considerable responsibility for British military unprepared-ness as the National Government was hampered by the opposition to armaments, particularly from the Left of the political spectrum, so that the critics of Chamberlain's policy could not always make a good case. Neville Chamberlain felt that he had to keep in step with public opinion, though he might have given more of a lead to the public. The British people were not ready for war in 1938, and the Dominions were not ready either. I believe the British government was right in not moving without support from the Commonwealth and Empire.

Again the historian is not equipped to pontificate as to who gained most from the eleven months' postponement of war. The gap between Germany and the Western powers may have widened even further, quite apart from the implications of the loss of Czechoslovakia. However, there were justified fears about the state of Britain's air defences, which were no longer quite so acute in September 1939. So, one has to look both at relative strength and at certain absolutes.

There were also some moral issues. It was difficult for Britain to cold-shoulder oppressive dictatorial regimes, because there were too many of them, not only the Nazi Germany and Fascist Italy, but a Stalin regime in the Soviet Union. Were Neville Chamberlain and Daladier making the best policy choice when they were lukewarm about involving the Soviet Union in the defence against Nazi Germany? Was that a crucial link in the chain of events leading to the Soviet decision in August 1939 to come to terms with Nazi Germany? How does one measure or compare the degree of repression? At what point does the use of force become inevitable for democracies because of the potential international threat of an oppressive regime? Does external aggression always follow from internal tyranny? I am simply raising questions without answering them to underline Chamberlain's difficulties and to discourage facile moral criticism of his policy of appeasement. And can a permanent peace be built on the destruction of a country of comparatively liberal institutions, whatever the treatment of minorities, in a part of Europe where human rights violations were the rule rather than the exception? Was a new reign of peace going to be ushered in with the persecution and oppression of dissident Sudeten Germans, Jews, and Czechs during the final agony of pre-war Czechoslovakia?

Neville Chamberlain was neither a villain nor a hero. He had solid reasons for not going to war in 1938. Chamberlain was ambivalent about Hitler, at times calling him "half-mad," or at others times showing himself as rather gullible about Hitler's trustworthiness. But Chamberlain was not as gullible about the Nazis as to neglect British rearmament after Munich. Thus the champion of appeasement made his contribution to Britain's eventual victory in the Second World War.

Notes

1   The editor remembers that this happened to friends who previously had found shelter in Austria and had to flee further on to England. Joachim C. Fest, *Hitler* (Toronto: Random House, 1974).

2   *Oxford Dictionary of Political Quotations*, 3rd ed. (Oxford University Press, 2006), 80.

Chapter Six

GERMAN REUNIFICATION

Presented April 21st, 1991, at the Deutschen Gesellschaft zu Montreal (German Benevolent Society of Montreal), founded and incorporated in 1865.

ON VISITS TO BERLIN, my native city, the last one in the summer of 1987, walking through the streets of West Berlin, before the advent of Mikhail Gorbachev's time (1989–1991) as leader of the Soviet Union, I sometimes let my imagination take over and wonder what Berlin would look like in twenty-five or fifty years. And then looking over the wall onto the Potsdamer Platz from an elevated platform, I could only see anti-tank blocks and watch towers occupied by armed East German soldiers. Once upon a time the square had been one of the busiest of central Europe, teeming with life; it was now emptied of life. In 1961, to keep its citizens from fleeing the country – about a thousand a month attempted to do so – this solid twenty-seven mile long wall was erected to keep her citizens in, and cut the city in two more effectively than the old wire fence had done: Additionally, a new dangerous electric barbed-wire fence was built all along the border between the two German Republics, made wide by a piece of mined, barren land several feet wide on the eastern side – a death strip – offering danger and spreading a desolated and frightening atmosphere. Sometimes at night an explosion was heard, a deer or a person had tripped on a mine. Just to drive along by train on the western side and to look at this border made one shudder. And in Berlin, on the western side of the wall, there were crosses in memory of those who had been shot while trying to flee.

How long would Berlin be a divided city? Would the Communists be able to undermine the special status of West Berlin? I have to admit it; I did not anticipate the removal of the Berlin Wall in 1989 and the crumbling of the East German regime, certainly not so soon.

The former German Democratic Republic in the East has now joined the German Federal Republic. Berlin is once more a united city. What had been impossible for decades was brought about within a few weeks. At no time since the beginning of the Soviet occupation in 1945 did the Communists ever give the population of East Germany the opportunity to express a verdict on the regime of the German Democratic Republic. The 1953 rising against the Communist government was brutally crushed by tanks running through the streets. The Federal Republic of Germany that was established in 1949 with Bonn as the capital eventually had to come to terms with the fact of the existence of another German state, the so-called German Democratic Republic in the East which was founded at the same time. This posed many problems, as the West

Infamous Wall on the Brandenburg Gate, 1961

Photo courtesy of Bundesarchiv, B 145 Bild

German government was freely elected, unlike the East German one. Besides, the Federal Republic claimed the right to represent the whole of Germany.

Now the two German states have been united by the accession of the *Länder* (provinces) of the former German Democratic Republic to the Federal Republic. The citizens of the East German *Länder* are descendants of the Germans of the Bismarck Empire, of the Weimar Republic, and of the Nazi regime. They all speak German, though their thought patterns have developed along somewhat different paths. Since the collapse of the Nazi regime at the end of the Second World War, West Germans and East Germans have lived quite separate lives and have had dividing experiences. The East Germans – together with some of the many expellees from the German territories further East of the boundary along Oder/Neisse rivers, as well as from century-old settlements outside the German Imperial borders like from the Baltic states, the Volga-Germans in Russia, and from the Siebenbürgen in the Austrian Empire, who had settled in the Soviet zone – went straight from

Berlin, 1963. J. F. Kennedy at Checkpoint Charlie
Photo courtesy of Bundesarchiv, B 145 Bild

twelve years of Nazi totalitarianism to forty-five years of Communist totalitarianism, living a total of fifty-seven years under dictatorial rule. By contrast, West Germans, which also absorbed millions of refugees from East Germany and of expellees from elsewhere, had enjoyed democracy, parliamentary government, and the rule of law. How did these different developments arise?

The background to the dissimilar developments lies in the opposition of the Soviet Union to Western democracy and capitalism ever since the Bolshevik revolution of 1917, right up to the beginning of the Gorbachev era a few years ago. It is true that during the Second World War there was a marriage of convenience between East and West, owing to the common threat from the Nazis. The agreements concluded between the Allies on the fate of postwar Germany were premised on the Allies' continued co-operation. Unfortunately, it was already clear before the fighting in Europe ended in May 1945, as I found out from messages while serving with the British army in Germany, that the Soviets were not prepared to collaborate. The scheme agreed to by the victorious powers, while each had their own occupation zones, was supposed to conclude a common policy to be formulated by the Allied Control Council, but that proved to be a dead letter. Each of the occupying powers, the Soviets, the Americans, and the British, later joined by the French, ran their zones according to their own models and predilections, following their own hobby-horses in everything from education to administration. Whether deliberately or coincidentally, the four parts of Germany were thus increasingly drifting apart. But at least the zones run by the three Western powers, and the ethos they preached, was of democracy and the rule of law until such time the Germans would be considered ripe for self-government. Still, even during the early stages of occupation, under direct military government – at least in the British zone, but largely also in the American and somewhat later in the French one – in a desperate situation with mass destruction of cities and severe food shortages, military government officials and Germans found themselves of necessity working together. I was involved in this collaboration in Hamburg and Schleswig-Holstein[1] in the organization of newspapers that could win the confidence of the German reader after the distortions of the Nazi period. And I believe this co-operation was the nucleus of what happened later in a much bigger way in the international organizations that linked Germans to their Western neighbours.

I am not for a moment going to assert that the Western Allies abstained entirely from actions that were morally and legally indefensible. But without justifying any wrong, we have to remember the bitterness caused by the Nazi measures during the war. In any case, within a relatively short time, in the Western zones, Germans were granted more and more freedom of action and self-government. This comparatively speedy development was due to the increasing tension between the Western powers and the Soviet Union. In 1949, the three Western powers gave their consent to the establishment of a West German state, the Federal German Republic with their capital in Bonn.

The historian can only hope to assess, in any meaningful sense, the development of a period after it has come to its end. The Federal Republic still exists, but the West German state on its own had come to an end. In my opinion, the Federal Republic during the first four decades of its existence, up to unification, was remarkable, indeed quite singular, in its achievements. Nobody who had lived though the Nazi regime could fail to be impressed by the degree of political freedom and the rule of law which had been established. Bonn owed much to Weimar, but the later regime was a great improvement on the former. Bonn tried to learn from the shortcomings of the Weimar Republic founded after the First World War. Thus measures were taken against the parliamentary representation of splinter parties through demanding a certain minimum percentage of the overall votes. Also, the head of the state, the federal president, is elected indirectly, by the federal parliamentary assembly (*Bundesversammlung*), rather than directly by the people. But with the Communist regime in East Germany, which was also founded in 1949 and constituted the German Democratic Republic, a fully-fledged totalitarian dictatorship developed. Any fusion of the two states could not be based on a compromise, but was bound to involve the abandonment of political principles by one side or the other. Konrad Adenauer, the outstanding first chancellor of the

Federal Republic (1949–1964), was criticized strongly by the Social Democratic opposition, led by Kurt Schumacher (1922–1953), for not following up approaches from Stalin in 1952 which might have explored the possibilities of German unification on the basis of complete neutrality. Apart from the hypothetical nature of the Soviet move in the Stalin era, Adenauer considered the price for unity too high,[2] and I believe rightly so, for it would have halted or at least slowed down the promising political and economic regeneration of West Germany, which was only possible in close co-operation with the West. West Germany was thus bound to be drawn into the Western network, but this could not but aggravate the gulf between the two German regimes. The Iron Curtain, politically, economically, diplomatically, and militarily, went right through Germany. However, this was not the fault of Adenauer, but of Stalin and his successors, until Gorbachev took over.

The postwar diplomatic and military situation in Europe does not in itself completely account for the success of the collaboration of West Germany with such countries as France and Italy. The drawing up of the occupation zones had effects hardly intended or foreseen by the Alliance or by any particular ally. The East-West, rather than the North-South, division followed from the advance of the allied forces and had the "advantage" of promoting the decreed destruction of the Prussian state, which had spread across the North and West of Germany and was now cut up among the four occupation zones, Poland, and Russia. The objective was to destroy Prussian militarism once and for all, though it can be debated whether it was mainly the Prussian ethos that was responsible for the worst sides of German militarism. While the Allies may not have been concerned so much with the religious aspects of these measures, their incidental effect was to destroy the main bulwark of Protestantism in Germany and to release the Roman Catholic population of the Rhineland and of Westphalia from its traditional role of the minority in a mainly Protestant state. Previously, Roman Catholics had lost out in Germany every time the frontiers were redrawn since the French Revolution. For the first time in a century and a half, Roman Catholics gained in 1945. Mainly Catholic Bavaria, which had been so discontented for much of the Weimar period, could now exercise a greater influence in a West German state than it had been able to do under the previous arrangement. A German state with a strong Catholic component could connect more easily than a Protestant one with Catholic France – however hemmed in by anti-clericalism – and with Italy. Could one go further and argue that Germany could thus reconnect with the mainstream of European culture from which the Lutheran and Calvinist Reformation had severed it? Obviously this is a matter of interpretation, and all I can do is advance a tentative hypothesis. In any case, collaboration of the Rheinlander Adenauer with De Gaul (in France) and with De Gaspari (in Italy) yielded a rich harvest culturally, politically, and economically, turning the Franco-German hostility of well over a century (*Erbfeindschaft*) into co-operation and friendship and enabled the Federal Republic to join the European Economic Community as an equal partner. The economic development which had begun with the painful measures of currency reform in 1948, when one hundred Reichsmark converted to ten Deutschmark, had been advanced considerably by Marshall Aid and received a further boost through becoming part of the Common Market. At the same time, the Federal Republic cultivated its relationship with the United States and joined the North Atlantic Treaty Organization.

Once somewhat settled, the Federal Republic did its best to make compensation for the crimes committed by the Nazi regime. Thus those who had suffered persecution because of their religion and race were paid restitution, also considerable aid was given to Israel. At the same time, the Federal Republic did not forget its own citizens who had been unlucky enough to have had their possessions on the wrong side of the Iron Curtain or who had lost them due to Allied bombing. "Equalization of Burdens" (*Lastenausgleich*) gave financial aid to victims from funds derived by levying taxes on those who had fared better. Restitution and "equalization of burden" underlined the moral mission of the Federal Republic, ranking high among the measures that helped to restore German prestige after the war and to leading Germany back into the community of nations. What also proved very reassuring to West Germany's neighbours was the restraint shown by the Federal German govern-

ment in the face of East German provocation, such as border shoot-
ings and the constant dissemination of false information and disinformation with the aim of destabilizing the Federal Republic.

When the German Democratic Republic collapsed, it shared this
fate with other Communist states in Europe. Communist governments realized that many of their citizens were only waiting for an
opportunity to escape from the country and therefore took enormous precautions to prevent illegal emigration. The East German
regime was in a more precarious position than some of its neighbours. When an East German managed to get out of the country, he
was in a better position to find a job than a Pole or a Czech because
he was entitled to enter and settle in West Germany as a German
citizen; he also did not have any linguistic obstacle to surmount.
Even more than Poland or Czechoslovakia, East Germany had been
dependent on the co-operation of its Communist neighbours to
prevent their country from being used as a springboard for emigration. Once the co-operation was no longer forthcoming in view of
the thaw emanating from Gorbachev's Moscow, the East German
government could no longer control emigration. The breakdown of
authority in one important respect undermined the credibility of
the whole regime and led to its downfall. What conclusion can we
draw from this sequence of events?

For one reason or another, economic or political, the East
German regime had failed to satisfy its people as a whole.
Doubtless some of the social and educational policies of the government were sincere attempts at betterment, but they were out-
weighed by the dark aspect of the regime about which communist
propaganda tried to delude us and which can now be well documented. One important failure must be attributed to the near
absence in the sphere of human rights. There was an extensive system of personal surveillance practiced by the state security service
(the *Stasi*) which accumulated an enormous amount of actual and
invented evidence incriminating individuals. The disposal of the
files, to which there is no easy solution, is going to pose huge difficulties for the future. The mistrust which had been sown will take
many years, if not decades, to disappear. The resignation of a number of politicians after allegations of assisting the state security

apparatus is evidence of this. Much of the administrative, police, and judicial system was so much involved in repression, that it has been discredited. Again, it will take a long time to sift the personnel, such as teachers, court judges, and policemen, so that all those who were guilty of injustice and inhumanity can be removed. Anybody, such as myself, who was involved in denazification, will not underrate the difficulties arising from the application of so-called laws which were in fact completely unjust. On the whole, categorization does not help, each individual has to be considered separately, but this in turn makes the whole process quite subjective and may sometimes even be unjust.

The treatment of political prisoners was often appalling. It is sad to think that Communists who had themselves suffered at the hands of the Nazis did unto others what they would not want to have done unto themselves. Recently, Erich Honecker, the former East German leader, was spirited out of Germany to the Soviet Union by his Russian friends because he had been imprisoned under the Nazis but now was involved in an inquiry regarding his responsibilities in the brutalities during his own regime. I am not so sure, whatever the merit of the proceedings, that his persecution under the Nazis serves as is a convincing argument. In any case, the methods used to keep East Germans in the country against their will, such as the order to shoot to kill escapees, were unacceptable.

For many years, East Germany was praised and was dressed up as a showcase of Communism. This theory has been thoroughly exploded. It is now clear that many East German factories were using out-of-date equipment, often creating health hazards for its workers. Environmental considerations were largely ignored. The much-valued full employment was in fact under-employment, with supplies often running out, and with serious overstaffing. An article in the German weekly *Die Zeit* recently pointed out that it is only a small minority in every country that supplies the innovative ideas leading to new methods and to the improvement of techniques. In a Communist country like East Germany, this minority had little chance to play any part.[3] This is only one of many disastrous consequences of people not being able to voice their opinion openly, to offer constructive criticism, and to tell the truth. The effect of

Berlin Potsdamer Platz in the Heydays (1929)
Photo courtesy of Bundesarchiv, Bestand Bild 183

brainwashing, too, will last for a great many years. There is, indeed, some evidence that current Communist propaganda may yet continue to celebrate some successes and impede the process of integrating the East German population into the Federal Republic.

Once the mass exodus from the German Democratic Republic started in the last months of 1989, particularly after the dismantling of the Wall, the Federal German government was under enormous economic pressure to take steps without delay to deal with the situation. For years reunification had been discussed in West Germany in theory, and I remember reviewing a book on it which struck me as quite remote from reality. So long as the Soviet Union rejected German unification, nothing could be done. The acid test was the degree of support the Soviet government might give to the East German regime. Before Gorbachev abandoned the traditional Soviet policy of coming to the "aid," that is military intervention, of any Eastern European Communist regime in trouble, all that a Western government could do was to make the best of a bad situation. While one may have reservations about certain aspects, on the whole, West German policy towards the other German state presented an admirable balance by accepting reality without excessively compromising principle. In retrospect, one can conclude that both Adenauer's establishment of close ties to the West, and Willy Brandt's *Ostpolitik* of an opening towards the East in the late 1960s and early 1970s, were well timed and contributed to eventual reunification.

The current coalition between Christian Democrats, lead by Chancellor Helmut Kohl, and the Free Democrats, represented in the government mainly by Foreign Minister Genscher, had to decide whether to accept the challenge of reunification – which history had dropped in their lap – or whether to refuse it. Nobody in the Federal German government was unaware of the huge problems and high costs of reunification. There was no pulling back, however difficult any financial quantification might be. Thanks to the determination of Chancellor Kohl, no time was lost in facing up to the long-term aim of unification and to the solution of urgent intermediate problems that could not be delayed. In carrying out the external aspects of the policy, Kohl was skilfully assisted by Genscher, the longest serving Foreign Minister of any leading country in the world. Thus the Christian Democrat–Free Democrat coalition rose fully to the historical occasion, which cannot be said for the opposition, the Social Democrats. The Social Democrat candidate for the chancellorship, Oskar Lafontaine, was without doubt correct in pointing out that the government underestimated the costs of unification and that increased taxes could not be avoided, in spite all of Kohl's assurances. It is indeed unfortunate that the chancellor was rash enough to commit himself to holding the line on taxes, and he has had to eat his own words since. That special tax levied to help the Eastern provinces is still collected today. But

Helmut Kohl (1930–)
Photo courtesy of Bundesarchiv, B 145 Bild

Lafontaine failed to provide any constructive alternative to Kohl's unification policy.

At one time it appeared as if Kohl was in too much of a hurry to get on with unification and was suspected of trying to secure party political advantage. This interpretation has been largely proved wrong. Kohl's instinct of striking while the iron was hot, even if he did not always carry out all the desirable consultation, particularly at home, nevertheless proved correct. The international constellation was particularly favourable so long as Gorbachev was still in his reforming phase and Sheverdnadze was his Foreign Minister.[4] We now know that the days for the Foreign Minister were numbered and that Gorbachev became increasingly dependent on the traditional Communist establishment. Not only did the West German government obtain the consent of the Soviet government, one of the four occupying powers with rights in Berlin, to unify both Germanys, but Moscow even agreed to the whole of the new German state now belonging to the North Atlantic Treaty Organization, NATO. And the Western powers, too, gave up their rights in Germany. The Soviet Union, however, was permitted to keep its troops on German soil for a limited period (until 1994) in view of the logistical difficulties of major troop movements, and they secured massive financial help from the German government to provide housing in the Soviet Union for the returning troops. Considering that not only the Soviets, but even some Britons, only until recently had reservations about the revival of Germany, and appeared quite happy to shelter behind the Soviet *niet*, the successful end of the negotiations with the four former Allies becomes all the more remarkable. Germany's integration into the European Community and into the North Atlantic Treaty Organization certainly helped to calm general fears abroad about a resurgence of German nationalism.

Turning to domestic factors, how realistic is this fear of German nationalism? What are the attitudes of West and East Germans towards their country and its history? Interestingly enough, it was the East German regime that rediscovered German and particularly Prussian history. When some of us visited the palaces of the Prussian court at Potsdam in 1987, when we still had to go though the unpleasantness of border controls, the official guides even had good things to say of the Prussian kings. The regime made history easy for itself by selecting readings that excluded the Nazi period. The communists regarded themselves as liberators of the East Germans from their enemies, the Nazis, and this construction was used by them, with somewhat doubtful logic, to avoid any restitution to the Jewish victims of Nazism.

Unlike the West Germans, East Germans could never in the nature of things achieve a relationship of mutual trust with the troops of their former occupying power, and as their attitude to countries like Poland and Czechoslovakia was affected by the mass expulsion of Germans from those territories, East Germany remained comparatively isolated and more "German" than West Germany. The official line about Socialist allies could not overcome these realities. After initially being very destructive, the East German regime appeared to have been somewhat more successful in getting the population to take pride in its more distant past. Through the control of the media, it was thus able to propagate a particular view of history, unlike the authorities of the Federal Republic, which operated in a pluralistic environment. There, even comparatively modest steps taken by the West German Federal Government, such as the creation of a German historical museum, were questioned in some scholarly circles, fearing that an official interpretation of history might emerge. This apprehension was due to the belief that the West Germans were not sufficiently familiar with their recent history.

This lack of knowledge certainly applies to many West Germans, particularly to the young. There are negative and positive reasons for this. On the negative side there is an undeniable feeling of being ashamed of the recent German past on the part of many people. In the years after the Second World War, children often questioned, though not necessarily openly, the actions of their parents in the Nazi period. Teachers found the treatment of the former regime in their class extremely difficult and often avoided it. A simplistic view of history, seeing it as a struggle between "progressive" and "reactionary" forces, often with some Marxist jargon about the class struggle thrown in, failed to do justice to the complexities of

German history. The contribution made by groups which did not fit in with a crude left-wing view of history, such as towards the nobility and the churches, was often overlooked. Travelling frequently about in West Germany, and particularly visiting universities and mixing with students, one often felt that an a-historical or even anti-historical attitude prevailed among many young people. The rationalization for this outlook was that nationalism was outdated. Indeed, clearly the national movements in Europe of the last two centuries often put forward oversimplified theories, and the extreme ones lead to the commitment of the most terrible excesses. But as we tried to explain in the British-controlled press in the British zone of Germany in the months after the end of the fighting, while nothing can justify an intolerant nationalism, there is such a thing as a positive love for one's country. Some common beliefs and ideals, indeed, are necessary to hold a country together, and an entirely negative view of one's history is self-destructive. Positively, many young Germans felt that European integration made national feeling outdated; in its extreme, that is accurate. But the sense of belonging to a wider European community does not supersede country and nation, but merely sets these in a proper context of co-operation with one's neighbours. In a sense, the new Europe represented by the European Economic Community is a return to the earlier concept of a Christian Europe, now in a secularized form, though at the same time drawing on the religious and cultural past. For its success, The European Economic Community requires the viability of the institutions of its member countries, including some basic agreement on what each nation stands for. And in our context, it needs the continued coherence of its German member state, now very much enlarged.

What are the tasks ahead for the new Germany? They are daunting. East Germany, for forty-five years a communist state, has been integrated into the constitutional and capitalist free market system of the Federal Republic. For the fusion of the two states was not achieved on the basis of a compromise between two constitutions, but on that of the accession of the German Democratic Republic to the Federal Republic of Germany. That this was possible without formal difficulties was due to the far-sightedness and confidence in the future of the German parliament who drew up the Basic Law for the Federal Republic in 1949 during the chancellorship of Konrad Adenauer, the Christian Democratic leader (CDU), and Theodor Heuss, the Free Democrat leader (FDP), who had become the first Federal President. It was specially stated in the preamble that the Basic Law was passed to provide a new order for a transitional period and that in doing so the German people represented by the West German Provinces (*Länder*) was also acting for those Germans who were denied participation – obviously a reference to the Soviet zone of Germany. The preamble finished with a call to the whole German people to complete the unity and freedom of Germany in free self-determination. Forty-one years later, the hope of the fathers of the Basic Law was fulfilled in the treaty between the Federal Republic of Germany and the German Democratic Republic on the accession of the East German Provinces (*Länder*) to the Federal Republic, as well as of East Berlin, which was to be amalgamated with West Berlin to form a united city and to constitute a *Land*. The treaty modified the Basic Law, among other things, stating that the unity and freedom of Germany had been completed. This is particularly important as Germany now gave up all claims to earlier territories and colonies. Germany formally, according to its constitution, ceased to be a revisionist power and accepted the frontiers of Europe as they are. The amended Basic Law of 1990 thus sets the Federal Republic apart from, for instance, the Weimar Republic, which never gave up the claim to the territories it lost to Poland. Chancellor Kohl appeared to dither for a time, but in the end came down on accepting the Polish frontier along the Oder/Neisse rivers; actually this was a legal issue, as only a united Germany could accept the final borders.

Whatever one's moral objections to the expulsion of the Sudeten Germans from Czechoslovakia and of the Germans from Polish territories, there is now no longer any substantial area outside Germany inhabited by Germans which could be claimed. The preamble to the unification treaty admirably summarizes the position; the new Germany wants to assume in peace and freedom as a member of the community of nations having equal rights, in a democratic social state based on the rule of law. In view of the past, Germany

especially recognized the responsibility it has for a democratic
development in the country which remains committed to peace
and to respecting human rights. The hope is that German unity can
make a contribution to the unification of Europe and to the establishment of a peaceful European order in which frontiers no longer
separate and in which all European people can live together in
mutual confidence. The treaty reaffirms the inviolability of frontiers and the territorial integrity and sovereignty of all states in
Europe within their frontiers. These sentiments cannot be simply
written off as political rhetoric. They mirror deeply held convictions.

The complexity of the fusion between the two states is reflected
in the treaty whose text runs to 244 pages.[5] One of the first matters
with which the treaty deals is a matter that has attracted a great
deal of international attention: the question of the capital city. The
treaty declares that Berlin is the capital of Germany, but that the
question of the seat of Parliament and government will be settled
after the unification of Germany. While Soviet troops are still sta-
tioned in the former German Democratic Republic, the question of
the move of the government to Berlin does not arise at the moment.
But where should the capital, in more than a formal sense, be in the
long run? There have been suggestions that the requirement of
Berlin as a capital might be satisfied by the move of the federal
president to Berlin. But it does not make much sense to have the
president in a different place from the chancellor. There is a lively
discussion going on in the German press about the relative merits
of leaving the real capital – which is the actual political centre in
Bonn – and later on moving it to Berlin, which would reflect a
deeper meaning of German history. Bonn symbolizes Germany's
reconnection with Western Europe, whereas Berlin would orien-
tate Germany more to the East. It would be a move from a Roman
Catholic to a Protestant capital, from the Rhineland, which admittedly since 1815 was part of Prussia, to the heart of Prussia itself,
but which as a *Land* does not exist anymore.

While I believe reunification was the only option, I am not
underrating the difficulties inherent in the process. To date, the
Federal Republic has been very stable. Any extreme movements of

right and left were short-lived in their electoral successes. The vast majority of the electorate voted for mainline parties which were solidly behind the democratic and parliamentary constitution and the rule of law. The "Greens" have posed certain problems as they are at least to some extent a political movement rather than a political party in the full sense, but they have as a rule operated within the constitution. They have even assumed governmental responsibility in some states as partners of the Social Democrats, though great difficulties have arisen in these coalitions.

However, there have been terrorist movements operating in West Germany, like the now defunct Baader-Meinhof gang, which became the *Rote Armee Fraktion* (Red Army Fraction or R.A.F.). Recently the civilized world was shocked by the news that this organization murdered in his home in Düsseldorf the Federal Trustee Officer for East Germany state properties (*Treuhand Stelle*), Detlev Rohwedder, who was charged with the task of privatizing East German state property. Only two years ago the chairman of the Deutsche Bank, Alfred Herrhausen, an outstanding, able man, was also assassinated by the R.A.F. Obviously the R.A.F. has been trying to capitalize on the discontent in East Germany with the economic and social consequences of integration. It is now known that West German left-wing terrorists up to some years ago used to find a haven in the German Democratic Republic. With this refuge no longer available, and the East German state security service no longer functioning, it was hoped it would be possible to eliminate these terrorist cells altogether, but this has not proved to be the case. Clearly, every effort must be made to crush terrorism completely. It is obvious from interviews with terrorists who have abandoned the cause that killing had become a means to an undefined end, or an end in itself.[6] Without wishing to minimize these activities, they have been able to impede the progress the Federal Republic has made and is making. But it is regrettable and indeed very sad that there is now serious discontent in Germany that the R.A.F. wishes to exploit. How is it that while the West Germans pour enormous sums of money into East Germany to straighten out a calamitous situation they did not cause, the people who are being aided are discontent with the donors and particularly with the government of Chancellor Kohl? Does this discontent reveal anything about the motives of those whose actions and demonstrations brought down the Communist regime in East Germany?

When the momentous change began to occur in the Central and Eastern European satellites of the Soviet Union, the reaction of most people in the West was relief at the overthrow of dictatorial regimes and at the ending of human abuses. There seemed to appear a clear division between oppressors and oppressed. We rejoiced at the defeat of oppressors. We felt like that about the downfall of Erich Honecker and the *Stasi*. We rightly admired the courage shown by the demonstrators in Leipzig, for instance, in the spring of 1989. In the elections, the East Germans cast their votes in the vast majority for moderates, and largely eschewed extremes.

Under the old dispensation, East German industry was sheltered by the Council Of Mutual Economic Assistance (COMECON), an economic organization prompted by the Marshall Plan of the Western powers. It lasted from 1949–1991 and had linked the USSR with Bulgaria, Czechoslovakia, Poland, and East Germany from 1950–90. It was joined by Mongolia in 1962, Cuba in 1972, and Vietnam in 1978, with Yugoslavia as an associate member. This system has now disappeared, and the pain of transition was setting in. Without the COMECON, East German industry simply could not function anymore because it was badly organized, its equipment outdated and hopelessly overmanned, which resulted in practically nonexistent unemployment, and the quality of most products was poor. It cannot compete in the world or even within a German market, and East Germans in one way, as customers, endorse this verdict, as they will buy goods made outside East Germany whenever they can. As workers and citizens in the East German territories now belong to the Federal Republic, they grumble about the consequences of the necessary reorganization. They have begun to blame Chancellor Kohl for broken promises. There is a serious danger of the West German backlash here. And West Germans are already asking the question whether the East Germans got rid of their Communist regime primarily because of its violation of human rights or because they wanted to share the higher standard of living of the West. Some support is given for the latter, materialist view by a revival of fond memories of the welfare state the Communists used to provide.

Speedy reunification was the right decision. There was no alternative, in spite of the different and diverse ways the two parts of Germany had developed over nearly half a century. In one sense, that of a meeting of minds, the situation may be more difficult in 1991 than it would have been in 1945. Most Germans in 1945 were open to the ideas coming from the West; many were only too happy to abandon the ideas of the Nazis and the discredited German nationalism of the recent past; having fallen for these ideas, they had been ready to revise and learn. At present, and at all levels of society, East Germans find it difficult to adapt to the new situation. They have not shaken off the effects of decades of Communist propaganda downgrading the achievements of the West German Federal Republic as materialistic and reactionary. Some of them may still hanker after what they regard as a third way, an intermediate solution between capitalism and statism, though in fact the Federal Republic, with its free enterprise system mellowed by a social security net, may have indeed followed this intermediate path. Unlike the Germans of 1945, the East Germans of 1991 lack economic realism, and fail to take into account that the state cannot go on subsidizing because the subventions have to be financed by the taxpayer. When it comes to economic enterprises, they find difficulties with basic capitalist concepts such as proper pricing. In many cases they have become accustomed for years to working only part of their shifts because their supply had ran out. For the moment, they now lack the positive attitude to work that Germans – including East Germans – had in 1945. All one can say at present is that in the short term there are going to be enormous problems and considerable frictions. It remains to be seen how these can be overcome. If they are dealt with as they ought to, the prospects look excellent.

So we end with what we began, with the constant interaction between events in Germany and the rest of Europe.[7] The historian can say no more.

P.S. A good twenty years after the collapse of the Berlin Wall and the subsequent demise of the Soviet Union, the opening of British Foreign Office Documents gives access to British policy overseas.[8] And the article published in the *Times Literary Supplement* of October 30th, 2009, "They wanted to be free," refers to a large number of monographers of the revolution of 1989.

Notes

1   Frank Eyck, *A Historian's Pilgrimage: Memoirs and Reflections* (Calgary, AB: Detselig Enterprises, 2009).

2   Hans von Herwarth, *Von Adenauer zu Brandt: Erinnerungen* (Berlin: Pyrinäen Verlag, 1990), 127–31.

3   M. Miegel, "Leistung lohnt sich nicht," *Die Zeit*, 22 March 1991.

4   "The Kremlin pushed to squashed revolts," *Calgary Herald*, 11 April 1991, A12.

5   *Presse Information der Bundesregierung*, Bulletin Nr. 104, 6 September 1990, 877–1120.

6   See, for instance, the interview with the former R.A.F. terrorist Werner Lotze in *Die Zeit*, 30 November 1990, 7–8.

7   Here I want to thank warmly my colleague at the University of Calgary, Dr. Erich Waldmann, Professor Emeritus of Political Science, for allowing me to draw on his extensive knowledge of contemporary Germany and on his excellent archives.

8   Patrick Salmon, Keith Hamilton, and Stephan Twigge, eds., "German Reunification 1989–1990," in *Documents of the British Policy Overseas*, series 3, volume 7 (London: Routledge 2009).

Chapter Seven

NATIONALISM AND INTERNATIONALISM

Presented September 25th, 1975, for the Humanities Association of the University of Calgary.

HISTORICALLY, the concept of both nationalism and internationalism has evolved over many centuries. Also, developments affecting one of the concepts usually have had effects on the other.

Before voicing any value judgment, let us – in as neutral a manner as possible – look at the two terms: Nationalism is one of the unsatisfactory and vague terms that the historian has to be prepared to accept. It can be used both in a neutral or moral sense, and in the latter often with strong disapprobation. I will use it in a neutral sense throughout, unless otherwise qualified.

Naturally, nationalism has as its object to further the interest of a possibly single nationality, i.e., a group of people sharing the same heritage, language, customs, etc. Tentatively, I suggest visualizing a nationality as a group of people, with or without a state and government of its own. Internationalism could then be the furthering of objectives going beyond one nation and benefiting more than one nation, spreading from a group of nations to a substantial region and finally to all mankind. International or supra-national organizations or units could take account of nationalities, or at least of countries or states, that to some extent would reflect the different nationalities within their borders, or they could ignore them.

The large empires of ancient times (eg., the Roman and the Persian empires) subjected countries to their rules, even if they invariably did not destroy all local administration. But certainly a vast institution such as the Roman Empire of ancient times was bound to see any further development of the political and religious institutions of the people under their control as a potential threat to its existence. In the days of the Roman Empire, the rulers often perceived a conflict between the rights of various peoples and the interests of the empire, a conflict or a possible conflict between the parts and the whole, between what was to develop as the national, on the one hand, and something larger, supra-national, on the other. But beyond that, we are not likely to get very much agreement. It would be very difficult to assert that Rome did better for all its subject peoples, or indeed did worse, based on any of the generally accepted criterion of today, such as the promotion of civilization and of more humane conditions. What about Roman treatment of the Jews?

Even if we find criteria of judgment on which we are agreed, which is doubtful, the application of these criteria is not easy. Some will assert that the Germanic tribes conquered by the Romans benefited from the higher civilization of their conquerors. But one should challenge this whole criterion and argue that peoples can develop best by developing their own institutions and customs, and indeed that there is something terribly patronizing about spreading civilization by means of the sword, which will lead to another important international reaction. How happy can we be, for instance, about forced Christianization?

A credit and debit balance or a profit and loss account between the advantages and disadvantages of the Roman, or indeed the modern British, Empire for the subject peoples is difficult to draw up. How much do the benefits of the Roman or British laws and the restrictions of warfare weigh against the loss of popular institutions and often of liberty and even life itself?

Regarding Christianity, the great persecutor of the early Christian Church was the Roman Empire, but it became its ally and protector in the fourth century, indeed it adopted Christianity as the state religion. From the Christian point of view, there were undoubted benefits in this development. However, the character of Christianity changed through this association with the power of the state – and not only to its advantage. Thus during the final phase of the Ancient Times, factors came into play which delayed the full development or even the possibility of the idea of nationality for about a thousand years.

The Roman Empire had deeply influenced Europe and the adjoining territories. Even after the fall of the West Roman Empire during the fifth century, the concept of a great empire ruling over a large part of Europe and other territories remained strong. Christianity was an international movement that did not halt at the frontiers of a state and could therefore not be entirely identified with one nation or country. But the division of the Roman Empire into West and East eventually led to the establishment of two rival Christian persuasions: the Latin one based on Rome and the Orthodox one based on Constantinople/Byzantium.

The memories, still alive, of the secular Romans Empire and the aspirations of the Latin Church represented by the Pope in Rome were combined in the creation of the concept of a new Empire (from AD 800 on) that was eventually called the Holy Roman Empire and later bore the suffix "of the German nation."

In the centuries that followed, this concept of the new Roman Empire – this time Christian – was not as devoid of meaning as it became by the time of its dissolution during the reign of Napoleon I in 1805. Under the medieval Christian system, church and state were closely interwoven; they represented two connected aspects of life. Charlemagne, Otto the Great, Fredrick Barbarossa, and the other emperors were to some extent the secular counterparts of the religious head of Western Christendom, the pope. They certainly did not have formal authority over all the territories in which the Latin rite was practiced. However, the empire was not confined to those regions which later formed part of Germany, but at various times extended beyond the regions of Switzerland and of Italy, Spain, today's Southern France, to the Low Countries, to Bohemia, etc. In Western Christendom, whether under the Emperor or not, Christianity of the Latin rite prevailed and constituted a strong bond between the different people. Latin was the language of the church, the language of the law, legal documents, and the learned. Thus an essentially common form of worship united England, France, the Italian territories, and what later became Germany. The division between Christians on the one hand, and Jews or Mohammedans on the other, was in many ways more important than that between, for example, the English and the French. Also, the establishment of the feudal system often cut across boundaries between peoples, their customs, and languages. Rulers, whether by conquest or by inheritance, were often not natives of the territories over which they assumed authority. There was little room in the Middle Ages for anything like territorially rounded states based on the people. Administratively its peoples were the vassals or subjects of a ruler, even possibly under a knight only. Territorial princes benefited and states were established primarily on dynastic lines, and only incidentally on those of nationalities. In many parts of Europe it would have been difficult for a man or a woman to say to what people he or she belonged. A break in this order in which nationality had played little part came with the Reformation. Western Christendom broke apart, and the empire gradually weakened.

For many centuries before the sixteenth century, there existed a vague international system in Europe. The Reformation destroyed whatever coherence remained in Western Christendom, affecting both the universal church and the supra-national institutions of the Holy Roman Empire. The structure of governments and society in Europe also changed as a result of new attitudes manifesting themselves in the Renaissance as the pace of trade and economic life in general quickened and as the strength of the feudal system declined accordingly. In the short run, the breakup or decline of supra-national institutions did not on the whole benefit the nationalities in Europe. Initially, the beneficiaries were the territorial rulers and the dynastic states. In the long run, however, the Reformation had important direct and indirect effects favouring the nationalities. The removal of universality in Western Christendom endangered the whole concept of orthodoxy, for there was not one but several orthodoxies. The exhaustion produced by the prolonged and bitter inter-religious strife had first effected some tolerance and then started to weaken the religious influence over society. Positively, in Protestant countries, the Reformation led to a greater interest in the native languages. In Germany, this was brought about through Luther's translation of the Bible into the vernacular and his hymns

enriching the use of the common language. As a further development two centuries later, the age of enlightenment brought the
flowering of secular German literature accompanied by the growing indifference to religion.

By 1789, with the French Revolution, the forces which had prevented modern nationalism from emerging were in decline. The
churches in Europe – Catholic, Protestant, and also Russian
Orthodox – were in disarray. This world was becoming far more
interesting than the next. With the division of the churches and the
decline of religion, the Holy Roman Empire had become a concept
empty of meaning. After all the bitterness generated by the Seven
Years War between the empress Maria Theresa and King Frederick
II of Prussia, there was now some co-operation between the
Eastern Powers (Austria, Russia, and Prussia). However, this limited international co-operation was used for the cynical annihilation
of Poland and its partition among them from 1772 onwards. But I
am not thereby implying that the Poland of 1771 was a national
Polish state.

The role of the monarchs changed under the influence of the
enlightenment. The workman like approach of King Fredrick II of
Prussia and Emperor Joseph II of Austria removed part of the aura
of mystery that had surrounded earlier rulers. The contempt for
tradition displayed by the reforming zeal of Joseph II of Austria did
much to undermine the special position of the monarchy with its
solid traditional elements. In a sense this special position had arro-
gated to itself by adapting the new ideas too keenly and by keeping
up with the times. This was as much a factor for the downfall as the
ineffectiveness of some of its latter-day representatives. The weakening of the monarchy allowed the nation to emerge.

It is no coincidence that modern nationalism was born in a revolutionary movement against a king (i.e., Louis XVI of France), of an
old-style territorial state, and that it won its spurs against an inter-
state coalition of monarchs to uphold the old order which gradually disintegrated because of their divergent interests. The kingdom
of France became the republic of the French people. The nation
could arise because the old form of representation by estates was
swept away to be replaced by equal rights for all citizens, leading

eventually – though not at once – to one-man-one-vote, and then to one-man-or-one-woman-one-vote. The rights of man or the citizen-within-the-state concept found their counterpart in the assertion of the right of a people to self-determination; that is, to determine in which state they would chose to remain or if they so wished to become independent, to form and join a national state of their own. The French did not keep republicanism and nationalism entirely to themselves but exported it with missionary zeal.

Many territories without organic unity could not withstand the onslaught, even after the republican plan of the programme had been abandoned with the advent of Emperor Napoleon I. The new French regime made conquests both morally and militarily. Italy was allowed to achieve a measure of national unity under French auspices. Nationalism spread not only by example, but also by reaction, like the national movements which followed. But contrary to the ideas the French applied to themselves, in their conquests they threatened the national aspiration of other peoples. When French nationalism was combined with the ambition of a Napoleon, citizens of many peoples in Europe felt that they had to resist, including the Spaniards, the Germans, and the Russians. Of equal importance was the co-operation called forth by the unbounded aspirations of the French emperor. Many statesmen in Europe, both in Britain and on the continent, perceived the danger that an unbridled nationalism could present to Europe, particularly if combined with the power of a leading state. The younger Pitt, Lord Castlereagh in Britain, the Austrian Count Metternich, the Prussian Reichsfreiherr vom und zum Stein, and Czar Alexander I thought hard about the European order which would secure peace for the war-torn continent and ensure some respect for international law. The balance of power was a concept of much more significance than later criticism has allowed. After the defeat of Napoleon I, the Quadruple Alliance of the victorious powers, soon joined by the defeated France, formed a concert of Europe, providing a rudimentary form of international co-operation among the great powers for a time. However, at once legitimate international aims became hard to reconcile with the aspirations of the nationalities. The powers were mainly concerned with maintaining the international status quo; they judged correctly that international stability would be undermined by some internal changes, particularly those due to revolution. When it came to endeavours of nationalities to form independent states, their realization obviously could not be accomplished without considerable changes in the political map of Europe, which would have its own impact on the balance of power and might impede the maintenance of peace.

The methods used by some members – for instance, the Italian national movement – did not garner much approval in ruling international government circles. These governments suspected at least the radical movements of following in Jacobin footsteps and of wishing by their actions a return to the instability and violence of the French revolutionary methods. The radical national movement in Italy reciprocated by using clandestine methods and resorted only occasionally to violence. It was a vicious circle from which neither the government nor the national movement could escape for long. In 1848, national movements became more respectable by linking themselves with moderate liberal constitutionalism and even, in some instances, with government.

In Germany, the enormous difficulties of defining national aims proved almost insurmountable. What criteria of the many used by national movements might be used to define what Germany was or ought to be? During the time of the Holy Roman Empire there were Germans settled in a wide range of ethnically different countries. There were Germans in Russia, in the Baltic states, and in Poland. There was Siebenbürgen within the Austrian Empire and the German part of Austria. There was a German population in Switzerland, France, and the Low Countries. On the religious front there was still the strict division between Catholics and different Protestant denominations. Natural frontiers were also not so obvious, which seemed somewhat easier in the case of Italy, but was troublesome over Tyrol. Not all difficulties could be faced at once. In the settlement after the First World War, Italy claimed her borders on both ethic and natural grounds. Eventually the powers had to accept the unification of Italy and of Germany, in some cases willingly, even supporting it, and in others, reluctantly. The aspirations of the nationalities were liable to cause tension between the great powers, not only over Italy and Germany – out of which one of their numbers, namely Austria, had to be forced – but also in the Balkans as the Ottoman Empire receded from southeastern Europe. In other cases, particularly over Poland, her borders changes too. All the powers in the area were determined to allow change.

However, from 1815 to 1914, Europe avoided prolonged and widely extended war because the great powers accepted the principle that change in European frontiers was a common concern to them all. These congresses and conferences were successful on the international level in preventing war, but they failed to deal with the underlying national problems in many cases. Where there was a conflict between the international demands or the balance of power and peace on the one hand and an aspiration of rising nationalities on the other, the international aspect was given priority. As a result, many nationalities stored up their grievances, real or imagined, particularly in the Balkans.

There, the Serbs were a case in point. Liberal and radical glorification of national struggle versus the oppressors, native or foreign, imagined or real, had not been lost on those Serbs who saw their progress towards full nationhood blocked by Austria. Gradually, terrorist organizations were building on Serbian soil with the connivance of at least some of the German authorities; that the weak government could hardly resist the machinations of "patriots," even if they had their grave doubts about their methods. In any case it was rather dangerous personally to resist the patriots because they might have a bomb to spare from those destined for the foreign oppressors. When everything seemed to be quiet and peaceful, the situation exploded in Sarajevo on July 28th, 1914, with the assassination of the Austrian Archduke Francis Ferdinand through the fanatical act of a South Slav nationalist, and war broke out in the summer of 1914.

It might have broken out at some other time, even without the assassination, for more general reasons because of the combination of this act of unreasonable nationalism with the breakdown of a minimum of international co-operation necessary to maintain peace. And this breakdown, particularly from 1908 onwards, was due to the increasing part played by matters of national prestige, national honour, and national economic policy, as well as colonial rivalries between the states in the formation of their foreign policy. In a sense, the rulers and their ministers, though they did not emerge as the result of a democratic process, were more responsive to the dictate of public opinion and increasingly emphasized national objectives. International understanding between the rulers, such as the three eastern emperors, became increasingly difficult to maintain in a climate of opinion in which their subjects had violent dislikes for each other on "racial" grounds, e.g., between the Germans and the Slavs. However, one cannot entirely blame national prejudice for the First World War. There were other important reasons for its outbreak, namely the ineptness of some of the rulers and ministers, such as the German Emperor William II and, in a sense, Ährenthal and Isvolsky, the foreign ministers of Austria/Hungary and Russia respectively, however intelligent they were.

After four years the First World War came to an end; Germany and her allies were defeated, and her empires broken up. The peace treaty of Versailles of 1919 made use of the apparent triumph of self-determination by public opinion. Nevertheless, the plebiscites needed international co-operation to determine the border for the new or extended national states. But not all problems and difficulties could be solved even in this way. The League of Nations from 1920 onwards, with changing memberships, took over an advisory and reconciliatory role through her assembly and council meetings that would be very different from the later United Nations organization. The name of the league reflected the hope of the nations for a better world in which the catastrophe of large-scale war could be avoided. Its weakness was that the United States of America and other great powers did not become members.

And generally the questions remained. What was the correct national unit for forming a state? External self-determination and internal self-government, in a sense, were two sides of the same coin. The Balkan remained troublesome, and the examples of Czechoslovakia and Yugoslavia in the interwar period showed that proper self-government was impossible to establish if true self-determination was not established by the state first. Short-sighted policies of some states towards minorities assumed that the old great powers and their successors in east and southeastern Europe would stay out of running the affairs of state and did not acknowledge that a power vacuum cannot exist for long, certainly not in any larger area of Europe. While the League of Nations did useful work in dealing with some important disputes, it was deficient in providing a bulwark against the major aggressors of the 1930s, partly because of the absence of the United States of America. The system of collective security failed its major test when the National Socialists in Germany were able to pick off one victim after another before the tide turned on them, and by then, the League of Nations was already defunct.

The unreasonable pursuit of national aims under the Nazis was apparently so successful in the short run because the people of Europe did not realize that they were endangering their very existence by pursuing their own narrow national aims. Was it better to have an international organization like the League of Nations, even if not comprehensive or inadequate, than having none? In some ways, yes. Co-operation between countries did not only exist at the diplomatic level, but also through other organizations that came into existence more or less with the League, such as the International Labour Organization and also the International Court of Justice at the Hague. They were all steps in the right direction, but some harm was done by over-emphasizing the international spirit still so imperfectly represented in practice by the League of Nations at the expense of old-fashioned national and traditional virtues such as patriotism and loyalty to one's country. A reliance upon the League to disentangle conflicts had developed that made it easy for countries to avoid making the sacrifices necessary to prepare their own defences. At the same time encouragement of hatred of other nations and the advocacy of aggressive designs against one's neighbours poisoned the atmosphere in Europe. However, the excessive nationalism – this perversion of nationalism – cannot and should not detract from the merits of the love of one's country and fundamental loyalty to it. Indeed, an enlightened pursuit of national interests demanded the occasional subordination of one country to higher goals. The national states of

Europe in the interwar years showed great shortcomings on both scores. A better balance between national interest and international requirements had to be found. Have we got it today?

So far I have given one of many views, as one historian out of a multitude. When dealing with the period since 1945, I can claim no "professional" privilege, whatever that may be, for the last three decades cannot yet be assessed by the historian. While in many countries in Europe and North America, little is left of that enthusiasm for and a belief in the superiority of one's own nation. Other regions of the world are now going through these earlier phases of independence with certain similarities to the European pattern.

On the whole nationalism in the world of today is becoming something mainly materialistic, a matter of bread and butter, full employment, low prices, and high wages. For economic and military reasons, states have formed groups with some sacrifice of sovereignty, like the European Economic Community (EEC) and the North Atlantic Treaty Organization (NATO), the Russian COMECON (Council of Mutual Economic Assistance) and the Warsaw Pact, the latter two now defunct. The world is divided into a number of power blocks, on the whole more along ideological and economic lines than on national ones. Blocks formed around the Soviet Union, the Peoples' Republic of China, the USA and Arab countries, OPEC (Organization of Petroleum Exporting Companies), and the less developed countries. There exists some co-operation between these groups, but often initiatives are directed against another group. This situation places limitations on what the successor of the League of Nations, the United Nations Organization (UN), can achieve. Still, UN membership is remarkably wide, much more so than the League of Nations at any time of its life. Also there exists now a whole set of international organizations connected in some way or another with the UN, such as the World Health Organization, UNESCO (United Nations Educational, Scientific, and Cultural Organization). Not only the maintenance of peace, but the survival of mankind in our environment depends on some subordination of narrow national interests in favour of international goals from which all will benefit. There comes to mind the complex and intricate question about nuclear weapons.

Nowadays I do not see nationalism in itself necessarily as a serious obstacle to the attainment of a minimum of international co-operation to the benefit of all nations. And I, too, think it would be a great mistake to downgrade and denigrate loyalty to one's people, as long as this loyalty is not blind and unreasonable. The nation, after all, is only the sum total of various families and clans. I regard loyalty to one's family and community group to be important and necessary. Why should we not also be loyal to the larger group, the nation? Indeed any meaningful international co-operation requires healthy and active members of the wider body to make it work. One of the most important duties of citizens, certainly in democracies, is to ensure that the kind of government he or she directly or indirectly elects co-operates properly with other countries. Similarly there are no objections to regional groupings. These can hinder wider international co-operation, but they can also facilitate it. However, some groupings based on certain ideologies have now become a greater obstacle to international co-operation than nationalism itself. Some of the ideologies have subordinated national interests to the goal of the ideology.

We have seen how nationalities played an increasingly important role after the decline of supra-international institutions from the end of the eighteenth century. But the shortcomings of modern nationalism led, particularly from the First World War onwards, to a new quest for some form of international co-operation. Today, groupings which are supra-national without being widely international hold sway to nationalism that is in decline in some Western countries but on the upsurge in some of the recently liberated countries. However, in the present political climate, no nation can stand alone, thus the trend towards supra-national groupings is likely to continue.

On the one hand, the deterrent of nuclear warfare limits recourse to extreme force. On the other hand, there is as yet no evidence that the differences between power blocks are being overcome. We must strive to keep the dialogue going, being aware of ideological differences. We must also recognize that nations are entitled to their different traditions and outlook, based on history, geography, religion, and ethnic stock. We must work towards creating a proper balance between a refreshing national diversity and the requirement of the international order. Perhaps we should also look at history to see whether there is anything we can learn from the achievements, as well as from the troubles, of international or supra-national organizations and groupings of the past, both secular and spiritual.

Chapter Eight

SAINT OR SINNER:
SOME REFLECTIONS ON
HITLER'S POPE: THE SECRET
HISTORY OF PIUS XII
BY JOHN CORNWELL

Presented March 16th, 2000, at Redwood House in Redwood Meadows, Alberta

ECAUSE OF THE NEAR INTOLERABLE tension and heart-breaking events in which Eugenio Pacelli, the later Pope Pius XII, was involved, it behooves us to research more thoroughly the facts and the ill reputation of his life.

Eugenio Pacelli was born into a family of senior Vatican officials in Rome in 1876, two years before the death of Pius IX , who never got over the shock of the loss of the Papal States during the long drawn out history of the Italian unification; he regarded himself as a virtual "prisoner in the Vatican." Pacelli was ordained in 1899 and served from 1904 to 1916 as assistant to Cardinal Gasparri, mainly in the codifying of canon law.[1] In August 1917 (during the First World War) Benedict XV undertook a peace initiative and sent Pacelli, raised to the rank of archbishop, to Munich as papal nuncio with the special task of taking soundings from the German government. Unfortunately, the powers there were not ready for peace. In 1920, Pacelli became the first papal nuncio to the German Reich, where he remained until 1929 when he was appointed cardinal. In 1930 he succeeded his former mentor Gasparri as Secretary of

Cardinal Eugenio Pacelli (1876–1958)

Photo courtesy of Bundesarchiv,

Bestand Bild 183

State, and on March 2nd, 1939, after the death of Pius XI, Pacelli became Pope Pius XII. He died on October, 9th, 1958. So for more than four decades, Pacelli was involved in dealing with problems arising from the troubled, and in many ways tragic, course of international events that began with the outbreak of the First World War in August 1914. Following the deceptive footsteps of Rolf Hochhuth's play *The Deputy*,[2] John Cornwell's book on Pius XII, with the title *Hitler's Pope*, was published in 1999.[3] This investigation, therefore, begins with the historical background of Hitler's rise to power and then turns to Pius XII's policy towards the Nazi regime.

For the first time in a century, the Concert of Europe failed to prevent a general European war in 1914. Over a period of four years the hostilities demanded enormous casualties. The severe problems encountered by Russia led to the October revolution in 1917 followed by the establishment of a Communist regime under Lenin's leadership that was hostile to religion. While in Germany, after the end of the war, the new Social Democratic German chancellor Friedrich Ebert wanted the decision about the future form of government to be left to the people.[4] But under the impact of revolutionary events, one of the other leading Social Democrats proclaimed a republic in Berlin on November 9th, 1918.

After Germany's defeat, the papacy, in a very far-sighted manner, drew the attention of the Allies to the great dangers that would arise unless a peace treaty could be reached "which Germans could accept and which would not be humiliating for them."[5] The Holy See was particularly concerned with the clause in which Germany (and her allies) had to assume responsibility for the war.[6] The Holy See also feared that excessive Allied demands for reparations would overtax Germany's economic capacity and might even be detrimental for the victors.[7] While the Treaty of Versailles of 1919 was fair in some other respects, most Germans found it difficult to live with.

From the beginning the fledgling German republic was under siege from both the Right and the Left. Bavaria went through a series of particularly disturbing events after Kurt Eisner, a Jewish journalist and independent Socialist from Berlin, had overthrown the monarchy there, just before the proclamation of the German republic in Berlin. His assassination by a right-winger, after receiving only a handful of votes at election time, led to another even more extreme left-wing revolution with red terror methods; this was followed in turn by a brutal crushing of the revolution by right-wing forces in a kind of "white terror." Like many others, Pacelli, who was in Munich at the time, was deeply shocked by the extreme left-wing takeover, and in a report to Rome commented unfavourably on Jewish participation in these events.[8] It would be unwise, however, as Cornwell did, to infer a personal anti-Semitic attitude from these remarks.[9] In general, Pacelli was certainly justified to worry about the events in Bavaria. The destabilization of the Bavarian situation made the state a haven for right-wing extremists, gave Hitler his first platform, and allowed him to get off all too lightly after his putsch in 1923. In Bavaria, as elsewhere in Germany, the Right, uncommitted to democracy and motivated by an extreme nationalism, did not face up to the military defeat that Germany had suffered. It attempted to square the circle by formulating a theory that Germany's brave and successful soldiers at the front had been stabbed in the back by the Jews, amongst others.

The new republican regime, rather than its imperial predecessor that was responsible for the disaster, was blamed for concluding the armistice on November 11th, 1918, and for accepting the terms of the Treaty of Versailles of 1919. The ruling classes, by and large, did not have the kind of loyalty to the new republic that they had shown earlier to many reigning dynasties. Additionally, the runaway inflation in the early 1920s deprived millions of Germans of their savings. But by 1924, political, economic, and social life had started to improve. Unfortunately, the world economic crisis of 1929 put new strains on the still vulnerable republic.

In the meantime, Pacelli, to seek understanding and harmony between the interests of various states and the Church, had been able to conclude concordats with Bavaria, Prussia,[10] and Baden, but a treaty with the Reich had eluded him. He worked well with the ruling parties, not only with the Catholic Centre party but also with the Social Democrats. He felt at home in Germany, with whose institutions and culture he had become familiar; he even learned to speak perfect German. As the first papal nuncio in Berlin, a Protestant capital, he gave considerable exposure to Catholicism. My father heard addresses Pacelli gave in the 1920s to the lawyers and to the journalists in Berlin. The nuncio's high intellectual calibre, sophistication, and humanity made a deep impression on my father. When Pacelli left Germany in December 1929, the country was once more in deep crisis.

The death in 1925 of the first Reich president, the Social Democrat Friedrich Ebert, was a grave loss for the Weimar republic. The new republic had been named after the place where the constitution had been adopted in 1919, which, unfortunately, stipulated the direct election of the head of state by the electorate instead of by parliament. Owing to disunity in the republican ranks, the Right won in the second ballot with the candidature of Field Marshal von Hindenburg, who had become famous through his victories on the Eastern front at the beginning of the First World War, but he was now nearing the end of his seventies. The death in 1929 of the right-liberal leader Gustav Stresemann, who had been the architect of the understanding with France at Locarno, and who had secured Germany's admission to League of Nations, removed, after Friedrich Ebert's passing, the only other statesman of the Weimar Republic.[11] Owing to the inability of the republican parties to agree on how to tackle the world economic crisis, it became impossible to find a parliamentary majority in order to form a government.[12] From 1930 onwards this led to a series of presidential cabinets, relying on presidential emergency decrees, which appeared to be the only way for government to function at all. To keep Hitler out in April 1932, the old Field Marshal, now in his mid-eighties, was re-elected president. But in July, the Nazis became the strongest party in the Reichstag nevertheless.

Pacelli, as papal nuncio in Germany and then as secretary of state at the Vatican, watched the rise of the National Socialists with grave concern. Their success was mainly due to Hitler's demagogy and to Goebbels's clever, if completely unscrupulous, propaganda methods. The Nazis, helped by the new media of the radio and the women's vote, exploited all the problems and fears of Germans for their own purposes. They promised to achieve national unity, to undo the "shame of the Versailles dictation," to make Germany great again, and to get people back to work. They vowed to fight Communism and any form of Marxism and to deprive all Jews and Jewish descendants, even if baptized, of their German citizenship.[13] Their brutality to those they regarded as their enemies was well known and their ruthlessness was recognized even by figures on the Right, like Hindenburg, who for many years refused to appoint Hitler as Chancellor. Hindenburg dismissed Chancellor Heinrich Brüning, a leading Catholic Centre Party politician and the head of the presidential cabinet since 1930, in 1932 as a result of a back-stairs intrigue. Franz von Papen, who had been a Catholic Centre party member of the Prussian legislature, was appointed chancellor, with General Kurt von Schleicher as Minister of Defence. The men of the Papen-Schleicher circle believed in an authoritarian regime, though without the brutality of a totalitarian dictatorship. They were strongly opposed not only to the Communists, but also to the Social Democrats who had so loyally supported the republic; they destroyed the Social Democrat government in Prussia by presidential decrees and brought Prussia under the direct control of the Reich. The Social Democrats did not resist, fearing the outbreak of civil war.[14] The meekness of the republican parties has often been criticized. They were losing ground to those parties determined to destroy parliamentary government and the rule of law. In the end, Hindenburg, after a short period with Schleicher as chancellor, on January 30th, 1933, appointed Hitler, the leader of the largest party in the Reichstag, as chancellor. The government formed a coalition with the Nationalists who completely underrated Hitler and the dynamics of his movement, and thought they could control the Nazis.

Pacelli, like Pius XI, never underestimated the strength of the Nazi regime. Pacelli had been taken to task for concluding a concordat with Nazi Germany in 1933. As a matter of principle, the Holy See never refused to discuss possible treaties with governments that wished to initiate them, such as that of Italy under Mussolini earlier on. The Lateran treaties of 1929 established for the first time since the Italian unification formal relations between the Italian State and the papacy. Though a dictatorial regime was strengthened by papal recognition, a number of problems were removed. An Italian Catholic could now be a good Catholic and a good Italian at the same time. The papacy could function more easily through recognition of the extra-territorial status of the Vatican, an area of 108 acres in all, and of certain buildings outside its borders; all this proved very useful in the Second World War.

Following Mussolini's example, Hitler signalled that he was interested in a German concordat with the papacy. As Pacelli had no illusions about the Nazi government, it appeared to him all the more essential to regulate relations with the new German state, especially as the determination of the new regime to do away with federalism affected the efficacy of the existing concordats with some of the states. In July 1933, the Holy See signed the concordat with Germany. The German government guaranteed freedom of confessing and publicly practicing the Catholic religion, including the celebration of divine service, preaching, confession (reconciliation), religious teaching, as well as the maintenance of some information media. This entitled the church to publicly proclaim a point of view diametrically opposed to Nazi ideology, for example on the racial question.[15] As was to be expected, the Nazi regime broke many stipulations of the concordat by frequently prohibiting publications. However, it entitled the ecclesiastical authorities to register protests, which, while largely ineffective, were still of importance. Above all, the basic organization of the Roman Catholic Church was maintained throughout the Nazi regime, even though the imprisonment and killing of many priests could not be prevented. The Catholic Church was unique in keeping its independence in

Nazi Germany and its international links, while the official Protestant Churches came under direct Nazi influence. Protestants who disagreed with the Nazi version of Christianity did not have the support of any officially recognized institution and were exposed to the full arbitrariness of the regime.

Naturally, the Holy See had to make concessions. Priests were no longer allowed to participate in political matters. In any case, under the Nazi regime only their own party members were going to be allowed to engage in politics. Therefore, I do not believe it is right to argue that the concordat sacrificed the Catholic Centre Party,[16] which was going to disappear in one way or another, like the Social Democrats, the left-liberals, trade unions, and others. Admittedly, the political parties did not show great dignity in this hour of trial, with most of them also accepting the Enabling Law, which in effect destroyed all constitutional safeguards.[17] But they were hard-pressed, not only by the terror exercised by the storm troopers who were all around them, but perhaps just as much by a feeling that they had lost their democratic legitimization; after all, a majority – roughly a third of the electorate – had freely rejected democracy and the rule of law.

Episcopal declarations on the incompatibility of Nazism and Christianity were withdrawn. A German Catholic could now, after the Reich concordat, so to speak join the Nazi party with a clear conscience, and numerous Catholics, including those who had served in the various legislatures, flocked to the Nazi party. All this is sad, and was a downside of the concordat. In 1933, Catholics were still influenced by memories of the measures against them in the 1870s, justified as a *Kulturkampf,* a struggle for culture against the dark forces of Rome, which had been waged against them by Bismarck and some liberals.[18] And they did not want to return to the ghetto. Thus they were all the more vulnerable to the Nazi clarion call for national unity.[19]

Pacelli was, however, quite clear in his rejection of National Socialism in an address to pilgrims at Fatima in 1935, referring to these enemies of the Church as "in reality only miserable modern plagiarists who dress up age old errors with new tinsel."[20] As Secretary of State, he played a vital part in the encyclical *Mit bren-*

nender Sorge (*With Deep Anxiety and Burning Indignation*) in March 1937 in which Pope Pius XI expressed strong opposition to the Nazi regime. "Printed copies were not distributed through the post, but delivered all over the German dioceses by private persons, on foot, using cars, motorcycles and bicycles. To give Pius XI's words the greatest possible effect, the bishops themselves, in cathedral cities, read the encyclical from the pulpits." The encyclical was, with Pacelli's help, written directly in German. After quoting from Cicero that "never is anything useful if it is not at the same time morally good," the encyclical continued:

> Since the State in its political life confuses what is useful with what is right, it misunderstands the basic fact that man as a person has God-given rights which are to be guarded from every attack that aims to deny, suppress or disregard them.

Warning against "counterfeit Christianity that is not the Christianity of Christ," the encyclical declared it is the duty of every professing Christian to keep his conscience clear of any blameworthy co-operation in so dreadful a work of corruption.[21] The Nazi regime reacted swiftly with repressive measures against the German Catholic Church.[22]

Pius XI died in February 1939 at a time of great international anxiety. The Sacred College had to decide who would be the best person to preside over the fortunes and future of the Roman Catholic Church in a period of grave problems, and possibly, even probably, of war.[23] Pius XI, an autocratic Pope, had groomed Pacelli as his successor, but the recommendation of an outgoing pope was not necessarily a blessing. No Secretary of State had been elected pope since 1667[24] "for the very reason that they were too identified with the policy of the predecessor."[25] However, at this time, when international events were crucial for the church, there was something to be said for breaking with tradition and entrusting with the papacy the cardinal who had been in the midst of diplomatic activities as Secretary of State. But did Pacelli have the right personality in a time of grave crisis? The only non-Italian curial cardinal, the French ecclesiastic Cardinal Tisserant, was absolutely convinced that he was "not the man for the situation [because he was] indecisive, hesitant, . . . more designed to obey orders than to give them."[26] In the end, Pacelli did not have any serious competition and was finally elected, though not unanimously.[27] He took the name of Pius XII.

The ambassadors respected the Pope; even revered him, his purity, his piety, his conscience. But as the tension mounted, they sometimes wished that his personality would be stronger. They admitted he had the qualities of prudence and balance to an exceptional degree. Occasionally they wished that he had less. The quality which they least admired was his eloquence: the baroque style, the flowery metaphors, and the grandiloquence, with an air of reciting rather than speaking.

In private conversation with the ambassadors, he was charming and natural, making them totally at ease, never anything but gentle.[28] Monsignor Tardini, an assistant secretary of state, found Pius XII "refined, amiable, obliging, and affectionate." He was deeply pious and ascetic, and he avoided confrontation:

> He did not like to give orders. He would rather persuade. He found it difficult to say no. When he had to take an unpleasant decision, he would cut the strong words from the draft letter, or add a gentle phrase. And his style was superabundant, with parentheses, amplifications and ornamentations.

In conversation, Pius normally had a slight stammer,

> but the effort to overcome it [in public] caused him to sound pontifical. Altogether he was a very gentle, cultured, shy, very controlled, very prayerful, [and a] lonely man with a yearning Christian heart. And he was the last Pope to have the mentality of "the prisoner in the Vatican." He wanted to keep the office unspotted by the corruption of the world, and therefore fenced in like a sanctuary, but fenced because to be close to God.[29]

How Pius felt about the Nazi regime comes out most clearly in his willingness, in the early winter of 1939, to act as a link with the

British government for a number of German dissidents desiring to overthrow Hitler. Some German generals were deeply troubled by Hitler's plans to invade Scandinavia and the Low Countries. The Pope personally knew their Bavarian intermediary General Beck, the former German Chief of Staff and, incidentally, a Protestant – who actually came to the Vatican and was also a leading member of the later plot. The conspirators wanted to make sure that the Allies would not take advantage of the confusion caused by an overthrow of the Nazis to inflict another Versailles treaty on Germany. In order to try and prevent further suffering for the peoples of Europe, the Pope took grave risks both for himself and for the Catholic Church in the Nazi domain, casting aside his usual prudence. With his long experience of international affairs he foresaw a prolonged and bitter war. The contacts, to which the British government responded positively up to a point, went on until just before the German invasion of Denmark and Norway in April 1940, when the conspirators decided the opportunity had passed. But they did give warning of invasion plans to the countries affected. Many of the same opponents of the regime were active in the July 20th, 1944, plot, which collapsed because von Stauffenberg's bomb failed to kill Hitler.

Was Pius right to engage in conspiratorial talks which conflicted with the neutrality between the powers on which rested the claim of the Holy See to be left undisturbed by the hostilities? In particular, was this not a breach of the Lateran Treaties of 1929, in which the papacy had undertaken not to interfere in political matters concerning Italy, a country now allied to Nazi Germany? And might the Pope not risk Axis occupation of the Vatican if his involvement was found out? Pius XII was not mistaken in his trust of the conspirators he dealt with, in many cases across denominational lines. In this instance, he judged correctly that he could rely not only on the good faith of the conspirators, but also on their silence, even when they were subjected to interrogation and torture. Cornwell speaks of the Pope's "almost foolhardy valor in his role of go-between."[30] I believe Pius was right to do what he did.[31] I am reinforced in this conclusion by my personal acquaintance with some of the conspirators and their circle.

When the Germans invaded the Low Countries in May 1940, the Pope sent to their rulers telegrams with his hopes and prayers for the re-establishment of their countries. The Vatican's efforts to keep Italy out of the war ended when Mussolini, in June 1940, decided to jump on the German bandwagon in the hope of sharing in the spoils of victory. The small area of papal sovereignty was now engulfed by Axis territory, which posed a potential threat to its survival. Maintenance of the integrity of the Vatican State was of importance not only to the Catholic Church, but also to the persecuted people everywhere in Europe, and especially the Jews. Many appeals for help were addressed to the Holy See and were answered wherever possible, often involving the intervention of the Pope himself. In June 1940, "some five hundred Jews embarked at Bratislava on a leaky Danube steamer headed for Palestine. Four months and untold deprivations later, their ship tried to enter the port of Istanbul," but was refused permission to land. Shortly afterwards, the ship was captured by an Italian patrol boat, and the Jews were imprisoned in a camp on the Island of Rhodes. One of the prisoners, who was sent out as an emissary, managed to reach Rome, was granted an audience with the Pope, and appealed to him for help preventing his group from being handed over to the Germans. Thanks to Pius's intervention, the refugees were transferred to a hastily improvised camp in southern Italy, where they were found safe three years later, in December 1943, by a Palestinian unit.[32] To me it is deeply significant that a group of Jewish Slovaks, who are likely to have experienced anti-Semitism from Catholics in their own country, turned to the Pope for assistance in their hour of need, and not in vain.

The papacy directed efforts to rescue Jews on a considerable scale, channelling money to those in need, issuing baptismal certificates to Jews for their protection, negotiating with, for example, Latin American countries to grant substantial numbers of visas to Jews, and making the Vatican information service available to them to put relatives in touch with each other.

Nazi persecution of the Jews in the countries controlled by them escalated further in brutality during the war. Using measures of wholesale extermination carried out with bureaucratic efficiency, it assumed proportions hitherto unimagined. In this connection, I shall mainly use the best known term "holocaust," in preference to the more correct "Shoah." One of the most important sources about the efforts to save Jews from the holocaust is the recently published book *Ne jamais désespérer* by Gerhart Riegner,[33] an old family friend, who was at the World Jewish Congress listening post in Geneva during the Second World War. Whenever he heard and could confirm another piece of harrowing news, he promptly approached any organizations that might be of help, such as governments, the International Red Cross, or the churches. He found a staunch supporter of efforts to save Jewish lives in the Secretary General of the emerging World Council of Churches, the Dutch Calvinist pastor W. A. Visser't Hooft, who was also in Geneva. Riegner was at first reluctant to contact the Roman Catholic Church because of the anti-Semitism of some of the national churches, such as that of Poland. But in March 1942, six weeks after the Wannsee conference had planned the holocaust, though before receiving the news, he approached the papal nuncio in Berne. From that time onwards, the World Jewish Congress was in constant contact with the Catholic Church and secured help in the first instance against anti-Jewish measures in Nazi satellite regimes in mainly Catholic countries. The Pope had the President of Slovakia, Joseph Tiso, a Catholic priest, called to order on the grounds that his anti-Jewish measures were incompatible with his Catholic faith and his priesthood, and managed to obtain a certain amelioration, though some mass deportations could not be prevented.[34] In Catholic Croatia, in spite of strong interventions by the Holy See, success was limited, as the Croat government submitted to German pressures to have the Jews deported;[35] mass extermination of Orthodox Serbs were also carried out in Croatia. One cannot help being surprised by what Cornwell calls the Pope's apparent benevolence towards the Croat regime.[36]

When it became clear around Christmas 1942 that the nightmarish scheme of the extermination of European Jewry was actually being carried out, the Pope expressed his deep sorrow about the fate of "hundreds of thousands of people who, through no fault of their own and solely because of their nation or their race, had been condemned to death and progressive extinction."[37] Here the Jews and Serbs were referred to, without actually being mentioned. The message displeased the Axis, but did not go sufficiently far to satisfy the Allies. When the Pope was asked why he had not used the word "Nazi" in his condemnation, he replied that then "he would have also had to mention the Communists by name," i.e., Russia, the then ally of Britain and the USA.[38]

The situation in Rumania, whose population belonged mainly to the Orthodox Church, was particularly difficult in view of the extreme anti-Semitism of its Iron Guard government, but the Vatican did avert some deportations.[39] The greatest successes in rescue were achieved in Hungary in June 1944, where the Pope sent a telegram in plain words to the regent, Horthy – who was not a Catholic.[40] The War Refugee Board set up by the Allies earlier that year was also able to save large numbers of Jews.[41]

When the Germans occupied Rome in September 1943, and the Vatican itself was in danger, Pius took prompt and energetic action to have as many Jews as possible spared deportation, which could not, however, be averted altogether. The Germans demanded a quantity of gold from the Roman Jews, and the Pope gave instructions to loan them any amount of which they were deficient.[42] Pius issued orders that all religious houses and other properties coming under some kind of extra-territorial arrangement should be opened up to any Jew who required protection. The SS appears to have been aware of this, but for once it did not intervene. According to reports, the number of Swiss Guards at the Vatican increased mysteriously at this time, to incorporate a number of Jews.[43] Numerous Italians, clergy and laity, all over the country helped to rescue Jews, at the risk and often at the cost of their own lives.[44] During and after the war, the Holy See received many heartfelt thanks from Jewish organizations for what the pope and the Catholic Church had done.[45] According to his private secretary, Father Leiber, Pius spent his entire private fortune on the Jews.[46]

Could the Pope have done more than he did? Should he have taken a stronger public stance? Even those who admired his qualities and his saintliness, like the British Minister to the Holy See, Sir D'Arcy Osborne, felt that at times he could have spoken out more clearly.[47] Pius XII did not quite possess the toughness his predecessor had shown towards the end of his reign. But there is another possible view, that the Pope feared that too public a stance might endanger his quiet efforts to rescue Jews. Each of us has to try to assess the facts and come to his own judgment of the man. I believe that Pius took his responsibilities very seriously, that he tried to guard against any misstep that might endanger his flock and the potential victims he was trying to save, and that therefore he felt that publicly he could not do more. This may well have been the lesson he learned from the deportation and killing of Jews and Jewish descendants in Dutch monasteries, including the Carmelite nun Edith Stein, which followed the public protest the Catholic Bishop of Utrecht, Johann de Jong, had made in July 1942 against the deportation of Dutch non-Aryans. It is believed that Jewish Protestants in the Netherlands were reprieved at that time because the Protestant Church, under threats, omitted its protest. It is said that Pius had drafted a protest against the deportation of Dutch Jews but burned it when he heard of the invasion of monasteries.[48]

Right from the beginning of the Nazi regime, there emerged a certain pattern of action, as demonstrated during the events leading up to the day of boycott of Jewish businesses in April 1933, which I remember so well from my life in Berlin. Nazi brutality that led to protests against this brutality were twisted and in turn regarded as provocation against the regime, which then were followed by yet more brutality. Also, after September 1941, the possibility of defeat spurred Hitler on to even greater bestialities. Perhaps his obsessed mind decided that he would at any rate leave one "achievement" behind, namely the destruction of European Jewry.

By means of this perceived sacrificial death of the Jews, he was fanatically steeling himself to achieve victory, or fight on to total destruction. At the same time, in his distorted and irrational mind, he imagined expiating the spilling of German blood and avenging a possible defeat. As the military situation worsened, he conducted and intensified this realization of vengeance with mounting determination as he advanced towards an apocalyptic end.[49]

The question of Pius XII's response to appeals for help for those threatened with extermination arouses strong feelings both among his critics and among those who support his canonization. We are not yet in a position to come to definitive conclusions, particularly as the papal commission consisting of three Jews and three Christians has only recently begun its work. In any case, all of us here will want to do justice to a person who had to make extremely difficult decisions in dealing with a criminal and irrational regime on which the lives of targeted victims and of his flock depended. Did Pius strive to do the best he could for those who were being persecuted? This is a judgment call which every one of us has to make for him or herself. In the light of my reading and of my experience of those terrible times, I have tried to do justice to Pius XII. I do not agree with Cornwell's description of Pius as "Hitler's Pope."

Of the various institutions approached by Jewish organizations, the efforts made by the churches compare well with those of other bodies, such as the International Red Cross (which did not or could not do very much) and Allied governments. Among churches, the help given by the Catholic Church, with its size and international network, stands out, thanks, I believe, to the central direction by Pius XII. As to the Allies, while their record during the war in relation to rescue operations leaves something to be desired, we are all deeply thankful that they won the war.

P.S. Now, further documents about Pius XII have been made accessible, and some are published.[50] On January 15th, 2005, the Catholic newspaper reported that in 1943 Hitler had ordered the SS general Karl Friedrich Wolff, who was in charge of the war theatre in Italy, to kidnap the Pope, an order that the German officer did not carry out.

> Wolff returned from the meeting with Hitler in Germany and arranged a secret meeting with the Pope. Wolff in civilian clothes and with the help of a priest went to the Vatican and assured the Pope he had no intention to carry the order out himself but warned the Pope to be careful because the situation in Rome was confusing and risky.[51]

Peter Godman's book *Hitler and the Vatican*[52] makes extensive
analytical and verbatim use of Vatican papers now available to confirm that at no time were Pius XI or Pius XII under any illusion
about the evil of Hitler's regime. But the Popes considered the communist regime of Russia to be even worse. General Ivan Agayant,[53]
head of the disinformation department of the KGB (the Russian
communist committee for state security) and Ivan Mikhail Pacepa[54]
of the secret service in Rumania, both eventually deserted to the
West where they published details of their destructive activity;
when under KGB command they were ordered by Nikita Krushev to
destroy the moral authority of the Vatican. They designed the
smear campaign that amounted to an attempted character assassination of Pius XII by initiating the Hochhuth play *The Deputy*. It was
first performed in East Berlin in 1963 and became widely known
and accepted as true. Earlier, in 1954, very possibly through KGB
infiltration in the Vatican, those secretly serving the KGB attempted to assassinate Pius XII, and in 1958, they succeeded.[55] The KGB
masterminded and its minions carried out the murder of Pope Paul
VI in August and Pope John Paul I in September 1978. In 1983, the
KGB was also involved in the assassination attempt of Pope John
Paul II. As for Pius XII, the Vatican has started the long process of
canonization.

Notes

1 Richard Cardinal Cushing, *Pope of Peace: Pope Pius XII* (Boston: Pauline Press, 1997); Richard P. McBrien, *Lives of the Popes: The Pontiffs from St. Peter to John Paul II* (San Francisco: Harper, 1997).

2 The play was first performed in 1963 in East Berlin by the communist Erwin Piscator. The play is a smear campaign, one might want to say an attempt at character assassination of Pius XII, initiated through devious ways by the General Ivan Agayants in the Disinformation Departments of the KGB, who in time defected and confessed to this. (There are also others with a similar story.)

3 John Cornwell, *Hitler's Pope: The secret History of Pius XII* (London: Viking Penguin, 1999); "Hitler's Pope," *Vanity Fair*, October 1999, 170, 192. On Cornwell's book see also Ronald Rychlak, "A Different Read: Vatican Chronicles," *Brill's Continent* 3, no. 3 (April 2000): 60–1, 120.

4 Heinrich August Winkler, *Der Lange Weg nach Westen* (München: C. H. Beck, 2000), 481; Winkler maintains Stresemann was the only statesman the Weimar Republic produced; however, the relative ratings of Ebert and Stresemann have not yet been finally settled.

5 Stewart A. Stehlin, *Weimar and the Vatican, 1919-1933: German-Vatican Relations in the Interwar Years* (Princeton University Press, 1983), 43.

6 Ibid., 43–4.

7 Ibid., 72.

8 Cornwell, 74–5; Max Levien, one of those mentioned by Pacelli, may not have been a Jew at all; see Richard Grunberg, *Red Rising in Bavaria* (London: Barker, 1973), 56.

9 Cornwell, 75.

10 Erich Eyck, *A History of the Weimar Republic* (Erlenbach-Zürich: Eugen Rentsch, 1963), 2:201.

11 Winkler, *Der Lange Weg nach Westen*, 481.

12 Karl Dietrich Erdmann, in Bruno Gebhardt, *Handbuch der Deutschen Geschichte* (Stuttgart, 1959), 4:163; Eyck, "The collapse of the Great Coalition," in *Weimar Republic*, vol. 2.

13 Wilhelm Mommsen, ed., "Article 4 of the program of the National Socialist German Workers' Party of 1920," in *Deutsche Parteiprogramme* (München: Isar Verlag, 1960), 548.

14 Eyck, *Weimar Republic*, 2:408–18.

15 Dieter Albrecht, "Der Heilige Stuhl und das Dritte Reich," in *Die Katholiken und das Dritte Reic, ed. Klaus Gotto and Konrad Repgen* (Mainz: Matthias Grünewald Verlag, 1980), 25–47; see generally Konrad Repgen, *Hitlers Machtergreifung und der deutsche Katholizismus: Versuch einer Bilanz* (Saarbrücken: Saarbrücker Universitätsreden, 1967), vol. 6.

16 Cornwell, 149; For a critical view of Catholicism, see Klaus Scholder, *The Churches and the Third Reich* (Philadelphia: Fortress Press, 1988).

17 Hans-Ulrich Thamer, *Verführung und Gewalt: Deutschland 1933–1945* (Berlin: Siedler, 1986), 272–81.

18 Frank Eyck, *Religion and Politics in German History: From the Beginnings to the French Revolution* (London: Macmillan, 1998), 370–1.

19 Rudolf Morsey, "Die Deutsche Zentrumspartei," in *Das Ende der Parteien 193*, ed. Erich Matthias and Rudolf Morsey (Düsseldorf: Droste Verlag, 1960), 281–453.

20 "This Rock," *The Magazine of Catholic Apologetics and Evangelisation* 8, no. 2 (February 1997); Cornwell, 172–3.

21 Robin Anderson, *Between Two Wars: The Story of Pope Pius XI (Achille Ratti), 1922–1939* (Chicago: Franciscan Herald Press, 1977), 84–7.

22 Cornwell, 183; The Nazis began an enormous propaganda campaign, though probably largely unsuccessful, to separate the Catholic laity from the clergy by reviving immorality charges against priests which had been suspended a year previously.

23 Owen Chadwick, *Britain and the Vatican during the Second World War* (Cambridge University Press, 1986).

24 McBrien, 363–4.

25 Chadwick, 40.

26 Ibid., 43.

27 Ibid., 46–7.

28 Ibid., 50.

29 Ibid., 51–2.

30 Cornwell, 380.

31 Harold C. Deutsch, *The Conspiracy against Hitler in the Twi-Light War* (Minneapolis: University of Minnesota Press, 1968); Peter Hoffmann, *The History of the German Resistance, 1933–1945* (Montreal & Kingston: McGill Queen's University Press, 1996).

32 Pinchas E. Lapide, *The Last Three Popes and the Jews* (London: Souvenir Press, 1967), 128–9. The Jewish author served in a Palestinian Unit with the British forces which landed in Italy, and found the refugees.

33 Gerhart Riegner, *Ne jamais désespérer: Soixante années au service du peuple juif et des droits de l'homme* (Paris: Cerf, l'histoire à juif, 1998).

34 Pierre Blet, *Pius XII and the Second World War*, trans. Lawrence J. Johnson (New York: Paulist Press, 1999), 177.

35 Blet, 178–81.

36 Cornwell, 260.

37 Saul Friedländer, *Pius XII and the Third Reich: A Documentation*, trans. Charles Fullman (New York: Knopf, 1966), 131.

38 Chadwick, 219.

39 Blet, 182–89.

40 Blet, 194–95.

41 Riegner, 130–45; see also Lévai (ed.), *Eichmann in Ungarn: Dokumente* (Budapest: Pannonia Verlag, 1961), 340.

42 Cornwell, 301–2; Eugenio Zolli, *Before the Dawn: Autobiographical Reflections* (New York: Sheed and Ward, 1954), 132–76. The author, who was Chief Rabbi of Rome during the German occupation, was baptized in 1945 and took the pope's principal baptismal name; for this see also *The last Three Popes*, 306–7.

43 Blet, 214–18; Chadwick, 288–89; Lapide, 132–35.

44 Lapide, 135–36.

45 Ibid., 132ff.

46 Ibid., 168.

47 Chadwick, 212–13.

48 Robert M. W. Kempner, *Ankläger einer Epoche: Lebenserinnerungen* (Frankfurt/Main: Ullstein, 1986), 421–22; Blet, 147–49; Lapide, 200.

49 Philippe Burrin, *Hitler and the Jews: The Genesis of the Holocaust*, trans. Patsy Southgate (London: Edward Arnold, 1994), 147.

50 Ronald J. Rychlak, *Hitler, the War, and the Pope* (Columbus: Genesis Press, 2006).

51 Dan Kurzman, *A Special Mission: Hitler's Secret Plan to Seize the Vatican & Kidnap Pope Pius XII* (London: Dacapo Press, 2008).

52 Peter Godman, *Hitler and the Vatican* (New York: Simon & Schuster, 2003).

53 John Barron, "KGB," in *The Penguin Books of Lies*, ed. Philip Kerr (London: Penguin Books, 1991), 420–23.

54 Ivan Michal Pacepa, "The Red Horizon: Moscow's Assault on the Vatican," trans Patrick McGill, *National Review*, 25 January 2007.

55 Jan Malina, "KGB murder of Pope Pius XII," *ISI forum*, June 27th, 2008; Rabbi David G. Dalin, *The Myth of Hitler's Pope:How Pius XII Rescued Jews from the Nazis* (Washington, DC: Regnery Publishing, 2005).

Chapter Nine

ON ANTI-SEMITISM
THROUGHOUT THE AGES

Presented Ash Wednesday, February 28th, 2001, at the Nazarene University College of Calgary; October 2nd, 2001, in the University of Calgary History Department; and at the Canadian Bible College in Calgary on November 14th, 2003, in the class "War and Society," led by Erich de Bruyn, on the Nazi persecution of the Jews.

THE TERM "ANTI-SEMITISM" was probably coined in Germany in 1879 by an anti-Jewish writer called Wilhelm Marr. It evidently denotes anti-Jewish sentiments, although Jews are not the only people regarded as Semites. It is clearly an attempt to link the Jews to the Middle East as a Semitic people, along with the Arabs, and to question their European legitimacy. For the earlier centuries, I will refer to anti-Judaism. I will try to deal with the subject as a historian but also as a German Jew who experienced Nazi persecution in his boyhood. I was forced to emigrate, eventually joined the British Army in 1940, and was baptized as a soldier. Hopefully, I can see things both from a Jewish and a Christian point of view while not being uncritical of either.

My main theme will be the relationship between Christians and Jews. The Roman rulers in the period of Jesus permitted the Jews in Palestine, the chief centre of Yahwism, a measure of political and cultural autonomy. This included the exercise of their religion; they had their subordinate local rulers and a high priesthood. However, for the Romans, toleration of monotheism, which in principle was intolerant to polytheism, and, in theory, invalidated other forms of religion,[1] made the concession of the Jews different from that granted to other rituals. Actually, the Jews were the only group in the Roman Empire that was exempted from what was regarded as an important religious duty, namely the offering of sacrifices to the gods, which included the emperor. A special form was eventually allowed and adopted for the Jews to express their loyalty to the emperor. The privileges extended to them did not cause too much of a problem for the Jews living in their own country, but by the time of Jesus, most Jews lived outside of the Palestine. For centuries Jewish settlements had been scattered over many parts of Asia, Africa, and Europe. So the exemption from the usual religious observance singled out a minority and was bound to cause friction with their pagan neighbours. This was all the more so, on account of quite a successful Jewish missionary activity among them, which worried the imperial authorities and lead them to expel the Jews from Rome in 139 BC. The Roman rulers of Palestine found their Jewish territories troublesome, and the Jewish authorities in Palestine, both secular and priestly, realized that the situation of their people was precarious and that any false move on their part might have serious consequences. They were worried about the religious excitement and missionary activity in the first half of the first century AD, which drew special and somewhat unwelcome attention to Judaism. Measures were taken by the authorities against the ultra-sectarian Zealots because of the political implications of their movement, with its readiness to proceed to insurrection when the occasion seemed ripe. It is against this very complex politico-religious background that the story of Jesus has to be seen. It is crucial in this context because Christian anti-Judaism arose from the way the Church interpreted the life and death of Jesus. For nearly two millennia, the Christian churches accused the Jews of deicide, of having murdered God, for being responsible for the crucifixion of Jesus. For most of this period, the Church confined the Jews to an inferior position on the grounds that, in their "obstinacy," they refused to accept Christ, which they ought to have done. Untold generations of Jews suffered discrimination, expulsion, and pogroms, which left in our present secular century persistent prejudices against the Jews.[2]

The historical Jesus lived as a Jew, in general as an observant one, even if he had his own views on some aspects of his religion. In this he was not unique in the Judaism of his time which was pluralistic and permitted a considerable variety of interpretations. These were regarded as "divisions within the framework of a commonly held faith," united by allegiance to the Law.[3] Thus, for example, the Pharisees were highly critical of the high priesthood, which they felt had become too political. While Jesus could not actually be counted among the Pharisees, though the gospels probably exaggerated his differences with them, he shared their criticism of the high priesthood of his day, and in this he went probably further than the Pharisees. Jesus, a Jew, naturally had friendships with other Jews, but, regarding the independence of his views, also had disagreements with some members of his community. These controversies are completely distorted if they are viewed as the almost single-handed struggle of a non-Jew against the Jews.

Jesus did not fundamentally object to the Jewish Law. He did not break it in any flagrant way with respect to food and the Sabbath, certainly not to the extent that would account for his eventual condemnation. Not only did he submit personally to the legal obligations incumbent on a Jew, but he more than once expressly urged obedience to the purely ritual and cultic precepts.[4] Jesus's "extraordinary emphasis on the real inner religious significance of the commandments was due partly to his natural bias towards the individual and personal, rather than the collective."[5] He stood out not so much by dissenting from the basic tenets of Judaism as by his interpretation, his striking formulations and parables. The Jesus of the Synoptic Gospels appears to the leading biblical scholar, Géza Vermès, "as a first-century AD Jewish holy man, portrayed as a preacher, healer and exorcist, delivering special moral exhortations concerning the impending arrival of the 'Kingdom of God.'"[6]

The titles "prophet," "lord," and "son of God" in biblical and post-biblical Jewish literature are in fact applied to charismatic holy men. Vermès emphasizes, however, that Jesus was an exception and incomparably superior to the minor charismatic figures of the post-biblical age:

Second to none in profundity of insight and grandeur of character, he is in particular an unsurpassed master of the art of
laying bare the inmost core of spiritual truth and bringing
every issue back to the essence of religion, the existential relationship of man, and man and God.[7]

Vermès cautions, however, against the application of the designa-
tion of Messiah to Jesus, "because of its most generally held sense of
a liberating king of the last days." For these reasons Jesus was disin-
clined to apply the notion to himself.[8] Vermès, who taught at
Oxford, is only one of several Jewish scholars who sees Jesus very
positively. It is pleasing to note that after all the terrible centuries-
long dissension, a much more positive view of Jesus has been developing in Jewish circles.

Why was Jesus arrested? What probably started the moves
against him was his action in the temple just before Passover, when
the Roman procurator Pontius Pilate normally came to Jerusalem.
The annual gathering of large crowds made both the Roman and
Jewish authorities apprehensive about possible unrest among the
people. In this very tense situation, Jesus's overturning of the tables
of the moneylenders in the temple was bound to be worrisome to
the authorities. What Jesus intended was not necessarily a purifica-
tion of the temple; he was not opposed to the required temple sacrifices, which needed commercial facilities to change money. Jesus
seems to have thought more in eschatological terms, that the end
of the world was at hand, that the old temple would be destroyed,
and that at the end of time a new and perfect temple might arise.
Jesus's words and deeds were taken at face value and therefore contained elements of a disturbance of the peace, which would have
given pause to the authorities. His claim to divine inspiration, as a
kind of prophet, was not in itself regarded as blasphemous. It was
the combination of word with deed, particularly the scene at the
temple in Jerusalem around Passover, which was difficult to over-
look. Pilate, who in any case was worried by the prevalence of disaffection among the population, may well have demanded some
action on the part of the Jewish authorities. It is plausible that the
High Priest and the Sanhedrin, the supreme Jewish body, anxious to

maintain the delicate religio-political balance that had been established, felt compelled to comply, and suggested Jesus's arrest to stabilize the situation. Pilate was a ruthless administrator who was eventually withdrawn in disgrace from Judaea by the Roman authorities because of the many complaints against him. The High Priest and the Sanhedrin feared that unless they satisfied the wishes of the Roman procurator, the remaining Jewish privileges would be abolished. Whatever were the technical modalities of Jesus's arrest, it appears to have resulted from a joint decision of some of the Jewish and Roman authorities.

Jesus was interrogated by the Jewish authorities, but there is now considerable doubt as to whether a formal trial by the Sanhedrin took place. Possibly Jesus was tried and convicted by the Jewish authorities for blasphemy, as Matthew and Mark report. More probably "he was turned over to Pilate by the chief priests as an evildoer according to Jewish law."[9] Crucifixion was not a Jewish but a Roman method of execution. It is likely that the charge against Jesus was that of sedition. His cross bore the inscription "King of the Jews," indicating his alleged claim as the cause for which he had been sentenced. In view of the turbulent state of the country and of past disaffection in Galilee, the fact that he was a Galilean with a following may have strengthened suspicions of him. Also in this period, anybody believed to be a Messiah would have been seen as a redeemer seeking to restore the Davidic Kingdom, who would be expected to be endowed with soldierly prowess, righteousness, and holiness. Actually, Jesus was completely innocent of plotting against the Romans. In his teaching he emphasized the importance of civil obedience to authority.[10]

Considerable doubts attach to the story reported in the Gospels that the procurator attempted to save Jesus from execution by offering to release one of the men sentenced to death, but that the *Jewish* crowd chose one of the other prisoners. According to Matthew, the crowd refused Pilate's intervening for Jesus, "with one voice the people cried, 'His blood be on us, and on our children'" (27:25). It was much later, when the Christian churches persecuted the Jews, that Matthew's words, interpreted by Christian preachers, assumed their terrible significance.

There is another way of looking at these events relating to the life and suffering of Jesus, the Passion seen in terms of faith. Jesus dwelled on earth as a Galilean Jew. He often talked in parables; his words had more then a literal meaning. When he had talked about the temple to be destroyed and rebuilt in three days (John 2:19–21, Matt. 26:16), he talked about himself. If Jesus had to die as part of his mission on earth, then the high priest and the Jewish authorities, and particularly Pontius Pilate, were the preordained instruments for a course of events over which they did not have any real control. This was recognized by Peter on Pentecost when he addressed his fellow Jews. He said that when Jesus had been given up to arrest "by the determinate council and foreknowledge of God" who used heathen (or pagan) men (meaning the Romans) to crucify and kill him (Acts 2:23). If at all, there was only a very limited Jewish responsibility for the execution of Jesus. The Jewish authorities acted in a tense and potentially explosive situation taking place under the shadow of the Roman Empire represented by the merciless Pontius Pilate, whose part in the execution the evangelists play down so as not to antagonize the Romans. Jesus died because he had done the wrong thing (cause a commotion) in the wrong place (the temple) at the wrong time (just before Passover).[11] As to deicide, quite apart from the problematic aspects of "killing God," those who sat in judgment on Jesus, so far as they were concerned, were trying a human being and not somebody who also had a divine nature. Since the Second World War there had been a turning away from this age-old doctrine. On September 1st, 2002, the Christian Scholars Group in the United States "reject[ed] this accusation as historically false and theologically invalid."[12]

The gospel writers produced a statement of faith and not a historical record. Their sincere religious views gradually made them emphasize more what separated them from Judaism than what they shared with it. Further, the successive generations of Christians became more and more removed in time from the period of Jesus's earthly existence, and the Jewishness of Jesus, that the fact that the apostles and his early followers were all Jews became increasingly submerged. Predominantly he appeared to them as "the first Christian" or the founder of Christianity who had been

executed because of Jewish hostility. That this was often the interpretation of the gospels does matter because later anti-Jewish
measures were based on these premises. The tragic antagonism
that ensued between the mother and the daughter religion, which
is to some extent reflected in the gospel according to John, was due
mainly to a new departure in Christian theology following the
destruction of the temple in the year AD 70. The fate of the temple
convinced Christians that all the promises of the Hebrew bible had
passed to them. The Christians thus "disinherited the Jews from
their own sacred books at the very moment when these provided
their only comfort."[13] The Hebrew bible, though accepted as the
word of God, is seen increasingly merely as a forerunner of the New
Dispensation, as foretelling the Coming of Christ. It was asserted
that through rejecting Jesus, the Jews had also lost any share in
God's promises to them, and the Jews are now represented as having plotted the killing of Jesus all along. The trial and crucifixion are
more and more reinterpreted in the light of later events, and two
separately established religions had developed, and became
increasingly at loggerheads with each other.

The mutually hostile atmosphere between Christians and Jews
was reflected in the Jewish anathema of the followers of Jesus,
which was probably instituted between AD 80 and 90. Neither side
distinguished itself by moderation or restraint. Still there were certain differences. The Christian campaign against the Jews created a
negative Jewish stereotype, whereas theologically the Jews largely
ignored the Christians. The Church's agitation against the Jews was
to some extent prompted by the continuing attraction of Judaism,
which had responded to the loss of the temple with the establishment of a network of synagogues and a remarkable development of
rabbinical teaching reflected, for example, in the Talmud. However,
in the long run, the Jews normally constituted a minority at the
mercy of the Christians' growing majority.

After a period during which Christians were themselves persecuted by the Roman authorities, Christianity became the state religion of the Roman Empire under Constantine in the first half of the
fourth century. It was now the turn of the Jews to be persecuted by
the Christian state. Christian theology, which had already acquired

strong anti-Jewish characteristics before Constantine's reign, almost seemed to require a caricature of a Jew composed of entirely negative features. In the post-apostolic period, the Fathers of the Church separated the promises of the Bible, which were now claimed for the Christians, from its curses and denunciations, which were henceforward applied to the Jews. The Jews themselves, well before and beyond Luther and right into our modern times, were blamed for the blindness and stubbornness which prevented most of them from giving up their religion for Christianity. One is at a loss to understand how the Jews were expected to accept Christianity with open arms when all this denunciation of their activity was going on.

In viewing negatively the attitude of the Church towards the Jews, we should not forget the many positive sides of Christianity. We should also be aware of the fact that the Jews were not the only group to suffer from the determination of the Church to enforce orthodoxy and uniformity. Christians regarded as heretics at times fared even worse than the Jews. But while the persecution of the heretics was – at least in some ways – aimed at individuals, the Jews suffered discrimination and pain as a group. However much a Jewish individual might distinguish himself by his human qualities, he was still judged as sinfully perverse in his obstinate adherence to a religion regarded as synonymous with error.[14] The measures taken against the Jews were, amongst others, their exclusion from the professions and from owning land; the special taxes imposed on them by the authorities, allegedly for their protection; their having to wear a special hat and dress to show that they were Jews; and their liability to expulsion from the territories on which they lived, which in some cases they could only escape by forcible conversion. Thus they were expelled from England in 1290, from France initially in 1394, and from Spain in 1492.

At various times the mob, which the teaching of the Church had turned against the Jews, took over, such as during the massacres and forced conversions of Jews at the time of the First Crusade towards the end of the eleventh century. The Jews are not free from black sheep any more than any other group of people. Gradually, over the ages, some less admirable qualities developed among some Jews as the result of persecution, such as a certain wiliness or cunning, often necessary to survive in adverse circumstances. Some of these characteristics persisted even in situations when the end of persecution made them superfluous, but human nature does not change that quickly. Also, the inability to practice many trades and professions forced the Jews into finance, with all its pitfalls, such as the encouragement of greed and the temptation of unscrupulousness. Under siege from the outside world, Jews tended to stick together, because they needed to do so; this in turn was often resented by the Christians as "exclusiveness."

So far, when the Church was mentioned, the Roman Catholic Church is meant. But after the Schism (the separation between East and West Rome in 1054), Jews under the Orthodox Church with the Patriarch of Constantinople did nor fare any better than those under the Pope in Rome. With the Reformation, alternatives to the Roman Church opened up, and there was now at any rate the possibility of better conditions for the Jews in Protestant countries. Indeed, Martin Luther at first stood up for the Jews. He believed that a Christianity more humane and more firmly rooted in scripture would lead to a large-scale conversion of the Jews. When that did not happen, even after the Reformation, he turned bitterly against the Jews. But Protestant powers, some of which were Calvinist, generally provided a more tolerant environment than Catholic authorities.[15] In England, the Puritan's mind regarded the Jews with favour as the ancient people of God. The more sanguine hoped that the newly purified forms of Christianity would convince them of the truth of the Gospel, where the Church of Rome had so miserably failed.[16] During Oliver Cromwell's regime, a synagogue in London was authorized in 1656, paving the way for Jews who had been forcibly baptized to practice their Jewish faith openly. But other Protestant territories followed the Catholic lead by confining the Jews to ghettos. The word "ghetto" is derived from the original quarter to which the Jews were confined in Venice from 1516 onwards.[17] The Catholic Church, which was on the defensive owing to the Protestant Reformation, actually tightened up its measures against the Jews.

Initially, mainly as a result of the massacres during the time of the crusades, for about four centuries, from the end of the eleventh century to the end of the fifteenth (i.e., to the end of the Middle Ages), Jewish migration had mainly moved eastward from France, the Rhineland, and Spain, towards Turkey and Poland. Then, with the reversal of this trend, came the terrible massacres of Jews by the Cossacks of the Ukraine from 1648, which was worse than anything the Jews had suffered for some time. This reversed the geographical direction of migration, which then for nearly three centuries moved from East to West. The two main groups among the Jews differed in their precise attitude to Judaism and the Christian environment: in very broad terms, the Sephardim from Southern Europe were more in favour of assimilation than the Ashkenazim from Eastern Europe, who remained more orthodox.

As the churches had been mainly responsible for anti-Jewish measures, one might expect that a diminution of church influence, such as during the Enlightenment of the eighteenth century, would benefit the Jews. Up to a point this was true, but the Enlightenment questioned all religions, including Judaism, and some of the enlightened philosophers were not particularly pro-Jewish. One aspect of the increasing toleration granted to the Jews in several European countries, such as the Austrian Empire in 1781, opened the ghettos but implied in a rather condescending way typical for the Enlightenment that the Jews were expected to change for the better. This had to do with moving them out of their traditional occupations like money lending, into something considered more productive. Over time, they shed the old restrictions and became prosperous in the newly opened pursuits, and this unfortunately gave new ground for envy and persecution for which they then were blamed. An even more sensitive aspect of toleration was the question to what extent Jews were expected to assimilate in their country of residence. Was their culture, and even their religion, at risk?

Similarly, the French Revolution of 1789 and the birth of a modern nationalism had both positive and negative aspects for the Jews. On the positive side, the French Revolutionary Assembly in 1791 gave equal rights to the Jews, removing the disabilities from which they had suffered because of their religion. But the new turn of events also raised some questions. Under the old order, the Jews had their own community organization, including their law and their courts of law, and within certain narrow limits were autonomous. They were in fact, in the countries in which they lived, normally regarded as a "nation" in the earlier sense. How would the new national state look on Judaism? Was it simply a religion, or would the Jews continue in each country as a separate nation? Could the new national state be sure of the loyalty of their Jewish citizens, who had their own religion and even their own laws? And would Jews feel that they could completely identify with the national state in which they lived to the same extent as their Christian fellow citizens did? Or did the Jews have some international bonds cutting across national boundaries? And does Judaism imply a Jewish nationhood, compatible or incompatible with the nationhood of the host country? These questions were always posed theoretically, but they have assumed even greater practical importance with the foundation of the Zionist movement in 1897 and later with that of the state of Israel after the Second World War. The answers lie in the eye of the beholder, and even Jews are certainly not agreed on them.

Actually, the new national state recognized only one nation, its own, and not separate "nations" such as the Jews. But overall, for the time being, the Jews gained for moving out of the ghetto. In many European countries, following the French example, the Jews received equal rights, at least on paper, including Germany, mainly during the second half of the nineteenth century. Through increased political control, the influence of the churches, with their religious anti-Judaism, was weakened. The Jews had in fact only been one of the groups to have suffered discrimination, along with, for example, religious minorities, such as the Roman Catholics and Nonconformists in Britain. Gradually, during the course of the nineteenth century, these Christian minorities and the Jews became entitled to full civic rights. The talents of all these minorities previously under civil disabilities became available to their societies. During the course of the nineteenth century, European Jewry, except in some of the Eastern countries, moved strongly into professions and other activities previously closed to them. As their faith had always emphasized learning, through above all the study of the Bible and the Talmud, Jews took easily to intellectual pursuits and were keen to undertake university studies and to enter the professions, such as those of law and medicine. They became prominent in business and banking. With this sudden opening of the floodgates, Jews began to enter the legal and medical professions in great numbers, in Austria, for example, at times constituting more than 40 percent of them.[18] This set up a backlash on the part of their Christian competitors. Through their business activities, Jews became associated in people's minds with excessive capitalism; they attracted the hostility of all those anti-modernists who believed they had been harmed by economic development. Generalizations about *all* Jews were drawn from examples of Jewish sharp practice, for example in business. Negative stereotypes did not fail to emanate.

This new anti-Judaism or modern anti-Semitism found the ground prepared by Christian condemnation of the Jews as murderers of God. In addition, unlike the previous territorial or dynastic state, the new national state emphasized the people or nation into which you were born, and into which you as an outsider could not be so easily assimilated. This led not far from racialism, that your descent determined whether you could be regarded as part of the people in the national state. Various racial doctrines went beyond a classification according to the colour of the skin, and some were holding that all Jews belonged to a separate race. But in the long run, racialism and Christianity were on a collision course, particularly if the baptism of Jews was not recognized. Many people joined in the new anti-Jewish hunt, particularly in the last two decades of the nineteenth century. Even in France, anti-Jewish feeling was strong as the Dreyfus affair, arising from the unjust condemnation of a Jewish officer for espionage at the end of the nineteenth century, showed.

A new element was now being added to the religious anti-Judaism, a modern anti-Semitism with a strong national, racial, social, and economic emphasis directed against the Jews. It is the combination of the traditional religious anti-Judaism with these new secular elements that proved so disastrous to the Jews. In countries like Tsarist Russia, where there was a strong alliance between throne and altar with a virulent anti-Judaism, Jews were treated particularly badly. They suffered periodic pogroms, one of the worst of these following the assassination of Tsar Alexander II in 1881. The word pogrom derived from a Russian word meaning destruction. Western European and German Jews at the time, while horrified, somehow felt this kind of thing simply could not happen in their modern civilized country. There was an anti-Semitic party in Germany, but generally Protestants and Catholics were less virulent in their anti-Jewish feeling and actions than their Eastern European Christian neighbours. This flared-up anti-Semitism set off a chain reaction. When Jews from the Tsarist Empire fled to western countries. These so-called *Ostjuden*, with their East European culture, created resentment in the countries further west in which they had settled, and so were setting off fresh anti-Semitic waves. Many of the Jews escaping from popular Polish Catholic, Ukrainian Greek-Catholic, and Russian Orthodox anti-Semitism favoured Germany for settlement because they regarded its people as comparatively tolerant.

During the early years of the twentieth century, anti-Semitism in Europe was in decline, but the comparative stability of these years was interrupted by the outbreak of the First World War in 1914; due to the breakdown of the international system, in the form of the Concert of Europe, that since 1815 had allowed a "balance of power," now a tragic sequence of events was ushered in. The war was fought with the utmost bitterness by the five great powers, and joined in April 1917 by the United States of America, for more than four years. The enormous casualties forced millions to get used to killing and violence, with lasting disastrous long-term effects after the end of hostilities. The Communist revolution in Russia in 1917 led to increased ideological confrontation. Jewish participation in the spreading of communism was noted by parties opposed to it. The emphasizing of the danger from the extreme Left was used by the right-wing forces all over Europe. This missed the essential point that the real alternative to Soviet Communism was not another dictatorship, but democracy. The interwar period of Europe was however troubled by doubts about the efficacy of democracy and the rule of law. Which leads to the history of Germany and the question how the Nazis got into power.

Germany was defeated in 1918. Its people had been led to believe, certainly after the victory over France in 1871, that victory on the battlefield denoted moral superiority. Did the reverse also apply? Did defeat on the battlefield denote moral inferiority? Propaganda in the sense of a distortion of the truth had a perfect solution: Germany had not been defeated on the battlefield but had been stabbed in the back by whomever one disliked – the Jews, the Socialists, the war profiteers on the home front, etc. The terms of the Versailles peace treaty of 1919 imposed on the German people were widely resented. The "war guilt" clause was certainly unwise, but other stipulations (such as the restoration of certain territories to France and Denmark) righted historical injustices. Also, the introduction of plebiscites in the causes of self-determination was quite reasonable and even far-sighted. In November 1918, the Weimar Republic,[19] named after the city where the constitution was adopted, displaced the imperial monarchies. The new government had to deal with many crisis: uprising and putsch, in 1920 the runaway inflation which destroyed the savings of the thrifty, an ongoing occupation of German territory, and enormous financial reparations to France. And then, just when some stability seemed to be at hand, the world economic crisis of 1929/30 and its high unemployment brought new uncertainty. The German parliament, the *Reichstag*, did not reach a clear majority, and the country could only be kept going by constitutionally allowed presidential decrees issued by the octogenarian President, Field Marshal von Hindenburg. Using the general discontent and misery of the masses, the Nazi propaganda machine went in overdrive and used the forged conspiracy theory of Jewish world domination in the Nos Kan–inspired forgery of the *Elders of Zion*,[20] which seemed to explain to the simpleminded the cause of the misery. The Jews had the worst of both worlds, they were suspected of having enormous power, and at the same time as a minority, they were at the mercy of their national oppressors.

In the last free election, the Nazis obtained 33 percent of the votes, together with the communists and German national party, that amounted to over 50 percent of voters rejecting democracy and rule of law. The situation changed at once. Germany had been a state based upon the rule of law, a *Rechtsstaat*.[21] Now it became a state based on injustice. Brutality was glorified and might was right. Communists, Socialists, and Jews were arrested outside the normal court system and the official penal system. Concentration camps were established with brutal guards and torture. The government declared a boycott of Jewish business on April 1st, 1933, which was called off the next day. Their means of livelihood had been restricted and then taken away[22] by excluding them from professional and business life.[23] After the *Kristallnacht* in 1938, they were forbidden to use public places and transport, their children were dismissed from school, and they had to wear the Star of David (*Judenstern*).[24] A look at statistics gives a clearer picture: in 1933 there were about 500 000 Jews in Germany, and after the annexation of Austria, another 185 000 were added, making a total of 685 000. Up to the outbreak of the Second World War, 410 000 had left the country one way or another; this is a high number considering the difficulties of receiving permission to enter another country.[25] That left about 275 000 behind. Before the war, the well-educated Jews and non-Aryan for various reasons had a better chance to getting out than those with lesser education and qualifications. The loss to Germany of educated and qualified people was considerable. The contribution of German refugees to the American atomic bomb is just one striking example. Under the cover of war and the German occupation of most European countries, many of them with their own anti-Semitic tradition, a great number of Jews were subjected to further persecution. These Jews hardly had any chance to find to any form of safety, and became subject to what was called the final solution – the Holocaust or Shoah, the murder of millions of European Jews (something like five or six million). Death certificates were not issued nor were other official records kept, so it is impossible to know the exact number of those exterminated in places like Auschwitz.[26] All this is a story almost beyond belief, but unfortunately well substantiated. Many Jewish families mourn their victims, including my own. The experience of those twelve years left an indelible mark on me, though my suffering cannot in any way be compared to those who had to stay to the bitter end. When I went back to Germany as a British soldier in April 1945 and saw the destruction of the country, I tried to find the answer to the question: How was all this possible.

The National Socialists under Goebbels's direction conducted a relentless propaganda campaign to exploit the grievances of Germans, both real and imaginary. He always told the truth, but in a disjointed form. Anti-Jewish slogans fitted in well with their glorification of German nationalism and of an alleged Aryan race superiority, purged of its Jewish elements. In their anti-Semitism, they found the ground well prepared by the contempt the churches had shown for the Jews since the simplistic interpretation of the gospels. However, Hitler's rise to power was not inevitable. In 1932 and early 1933 it was touch and go whether he would be appointed chancellor. The rabid anti-Semitism of the Nazis, who clearly stated in their party programme that those of Jewish descent could not be German citizens and were subject to expulsion, helped them to become the largest party in the Reichstag. They coined the "non-Aryan" category to denote anybody who had Jewish blood, even it he only had one grandparent of Jewish descent. It was thus an important factor for getting the Nazis into power. Past errors in Christian theology, combined with the growth of a fanatical nationalism and racialism, led to the series of horrible events from 1933 onwards. But Jews were not the only ones that were persecuted; political and religious dissidents or anybody that did not fit in became subject to the same lawlessness. Hatred of the Jews, a key element in this chain of events, proved self-destructive to its German propagators, leading to the Second World War with massive bombing of Germany, enormous German casualties, the expulsion of millions of ethnic Germans from neighbouring countries, the loss of many German territories in the East, and for some forty years to the occupation and division of Germany as well as to Communist rule in her eastern part.

If my reasoning about the basic responsibility of the church for all this becomes more widely accepted, it would be important that we should do all we can to make sure that *all* Christian churches in their divine services provide some historical explanation whenever those parts of the New Testament are read which might be interpreted as condemnation of the Jews or which invite contempt for them.

Notes

1   Rodney Stark, *One True God: Historical Consequences of Monotheism* (Princeton University Press, 2001).
2   Gésa Vermès, *Jesus and the World of Judaism* (Minneapolis: Fortress Press, 1983), 47.
3   Ibid., 48.
4   Géza Vermès, *Providential Accidents: An Autobiography* (Lanham, MD: Rowmann & Littlefield Publishers, 1998), 212.
5   Ibid., 293.
6   Ibid., 246–47.
7   Ibid., 216.
8   James William Parkes, *The Conflict of the Church and the Synagogue: A Study in the Origins of anti-Semitism* (New York: Athenaeum, 1969), 84.
9   E. P. Sanders, *Jesus and Judaism* (Philadelphia: Fortress Press, 1985), 318.
10 Matt. 22:16–22; Mark 20:13–17; Luke 21:20–26.
11 Sanders, 216.
12 SIDIC #1-3, 2003, p. 41. See also in Frank Eyck's papers the unpublished essay of Sr. Margaret Mcgrath, "The Thorny Question Of Mission," JCST 6001, Lawrence Frizzell, December 2003, Frank Eyck, Special Collection of the University of Calgary Library.
13 Parkes, 84.
14 Frederick M. Schweitzer, *A History of the Jews: Since the First Century A.D.* (New York: Macmillan, 1971), 73.
15 Cecil Roth, *A Short History of the Jewish People* (London: East and West Library, 1948), 298.
16 Ibid., 298.
17 Ibid., 247.
18 Robert Gildea, *Barricades and Borders: Europe, 1800–1914* (Oxford University Press, 1987), 310.
19 Erich Eyck, *History of the Weimar Republic*, trans. H.P. Hanson & R.L. Waite (Harvard University Press, 1963).
20 United States Holocaust Memorial Museum, *A Dangerous Lie: The Protocol of the Elders of Zion* (http://www.ushmm.org/wlc/en/article.php?ModuleId=10007058).
21 Edith Stein in a letter to Pope Pius XII, April 12th, 1933, pointing to lawlessness of the new government, SIDIC #1-3, 2003, pp. 32–33.

22 Monika Richarz, *Jüdisches Leben in Deutschland* (Stuttgart: Deutsche Verlagsanstalt, Veröffentlichung des Leo Baeck institutes, 1979), 3:41ff.

23 Ibid, 3:47.

24 Ibid, 3:57–58.

25 Gebhardt, 4:209.

26 "Remembrance for Peace," SIDIC #1-3, 2003: pp. 23

Chapter Ten

NATIONAL SOCIALISM: A PSEUDO-RELIGION?

Presented February 24th, 2004, in Irving Hexham's course on "Method and Theory in the Study of Religion."

THE NATIONAL SOCIALIST REGIME from 1933 to 1945 was barbaric. Thus the historian has to try and explain how Germany – a country that was a leader of European civilization before 1933 and had a well-established rule of law, though not a long democratic tradition – could be taken over by a brutal regime.

Adolf Hitler and his National Socialist party owed their importance, above all, to their success at the ballot box, in free elections, by becoming the leading political party before Hitler's appointment as chancellor in January 1933, achieving about 37 percent of the vote at their most popular, then dropping back to about 33 percent in the last free election. They did not obtain a majority any more than any other political party during the republican period between 1918 and 1933. But how did the National Socialists achieve their success?

In answering these and other questions about the Nazi regime, the researcher has to apply the same strict standards of evidence and judgment as to other historical events. Once he has in this way established the sequence of events, only then can he apply moral judgments, or should he abstain from applying any kind of ethical values altogether? Different answers have been given to this question. To my mind, the historian should clearly characterize crimes – such as murder, or mass murder – as such. But he should think carefully before criminalizing *en bloc* political actions, such as going to war, without paying sufficient regard to the complexities of international law and the particular circumstances.

While we try to understand the rise to power of Hitler and his National Socialist Party, we must remember that understanding is not necessarily the same as justifying. Three events played a major part in paving the way for the National Socialist regime:

1. The outbreak of the First World War in 1914
2. Germany's defeat in 1918 and the Peace Treaty of Versailles in 1919
3. The proclamation of the Republic of Germany in 1918

In view of the crucial, indeed essential, part Hitler played in the Nazi regime and the rise of National Socialism, we should look at his early life. Adolf Hitler was born in 1889 in Braunau, Austria, on the Inn river at the border with Germany, into a German-speaking, Roman Catholic, lower-middle-class family as the son of a customs official. He certainly did not come from the money-less proletariat. He was a poor scholar and whiled away the early years of his life, not settling down to any definite occupation and for a time was a drop-out in Vienna, a city rampant with anti-Semitism. This anti-Jewish feeling, which began in Hitler's mind to acquire racial over-tones and drew on the anti-Judaism the Christian churches had been propagating for nearly two millennia, is denied by some schol-ars, but I have to inform you of this interpretation. As a strong German nationalist, Hitler was unhappy with the multinational compromises of the Austro-Hungarian monarchy under Habsburg rule, and in 1913 he moved to Germany, settling in Munich, the Bavarian capital. He did not register for military service in Austria, as was his duty, and narrowly escaped serious trouble when this was discovered. In August 1914, on the outbreak of hostilities, Hitler, like many others, volunteered with great enthusiasm for the German army and was accepted. Strictly speaking, he should have been returned to Austria as an Austrian subject, but the army "made him," in a sense, for now the drifter began to acquire a sense of purpose; also he was taken care of and had the comradeship of other soldiers. He was employed as a message runner at the front, a service fraught with danger, and was twice awarded the Iron Cross for bravery. He rose to the rank of corporal. Hitler was wounded during his service, though, as elsewhere, the details are not necessarily quite those given in his book *Mein Kampf* (*My Struggle*). He was deeply shaken by Germany's military defeat and by the political changes that followed, including the left-wing putsch in Munich made by the completely unrepresentative German Jewish journalist from Berlin Kurt Eisner. While still serving as a soldier in Munich, he witnessed the dramatic course of events in the Bavarian capital that culminated in a quasi-Communist take-over (*Räterepublik*), and the ensuing re-conquest of the city by the authorities. Hitler's role in these events is not quite clear; he may for a time have gone along with left-wing feelings in his army unit. He got his first great opportunity when he was employed by the army as a political propagandist against the Left, particularly among the troops. Hitler now realized that he had oratorical gifts, and these were generally appreciated by his superiors. Ian Kershaw, in his excellent Hitler biography, states that Hitler got his chance to rise to prominence as a result of "a lost war, a revolution, and a pervasive sense of national humiliation." Hitler's message did "capture exactly the uncontainable sense of anger, fear, frustration, resentment, and pent-up aggression of the raucous gatherings in the Munich Beer Halls."[1] I believe the potency of Hitler's demagogy may have been enhanced by the bitterness and hatred he had accumulated during his years as an underdog and by his inability, in general, to form close personal relationships. His political activity became the centre and the whole purpose of his existence, literally the one thing for which he lived.

Hitler's ideology was strongly nationalistic and anti-Semitic. He never entered deeply into political and economic problems. As Kershaw points out, "ideas held no interest for Hitler as abstractions. They were important to him only as tools of mobilization of public opinion."[2] Drawing on the kind of *völkisch* (meaning belonging to a certain people and or race) ideas in vogue in Central Europe at that time, Hitler had a simplified and somewhat irrational view of the world (*Weltanschauung*) that blamed the ills from which Germany was suffering on war profiteers, Marxists, Socialists, and

Jews stabbing the brave army in the back. The painful social adjust-
ment to industrialization was blamed on the dark forces of "capital," including a Jewish conspiracy and the serfdom imposed by the
charging of interest (*Zinsknechtschaft*). In September 1919, as an
army informer, he was ordered to keep an eye on political organizations in Munich; he attended a meeting of a small right-wing group,
the German Workers' Party (*Deutsche Arbeiterpartei*), which he
soon joined. In July 1921, now as a civilian, he assumed leadership
of the National Socialist German Workers' Party (*National-
sozialistische Deutsche Arbeiterpartei*) and put it under his strict
personal control. The name implied that the party wanted to
appeal to all those of German stock, and in particular to workers in
the name of a non-Marxist socialism, whatever that meant. An article of the party programme laid down that persons of Jewish
descent were not entitled to be German citizens and could be
expelled from the country if necessary. Jews apart, the all-embrac-
ing formula allowed Hitler to secure allies in many disparate quarters, including the right-wing officer class, among them General
Ludendorff, one of the German heroes of the First World War. In
these endeavours, Hitler was certainly helped by his military service and by the award of the Iron Cross. His ideology put forward a
crude theory of the Germans as the master race, superior to Jews,
Slavs, and Gypsies, and claimed, absurdly, the need of more living
space to be gained at the expense particularly of the Slavs. Strongly
influenced by Social Darwinist theories he had picked up in the
popular literature he read, the world to him was a kind of struggle
in which only the fittest survived. Eugenics fitted in here, breeding
a thoroughly fit master-race, a social order in which the physically
or mentally handicapped had no place. In all this, the atmosphere
on the front during the war, what was called the "killing ground," as
well as what he had made of his experiences in Vienna, helped to
shape his outlook.

At the outset I drew attention to the importance of the First
World War in understanding the atmosphere of the time in which
Hitler and the Nazi movement thrived. Previously, for practically a
century before 1914, co-operation between the European great
powers, then called "the Concert of Europe," had prevented wars

involving all of the powers. Mercifully, the wars that actually took place were comparatively limited and short. The ability of governments to resist the pressure of an increasingly strongly nationalistic public opinion declined as this nationalism became more powerful and indeed in some cases began to affect rulers, such as the German emperor William II. And once war had started between all the five major European powers, this nationalism on all sides prevented an early termination of hostilities on the basis of compromise. To keep up the fighting spirit, governments found it necessary to make promises to their population that were impossible to keep, such as "creating a world fit for heroes to live in." And once the enemy had surrendered, public opinion in the victorious countries demanded a harsh peace, including massive reparations, to compensate their population for the sacrifices they had made. There was thus the peril of endangering the future peace by inflicting peace terms on the Germans they were bound to regard as emotionally and physically unacceptable, thus turning them into irreconcilable revisionists.

Although it was the imperial government that had lost the war, it was its successor, the government of new *Weimar Republik*, that had to sign the armistice on November 11th, 1918, and the peace settlement of Versailles the following year, thereby incurring the odium for these events in the eyes of German public opinion. The new republican leaders thus laboured under a disadvantage from the beginning, being unjustly targeted as traitors betraying their own country. The French government, in the early years after the war, was blind to the dangers to its own interests for the enormous strain their demands, such as the excessive reparations, put on the fragile new German regime, which caused unemployment in their own country. Finally, the psychological effects of a world war lasting more than four years and enormous casualties cannot be overstated. The individual's threshold against killing had been lowered. There was some romanticizing of the comradeship in the trenches, certainly in Germany, and for a time in France, too. The war also left a heritage of paramilitary organizations, for example the German *Freicorps*, which were former army units no longer under the direct control of the government but under the political parties' affiliates, such as the Nazi SA (*Sturmabteilung*, the Storm Troopers) and SS (*Sturmstaffel*). The experiences of the First World War and its legends lived on in Germany after 1918 through Hitler's own activity and through the prestige which some generals had acquired during the war, such as Ludendorff, one of Hitler's early promoters, and even more fatefully through Hindenburg, who was elected president in 1925 and who, as we shall see, appointed Hitler chancellor in 1933.

In Germany after the First World War, the instability caused by the enormous loss of life and devastation of the military defeat, by the severe economic and social problems facing the population in the postwar years, and by the alienation so many felt as a result of the proclamation of the German Republic in Berlin, were all grist to Hitler's mill. One area strongly affected by these constitutional changes was the mainly Catholic Bavaria, with its particularist tradition and its strongly retained attachment to its royal dynasty, the Wittelsbach, and, last but not least, its resentfulness about receiving directions from the mainly Protestant German capital.

At this point it is useful to deal briefly with the events that brought Hitler to power. There was the terrible year 1923 when the French occupied the German Ruhr territory to enforce demands for reparations, the height of the raging inflation in Germany that wiped out hard-earned savings, and the Hitler putsch in Munich in November. The theatrical putsch failed, as it was bound to do. That Hitler escaped severe punishment he owed to the help he received from many right-wingers in Bavaria fanatically opposed to the republican regime in Berlin. Hitler was able to use the court-room for propagating the Nazi cause. The court order for his deportation to Austria was rejected by that country, of which he was still a citizen, not yet having acquired German nationality. The resulting stay in the Landsberg fortress, a comparatively honourable form of imprisonment, was comfortable. He could receive his party friends and use the time to begin writing *Mein Kampf*. After a few months, he was released from imprisonment.

The world economic crisis starting in 1929 was also a great boon to the Nazis. It was partly against the background of this crisis that the German parliament, the *Reichstag*, was no longer able to provide the basis for a stable government from 1930 onwards and that the slide into non-parliamentary government began. The country's business was carried on by decrees signed by the president under the emergency powers granted to him under article 48 of the constitution. The self-exclusion of a freely elected parliament, because there were too many small parties that could not reach agreement to form a majority, led to the intrigues of the circle around the by-then very ancient president von Hindenburg who had resisted Hitler for some years. In fact, Hindenburg displayed a certain disdain for Hitler by referring to him as "that Bohemian corporal," but by 1932, at eighty-five years of age, Hindenburg could only work part of the day. All this resulted in the supersession of the Catholic Centre Party leader in the Reichstag, Chancellor Brüning, by von Papen, a nonentity renegade from the Centre Party without any parliamentary following. He was in turn succeeded by General Schleicher, the Minister of Defence, comparatively a political dilettante, who had exaggerated hopes of being able to stop Hitler. However, as a result of yet another intrigue in the presidential entourage, Schleicher, after only a few weeks in office, was replaced as chancellor by Adolf Hitler on January 30th, 1933. Nominally, Hitler was in charge of a coalition government with the right-wing German National Party of Hugenberg. Hindenburg's advisers adopted this course in the belief that Hitler, the leader of the largest political party in the Reichstag (33% of the votes), could be harnessed by putting him into office as coalition partner of the more traditional conservative German nationalist party. Here once more Hitler benefited by being underrated outside his own party. Hugenberg and the other ministers were no match for Hitler and his party, which had a dynamism the other political parties lacked. In a sense, Hitler had come into power legally, though he had used loopholes in the law and twisted them somewhat to suit his own ends. Now he began his revolution in earnest, perhaps starting with a constitutional form, but ultimately resorting to illegality, indeed removing any rule of law and any opposition or alternative to the Nazi party.

Contrary to an opinion I have often encountered, it was clear from day one which way the wind was blowing. To me, as an eleven-year-old schoolboy, brought up in a cultured professional Jewish home in Berlin, the whole situation changed at once. I sensed that my parents could no longer fully protect me. Those who kept their eyes open and were better informed felt the pressure of the "street," of the Nazi storm troopers (SA) having their marches. It was clear that one had to keep out of their way, and that one had to be careful about what one said. At school, some masters wore their party badges, and some even appeared in Nazi uniform. I was comparatively fortunate in my school, the College Français (*Französisches Gymnasium*), which the electors of Brandenburg (the future kings of Prussia) had founded for the French Protestant refugees who had flocked to their territory after the measures taken against them by King Louis XIV in 1685. The school had a tradition of tolerance and a certain *esprit de corps*. We had both Nazis and, interestingly enough, even openly anti-Nazis among the teachers. Actually, at the time, I had never heard of a Nazi teacher denouncing to the authorities a colleague opposed to the regime. The principal, Gerstenberg, was displaced as a "non-Aryan" (i.e., of Jewish descent). But his successor Roethig, a member of the Nazi organization NSKK (*Nationalsozialistisches Kraftfahrkorps*), was consulted by my parents as to whether I should stay at the school or emigrate. While at first he strongly supported my remaining at the school, some time in 1935 he told my parents to have me sent abroad as soon as possible to be brought up there. For technical reasons, my parents were able quite legally to transfer funds to pay for my initial schooling in England. I may partly owe my survival to that principal.

In the initial period, the Nazis directed their strongest measures against their political opponents, particularly against the Communists. Having taken over key ministries, they controlled the police. They also made the secret police, the Gestapo, a feared institution. Arbitrary arrests, without any court order, were made on a considerable scale. On February 27th, 1933, a deranged psychopath Dutchman named Marianus van der Lubbe, formerly a Communist, acting on his own, set fire to the Reichstag. The Nazis did not allow the fire brigade to quench the blaze and interpreted it as a signal for a Communist uprising, which was used by the Nazis to increase their support in the Reichstag election due in early March 1933. Even with all the terror, the Nazis did not get a majority, just 43.9

percent of the votes. There was intensified oppression. One opposition party after another was excluded from the Reichstag, whose freedom to debate was curtailed by pressures from the "street." The Nazis demanded that the new Reichstag pass an Enabling Law (*Ermächtigunsgesetz*), which gave the government additional, though even then somewhat restricted, emergency powers. Our family friend Theodor Heuss, later the first president of the German Federal Republic in 1949, then a liberal member of the Reichstag, advised his by-then very small parliamentary group to oppose the measure, but followed party discipline when the majority of the group decided to accept it. The Nazis did not adhere even to the wide limits of the Enabling Law. There is something to be said for a view that in any case, with or without the Enabling Law, the Nazis were going to do what they wanted. They certainly proceeded to consolidate their hold on power, abolishing all political parties except for their own, which they called a movement. The Hitler Youth became the sole youth organization. By and large, the information media could only say what the government allowed them to say. Many of the quality independent newspapers of the republican period were forced to close, often by brutal methods. The propaganda machine under Josef Goebbels, the Minister of Propaganda and Popular Enlightenment, incessantly churned out its poisonous venom against all the alleged enemies of the regime, from the Communists to the Jews.

Perhaps the only independent institutions that the regime treated with somewhat unusual caution were the churches. Initially, Protestant leaders, who represented the majority of Christians in Germany, gave considerable support to the regime, even some of those who became its most bitter enemies. But not all of them were by any means prepared to toe the Nazi line and join the Nazi movement inside the Protestant Church consisting of what were called *Deutsche Christen*, German Christians. These adopted a great deal of Nazi ideology, including its quest for a cleansing of Christianity from its Jewish elements. Soon, courageous men like Pastor Martin Niemöller founded their own organization, the Confessing Church (*Die Bekennende Kirche*) which eventually led to Niemöller's lengthy incarceration in the Dachau concentration camp, as the "personal prisoner of the Führer." Thankfully, he survived. But many others did not, and the intercessional prayer list of the village church of Berlin Dahlem often mentioned more than fifty names. The Catholic Church in 1933 concluded a treaty with the Nazi Regime, a concordat, about the wisdom of which there is not yet any agreement among scholars. The Nazis reserved a final reckoning with the churches for their moment of victory, which fortunately never came.

You may ask, how were the Nazis able to carry the population with them on their course of monopolizing power, their increasingly more vicious persecution of the Jews and their perceived enemies, and eventually their pursuit of war? The Nazis always paid great attention to carrying the masses with them, helped by their incessant propaganda. In the early years, as the world economic crisis was receding, as public work projects, such as the construction of the *Autobahn*, rearmament, and the expansion of the armed forces created more jobs, contentment with the economic situation grew. It was assumed that Germany's eventual victory would take care of the accumulated public debt. In the meantime, the financial wizard Hjalmar Schacht, a renegade liberal, kept things going by tightly controlling foreign currency movements in which Germany was involved. As for the elites – in the army, the civil service, and business – they largely co-operated. Indeed, if they had not done so, the regime would soon have collapsed from its organizational flaws. For contrary to a widespread belief sometimes voiced: "If we only had a Hitler to put things right," dictatorship, with its suppression of public discussion and contempt for democracy and the rule of law, is not an efficient way of running a country. This certainly applied to the National Socialist specimen. From the time of his foundation of the National Socialist Party, Hitler always kept all decisions to himself. The efficiency of the Nazi regime was handicapped by a duality between the official government machine and the party. Often in the party, too, perhaps on the principle of "divide and rule," there were overlapping responsibilities. Hitler was not interested in the details of administration and long-term bureaucratic planning and was too lazy to be bothered with reading complicated government position papers, and relied on his intuition to make the appropriate decisions. He was encouraged in his indolence by the adulation of his genius on the part of his followers, who regarded him as a kind of saviour – until the whole system collapsed in ruins. Instead of being close to the government apparatus in Berlin, he spent a lot of his time at his retreat in the Bavarian Mountains at Berchtesgaden. There he had to be sought out to obtain his approval, which was often simply given in a nod, for example when later his decision was sought as to whether only East European or all German Jews should be murdered, or whether women and children should be included along with the men. Hitler also personally authorized the programme of killing the mentally incurable, though the regime took some notice here of protests from the public and particularly the churches. Precise figures of the number of those killed are not available, but a conservative estimate would have considerably exceeded one hundred thousand people.

Hitler tolerated radical pressure from the "street," which came from party organizations, for example from the SA, so long as it did not threaten his own position. But early on, when the leader of the SA, his old comrade Röhm, was becoming too independent of him, and when the German army put pressure on Hitler to curb the military ambitions of the SA, he had Röhm killed in the notorious Night of the Long Knives on June 30th, 1934.

Hitler used the opportunity to rid himself of a whole list of others with whom he had wanted to settle scores, including his predecessor as chancellor, General Schleicher, who had tried to foil the Nazi assumption of power and whom he suspected of still intriguing against him. Hitler had a long memory, killing also the former Bavarian General State Commissar, Gustav von Kahr, who had refused his co-operation during the November 1923 Munich putsch. I still remember the grief of my father, a lawyer and leading legal commentator in the republican period, over all this. Right from the beginning, the Nazis had maltreated political opponents they arrested, often shooting them. Now they had trampled on human rights in a massive action which was, at least up to a point, and with the usual distortion, reported in the information media. The German Minister of Justice, Gürtner, defended Hitler's action as being in accordance with the law. The leadership of the German army did not protest against the murder of Schleicher, one of their generals. Indeed, they must have been rather pleased that with the curbing of the SA, a rival to their monopoly of military power had been removed. Hitler's power was increased even further by the death in August 1934 of President Hindenburg, whose office he usurped.

The Nazis had successes in their foreign policy too. In 1935, the population of the Saar territory voted for their return to Germany after a period under the control of the League of Nations. This happened in accordance with international treaties. Also in 1935, the National Socialist government felt strong enough to openly declare their rearmament plans and to introduce conscription in violation of the Treaty of Versailles of 1919. The following year, in 1936, Germany remilitarized the Rhineland, which had been demilitarized since the war, originally under the peace treaty. And demilitarization had been confirmed by the voluntary agreement of Germany in its treaty with France at Locarno in 1925, which at last brought about better relations between the two countries. The French were entitled to resist the occupation of the German Rhineland by German troops but did not take any military action. In the spring of 1938, Germany annexed Austria, in breach of the prohibition of an *Anschluss* stipulated in the peace treaties. Hitler's position in Germany was enormously strengthened by Britain and France now accepting changes in the peace settlement as a result of his policy of force, which they had earlier refused to the republican regime in negotiation. Hitler had tested the waters. With the annexation of Austria he had undermined the whole territorial settlement in Central Europe. In accordance with his continued cynical use of the principle of self-determination (which was denied to others), he now claimed the Sudetenland, the part of Czechoslovakia inhabited by a mainly German population. Some of the German generals were critical of Hitler's determination to force the issue even at the risk of war. However, Britain and France caved in with a policy of appeasement, and in the Munich treaty at the end of September 1938, Czechoslovakia was forced to surrender the Sudetenland. When in the spring of 1939 Germany took over the rest of Czechoslovakia, even Neville Chamberlain, the British Prime Minister, realized that the policy of appeasement had failed.

As soon as Czechoslovakia had vanished, Hitler started on Poland. Once again, he played the self-determination card, this time over the previously German Danzig, a *Freistaat* (free state) under a protectorate of the League of Nations, in which Poland was, however, given certain administrative functions, while the population was mainly German. Britain had in the meantime guaranteed Poland. In August 1939, in a cynical move on both sides, Hitler and Stalin, whose ideologies had apparently been in irreconcilable conflict, concluded a pact in which they agreed to divide up Poland between them. So much for the Nazis as a bulwark against Bolshevism. The Second World War is the story of the Germans overrunning one country after another, including Poland in 1939, Denmark, Norway, Belgium, the Netherlands, and France in 1940, and Yugoslavia and Greece in 1941. The principle of self-determination did not apply to other nations besides the Germans. In June 1941, Hitler invaded the Soviet Union, but there, after initial successes, the Germans got bogged down. Throughout the invaded countries, the Germans ruled barbarically. It was bad enough in the West, but even worse in the East. Mass murder was rampant, and the cover of war was used to carry out the mass extermination of Jews, above all in the gas ovens at Auschwitz. However sad to state, there is no way around attributing some responsibility for the holocaust to the German army, which, even where it was not directly involved, held the ring.

There were the German bureaucrats, such as those who attended the Wannsee conference at Berlin in January 1942, who participated in the process, and the German business firms that supplied the gas ovens. Some scholars go so far as to conclude that the elites in general went along with Nazi crimes. A great deal of research has been done on the connections between the German army and the Nazi regime, and I myself visited the exhibition "Crimes of the Wehrmacht" in Munich during October 2002. It was hard to take, but the facts speak for themselves. At the same time it is best to refrain from a blanket condemnation of the German army. Thankfully, many German soldiers were not involved in the barbaric acts, and somebody like our good friend Hans von Herwarth, Germany's first ambassador to Britain after WWII, who had a non-Aryan grandmother, which made him "of Jewish descent," sought refuge in the Wehrmacht. We can also be sure that he never participated in any action in the war which he could not justify to his conscience. He was, incidentally, saved from active involvement in the abortive so-called generals' plot of July 20th, 1944, through a fortunate circumstance. On that day the telephone rang at the home of the Herwarth's, and von Stauffenberg, who had set off the bomb that should have killed Hitler, was on the line. Elisabeth von Herwarth, who answered the telephone, expressed regrets that her husband could not himself take the call as he was asleep, having just returned from the front, completely exhausted. Thus Hans von Herwarth escaped the terrible revenge the regime exacted from the failed insurrection. I knew a number of those who participated in the plot: Dr. Franz Kempner, who had been head of the presidential office under the first republican president; Friedrich Ebert, a Social Democrat; and Dr. Fritz Elsas, a former Deputy Mayor of Berlin. They were acquaintances of my father's whom we used to meet together on our walks in the Tiergarten in Berlin. Both were executed. Kempner was hidden in Berlin after the failed plot by a dear old family friend of ours, Editha Rau, and her husband, incidentally a senior official at the German ministry of Transport. Frau Rau, one of the finest people it was ever my privilege to know, the daughter of a Protestant Prussian officer, went to see Kempner the night before his execution. When I visited our friends in Berlin as a British soldier in the spring of 1946, Frau Rau told me what dilettantes the conspirators had been. Nevertheless, she and her husband had the courage to hide one of them. The other member of the plot to whom I have referred was Fritz Elsas, the former Deputy Mayor of Berlin. After the failure of the plot, members of his family were also arrested, as was the custom of the Nazis (*Sippenhaft*). Ludwig, the son of Theodor Heuss, the first president of the Bonn Republic, succeeded somehow in talking the prison warden into releasing Mrs. Elsas and Hanne, her daughter, from prison; a few minutes later, when the authorities became aware of the unintended release, they had already left with great speed. Ludwig and

Hanne married very soon after the war. I saw the Elsas's daughter when I visited President Heuss and his wife near Bonn in the summer of 1950. I also met one of the survivors of the plot, the army officer Fabian von Schlabrendorff, a descendant of the trusted adviser of the Coburg dynasty and the British royal family, Baron von Stockmar. He was a fine man. Later I heard through a mutual friend that Schlabrendorff, as a believing Protestant, worried whether the attempted tyrannicide could be theologically justified. Altogether it should be remembered that a not insignificant number of Germans suffered the ultimate penalty for their opposition to the Nazi regime. It is incredibly sad that the executions by the Nazis following the failed putsch went on right to the end of the regime. One of the last casualties of National Socialism was Hitler himself, who committed suicide in his Berlin bunker on April 30th, 1945, still unshaken in his belief that he had been right after all.

Was National Socialism a pseudo-religion?[3] National movements are liable to use rather sentimental religious terms. Thus Germans used to refer to the sacred fatherland. The then national Anthem proclaimed: "Germany, Germany above all, above all in the world" (*Deutschland, Deutschland über Alles, über Alles in der Welt*). The Nazis exploited a romantic German longing for some kind of revival of the thousand-year-old Holy Roman Empire of the German Nation, which they unhistorically regarded as the precursor of modern Germany and at the same time also popularized some pre-Christian Germanic heathen traditions. They used symbolism for their mass rallies, including the consecration of flags. As we have seen, Hitler was elevated into a kind of superhuman figure, a saviour of the German people, which Christians ought to have rejected as blasphemy. There is a painting, then widely distributed as a postcard, of Hitler on horse back as Knight of the Holy Grail; he never rode a horse (in fact he was scared of horses). Altogether, the Nazi movement simply misused religion for its own secular political purposes. To the extent that religions promote ethics, the Nazis in fact rejected moral laws and believed in the principle that might is right. It is extremely dangerous to use religious terminology in secular affairs, for it is liable to inhibit people's ability to view things rationally and to form independent critical judgments. Germans and the world in general paid a terrible price for being blinded by Nazi propaganda and only waking up too late to the true meaning of National Socialism.

Notes

1   Ian Kershaw, *Hitler, 1889–1936: Hubris* (London: Penguin Books, 1999), 132.
2   Ibid., 137.
3   Karla Poewe, *New Religions and the Nazis* (New York: Routledge, 2006).

Chapter Eleven

ZIONISM AND THE ESTABLISHMENT OF THE MODERN STATE OF ISRAEL

Presented at the Middle East forum at the Nazarene University College (now The Ambrose University) in Calgary on February 4th, 2002.

THE ZIONIST MOVEMENT held its first congress in 1897, at Basel in Switzerland. The congress passed a resolution according to which Zionism sought to secure a publicly recognized and legally secured home in Palestine for the Jewish people. Palestine was Zion to the Jews, the Promised Land, where they had had their own state more than two millennia ago, and from which they had emigrated elsewhere.

In 1897, Palestine was in Muslim hands, inhabited by Arabs and sparse Jewish settlements forming part of the Ottoman or Turkish Empire. The initiative for the congress and for the resolution emanating from it came mainly from Dr. Theodor Herzl, a Hungarian-born Jewish journalist who in the previous year had published a book called *The Jewish State (Der Judenstaat)*. In this tract he argued that the emancipation of the Jews and the bestowal of equal rights on them starting from Emperor Joseph II's reform of 1781, and growing onwards during the nineteenth century, had created new problems and required new solutions. The emancipated Jews, who had previously been barred from many occupations, now entered into fierce competition with the Christian middle classes, engendering fresh anti-Jewish feelings. Basically, Herzl and other Zionists were pessimistic in their outlook for the future of the Jews in

Europe. Herzl himself served as a Paris correspondent of an important Viennese newspaper in the 1890s and saw the growth of French anti-Semitism first hand. The hope for a gradual amelioration of conditions for European Jews had also received a serious setback through the pogroms in Russia following the assassination of Tsar Alexander II in 1881. Anti-Jewish sentiments stirred up for centuries by the Christian churches had prepared the ground for a reinforced, partly secular movement against the Jews and called itself anti-Semitic to emphasise the distant Middle Eastern origin of the Jews. The term is inaccurate, for it was not directed against such Semites as the Arabs. In view of a nationalistic and even racial anti-Semitism, the Zionists saw no future for the Jews in continuing as a minority in Christian countries at the mercy of the Christian majority. To them, a long-term solution required the establishment a national home where Jews would no longer be a tolerated minority.

Herzl has been called a "grand simplifier." He never carried out detailed research and analysis of the conditions of Jews in various countries. He never really faced up to the fundamental problem that the Jews in Palestine, a "people without a land," were not coming to "a land without people." Herzl tried to negotiate with the imperial masters of Palestine, the Ottoman rulers, but the negotiations with the Sultan came to nothing, as did other schemes for Jewish settlement, such as in Cyprus, or in East Africa. Significantly, in what was to become Kenya, the European settlers at that time expressed opposition to the proposed Jewish immigration.

It is noteworthy that Herzl was accepted even by crowned heads, such as the German emperor William II, as a kind of leader of the Jewish people, or at least as their spokesman. Actually in world Jewry the Zionists were a minority, and a century ago a small minority. In general, Jewish religious leaders were opposed to human endeavours to bring about a return to the Promised Land, which to them was something reserved to the divine will. While the Zionists had a certain religious motivation, their ideas contained important secular elements in terms of nationalism and staunch socialist ingredients. Strong opposition to Zionism also came from another quarter. The assimilated Jews of Western and Central

Europe, for example, were firmly rooted as citizens of the countries they lived in. They did not accept the pessimistic Zionist analysis of their future. Herzl died in 1904, but in spite of the impetus he had given to the movement, Zionism did not make any striking progress in the next decades. The existing small-scale Jewish settlements in Palestine only grew slowly.

The First World War marked an important stage in the progress of Zionism. At first the outbreak of hostilities created difficulties for the movement. Many of the leading Zionist personalities were German Jews, and some of the offices were in Germany. Important Zionist publications, such as Herzl's *Jewish State*, first came out in the German language. However, Dr. Chaim Weizmann, a Polish Jew who was developing a high profile in the movement, resided in Britain. As a distinguished biochemist, he rendered great service to the British war effort. Organizationally care was taken initially to adopt a neutral stance. Obviously, it was important in the interests of Jewish citizens of the various warring countries not to identify Zionism too closely with one side or the other.

Dr. Weizmann was a highly cultivated personality of great integrity and extraordinary radiance.[1] Partly through his war work, he was in touch with many of the leading personalities in Britain, including the Liberal David Lloyd George, who as Prime Minister of a coalition government took the country to victory, and the Conservative Foreign Secretary, Arthur Balfour. Both were strongly influenced by Weizmann and gave their support to Zionism. Interestingly enough, some of these leading gentile pro-Zionists shared certain prevailing prejudices against the Jews. But as believing Christians they were strongly moved by biblical prophecy. Also their sense of justice made it incumbent on them to try and correct some of the wrongs they felt had been done to the Jews by their churches. All these aspects were important factors in the support they were to give to Zionism, but they were also guided by their perception of British interests. Apart from the entry of the United States into the war, 1917 was a very difficult year for the Allies, with, for example, the overthrow of the regime of their Tsarist ally in Russia in the February Revolution. The extent to which a weakened Russia, now under a moderate constitutional regime, could still make an appropriate contribution to the general war effort, and indeed it was questionable whether the country would be able to stay the course, was only one of many worries for the Allies. In general, the war was not going that well militarily, and victory was not yet in sight. The British government, for one, entered into a number of understandings apparently demanded by the general strategic situation at the time. France as a battlefield was under enormous pressure. Accordingly, the British felt that they should encourage the French government by coming to terms with it concerning future spheres of influence in the Middle East. This was done in the Sykes-Picot agreement, which endorsed French claims to parts of Syria. To weaken Turkey, Germany's ally, Britain appealed to the Arabs to revolt against Ottoman rule. This led to the contacts between Sir Henry McMahon, British High Commissioner in Egypt, and the Sheriff Hussein of Mecca, the head of the Hashemite dynasty from which the late King Hussein of Jordan was descended. Into this minefield of understandings understood differently by the various participants, there was now inserted an important British statement on Palestine, the Balfour Declaration, which promised the Jews a national home in Palestine.

Weizmann certainly played a key role in bringing the British government to issue the declaration. He convinced ministers that the Jews ought to be treated as a people entitled to their national home. There were vague hopes that a Jewish community in Palestine would act as a link between Europe and Asia. The ministers probably had an exaggerated opinion of Jewish influence in the world they wanted to secure for the Allied war effort. There was also a fear that the Germans would anticipate the British in holding out their hand to Zionism, although it is difficult to see how much room to manoeuvre the Germans had, even as the sultan's ally. Finally, even more absurdly, it was hoped that by giving support to Zionist aspirations, Jewish influence would help to keep Russia in the war. In fact, the declaration came too late for that in any case, being published on the day in November 1917 that Lenin took over power in Russia, prior to disengaging the country from the war. Finally, while Britain during the conflict had not yet formulated a definite strategic policy for the postwar period, it was clear that

Palestine might play an important part as a British military base; the support of a Jewish community there, it was felt, might be helpful.

The discussions with the British government prior to the issue of the declaration brought out the strong differences of opinion within the Jewish community. While Herbert Samuel, a Jewish liberal minister, was an enthusiastic supporter, the incoming Secretary of State for India, Edwin Montagu, expressed his fear of a return to the ghetto. For the assimilated Jew, the Zionists were emphasizing aspects of Judaism, like being a nation, that they had always deliberately de-emphasized as it undermined their claim to be nationals of the countries in which they lived. British ministers in response to Zionist ideology, and without any ill intent, also used the term of the Jewish race, a concept that in the Nazi period was to have fatal consequences for millions of Jews, baptized Jews, and those partly descended from Jews.

The declaration was issued in a letter the Foreign Secretary, Arthur Balfour, wrote to Lord Rothschild as a leading British Jewish personality. The key passage stated:

> His Majesty's Government view with favour the establishment in Palestine of a national home for the Jewish people, and will use their best endeavours to facilitate the achievement of this object, it being clearly understood that nothing shall be done which may prejudice the civil and religious rights of existing non-Jewish communities in Palestine, or the rights and political status enjoyed by Jews in any other country.[2]

The qualifications were important, but it remained to be seen to what extent the rights of the Palestinian Arabs were compatible with the establishment of a Jewish national home in the short or the long run. A leading anti-Zionist British Jew was scathing about the other qualifications in the declaration: "Henceforth we are only temporary sojourners here [in Britain] enjoying a political status which we obtained by some oversight . . . What a triumph for the anti-Semites."[3]

In 1920, the recently founded League of Nations entrusted the
mandate for Palestine to Great Britain, in terms which included the
promise of a national home for the Jews. These developments took
place in a period of transition between the old colonialism and the
new nationalism of which, in a sense, Jewish nationalism was part.
But at the same time, Jewish aspirations in Palestine required the
help of a colonial power at a time when colonialism was losing
power.[4] Britain could not completely ignore the opposition of Arab
rulers and of Palestinians to Jewish immigration. Weizmann did try
to come to an understanding with the Hashemite dynasty, but to no
long-term avail. The difficulty of reconciling all the different British
and French understandings and the commitments they had made
to Arabs and Jews, whose contradictions were admitted by Balfour
himself in August 1919,[5] made Arabs and Jews feel that they had
been misled. The development of Arab nationalism in the Middle
East, which had been encouraged by the Allies as a weapon against
their Turkish enemy, was in any case bound to have effects on the
position of non-Arabs in the area. The Arabs suspected the Zionists
of aiming at becoming a majority in Palestine, outnumbering the
Arabs. This was a realistic fear, because at the heart of Zionism was
the Jewish experience as a persecuted minority in many countries
in which they had lived. Surely for the Zionist dream to be fulfilled,
the Jews had to become a majority in their national home. And
what guarantees did the Arabs have that the Jews would not go one
step further and try to convert their national home into a national
state? The transplanting of a population from one part of the world
into another, into a territory already inhabited, was extremely rare,
even unique. Would other countries have accepted a population of
a different culture and religion? At any rate, in 1921, the murder of
twelve men and women in a Zionist hostel in Jaffa by some Arab
desperadoes led to serious intercommunity strife. There were more
than three hundred casualties, with nearly a hundred persons
killed, about half Arabs and half Jews.[6]

It became clear that the Balfour Declaration, far from facilitat-
ing British rule in Palestine, had only aggravated its difficulties.
Britain, as the mandatory power, tried to be fair to both sides, earn-
ing little thanks from either. In order to keep the area quiet, Britain

limited Jewish immigration into Palestine and imposed restrictions on Jewish land purchases from Arabs. Although there were continued Arab complaints about the loss of land to the Jews, many landowners did in fact sell land to Jews of their own free will. Jewish money helped the region to greater prosperity in the interwar years, and there was also a considerable increase in the size of the Arab population in Palestine. The determination of many Jewish enterprises to employ only Jewish labour also caused resentment.

The restrictions on Jewish immigration into Palestine, always resented by the Zionists, led to increased tension with the British authorities just as the tragedy of the German Jews began to unfold in the Nazi period. In a sense, the advent of Adolf Hitler as German chancellor in January 1933 was a defeat for the Jewish optimists who had believed in assimilation, and seemed to confirm the correctness of Zionist pessimism about the degree of Jewish acceptance in their countries of residence. But some qualifications have to be made. Events are rarely mono-causal in their origins, and the Nazis benefited from a general atmosphere of crisis in Europe after the First World War. Furthermore, while the Nazis eventually dominated vast tracts of Europe and indeed found many willing helpers outside Germany, too, there was fortunately, both within Germany and elsewhere, a revulsion against their anti-Semitic measures.

Attempts to solve the tension between Arabs and Jews in Palestine before the Second World War – for example the recommendations of the British Peel commission in 1937 – unfortunately failed to find acceptance. A fresh Arab rising in Palestine beginning in 1936 was ominous, and the clouds of war began to thicken. The British government in this situation wanted to do everything to safeguard its lines of communications in and through the Middle East. In September 1939, Britain declared war on Nazi Germany and, from the summer of 1940 to Hitler's invasion of the Soviet Union in June 1941, faced the Nazis alone. Britain was fighting for the Jews, too, but unfortunately, in order to keep the Arabs in the Middle East as quiet as possible, Jewish immigration into Palestine was restricted at a time of direst need. The Jewish refugee passengers on boats trying to flee death at the hands of the German Nazi regime, who were refused landing in various countries, including

Palestine, had to pay the price for immigration restrictions regarded as necessary to win the war. The British base in Palestine, so
important for the war effort, particularly when Rommel had penetrated into Egypt, remained quiet.

The seriousness of the situation can be seen in the involvement
of the Mufti of Jerusalem, Haj Amin El Husseini, in "the German
attempt to seize Syria and Iraq in conjunction with Rashid Ali's
[Baghdad] putsch in 1941,"[7] which could fortunately be frustrated.
The Mufti then fled to Berlin and supported the Nazis in their extermination of the Jews, "protesting successfully to Hitler at some
small alleviations in regard to children."[8] A risky Palestinian policy
antagonizing the Arabs through increased Jewish immigration
might have endangered victory over the Nazis, with terrible consequences for the surviving European Jews.

Sadly, the restrictions on Jewish immigration into Palestine
brought the Zionist movement, including the Jewish Agency in
Palestine, into direct conflict with the British authorities, even
before the war was over, and indeed while a Jewish unit was serving
with the British Army against Nazi Germany. The moderate Chaim
Weizmann, who believed in gradual progress, was losing ground in
the Zionist movement to the younger generation, and in particular
to David Ben-Gurion. Born in Russian Poland, Ben-Gurion came to
Palestine in 1906 and, unlike Weizmann, settled there. Ben-Gurion,
who rose to the leadership of the Jewish Agency, supported a more
determined, and if necessary also anti-British, policy. The Jewish
Agency in effect had its own army, the Haganah, which was at times
utilized by the British and could not therefore be easily banned by
the authorities as an illegal organization. That the Jewish Agency in
Palestine and other Jewish organizations did their best to circum-
vent immigration regulations during the desperate situation in
which many Jews found themselves is not surprising. That they participated in the smuggling in of immigrants is understandable, but
by doing so, the Jewish Agency was risking its semi-official status.
There were also other paramilitary organizations that initially
operated independently of the Jewish Agency and the Haganah.
These included the Irgun Zvai Leumi, commanded from 1943 by a
Polish Jew named Menachim Begin,[9] and an organization best

known as the Stern Group, whose chief of operations was Yitzhak Shamir;[10] both Begin and Shamir were future prime ministers of Israel. In November 1944, two young men of the Stern Group murdered Lord Moyne, British Minister Resident in the Middle East, who was suspected, probably wrongly, of being hostile to Zionism, in Cairo.[11] This aroused the "indignation of those many Jews who held to the long liberal tradition . . . little heard of in this time of strident nationalism."[12] The Jewish Agency took strong action against the terrorists.

It fell to Ernest Bevin, the trade union leader who was Foreign Secretary in Clement Attlee's postwar Labour government, to try and find a solution to the Palestinian question. Partly because of some unwise remarks, Bevin was regarded as an enemy by the Zionists. In his Bevin biography, the eminent British historian Alan Bullock[13] concluded that Bevin tried his best to reconcile the various interests – British, Jewish, Arab, American, to name a few – in the context of the newly founded United Nations and its charter. He was handicapped not only by the long history of incompatible commitments, but by the unreliability of American policy. Bevin rightly very much wanted the United States to participate in a solution, but he could never be quite sure of the Americans, as the Zionists were constantly putting electoral pressure on President Truman to obtain more favourable terms. The Jewish lobby was only following the practice of other interest groups. But these manoeuvres may have prevented the solution of an almost intractable problem investigated by a number of commissions and persons.[14] Bevin almost despaired of the United States so far as the Palestinian question was concerned, while at the same time realizing how dependent Britain was on American help for its economic survival.

A solution acceptable to both Arabs and Jews was extremely difficult to find. Unfortunately, relations between the Jews and the British as the mandatory power in Palestine got increasingly worse. From November 1945 to some time in the summer of 1946, the Jewish Agency, despairing of the negotiating process, allowed its military arm, the Haganah, to participate in a united resistance movement with the Irgun Zvai Leumi and the Stern Group against the British, but each organization kept its independent existence. A number of terrorist acts were carried out, including the blowing up of the British Secretariat and Army Headquarters in the King David Hotel in Jerusalem in July 1946, in retaliation for the arrest of several hundred members of the Jewish Agency and the Haganah; ninety-one persons were killed and forty-five wounded.[15] According to David A. Charters in *The British Army and Jewish Insurgency in Palestine, 1945–47*, "the Haganah approved the bombing in general, if not specific, terms as an action of the United Resistance Movement."[16]

I believe it was Jewish terrorism that clinched the determination of the British government to abandon the mandate by a certain date and to hand over the whole question to the United Nations, irrespective of whether a definite settlement acceptable to all sides had been reached. In November 1947, the General Assembly of the United Nations voted in favour of partitioning Palestine by a vote of 33 to 14. The proposed Jewish state was to receive roughly fifty-five per cent of the land area of Palestine. The departure of the British administration and troops took place in May 1948. On May 14th, 1948, the Zionist leader David Ben-Gurion and his cabinet proclaimed the independence of the Republic of Israel. But in the chaos created by the withdrawal of the British without any transitional arrangements, the new state was not to be born peacefully. Already in the half-year between the partition resolution of the United Nations and the establishment of the State of Israel, large numbers of Arab irregulars had penetrated the area allotted to the Jewish state. This was followed from May 1948 by the invasion of organized armies of the neighbouring Arab states: Egypt, Trans-Jordan, Syria, Lebanon, and Iraq. The Jewish troops fought bravely and successfully, indeed conquering additional territory. By July 1949, an armistice had been concluded between all the warring parties. Trans-Jordan, renamed Jordan, occupied territory west of the Jordan River, which has become known as the "West Bank," and shared Jerusalem with Israel; the New City was in Jewish and the Old City in Arab hands. The armistice frontiers, meant to be temporary, often were not viable.[17]

The fighting of these years left enduring problems, among them that of the Arab refugees from what now became the state of Israel.

The refugee question remains one of the main obstacles to a settlement between the state of Israel and the Palestinians. I have been a refugee myself, and at any time I feel with refugees in any part of the world. The refugee problem arose largely during and through the fighting, mainly in four clearly identifiable periods linked to corresponding stages in the war between December 1947 and November 1948. Each side has blamed the creation of the exodus of refugees on the other, which is bound to be an oversimplification. Probably neither side is entirely guiltless of having contributed to the problem.[18] In any case, there is no possible justification for what Sachar calls "a particularly brutal and irresponsible act of the Irgun Zvai Leumi." He writes:

> On April 9, 1948, these terrorists occupied the Arab village of Deir Yassin and slaughtered, without mercy, several hundred Arab men, women, and children. However much the Israeli government deplored this act, repudiating it publicly and imprisoning the Irgun leaders responsible for it, the effect on Arab morale was decisive. By the end of 1948 the majority of the Arabs of Palestine had fled the area under Israeli military control. They huddled now in squalid refugee camps.[19]

These Palestinian refugees were now dependent on help from the neighbouring Arab states. Perhaps one may well ask whether these states have done enough to make the refugees welcome in their countries, as the West Germans did with other Germans expelled from Poland, Czechoslovakia, and Russia after the war, quite apart from those who fled from East Germany.

This leaves the question of how the State of Israel has fared since the end of 1949, and the following part of this session will examine its successes as well as the areas still posing problems. Does the history of Israel since 1949 point to systemic problems in the sense that the problem with the Arabs may be insurmountable? Or could more be done by both sides to find a solution?

Notes

1   Chaim Weizmann, *Trial and Error: The Autobiography of Chaim Weizmann* (London: Jewish Publication Society, 1949).

2   Leonard Stein, *The Balfour Declaration* (London: Valentine Mitchell, 1991), 5.

3   Lucien Wolf, quoted by David Vital in, *A People Apart: The Jews in Europe, 1789–1939* (Oxford University Press, 1999), p. 698.

4   Christopher Sykes, *Cross Roads to Israel* (London: Collins, 1965), 345.

5   Ibid., 16ff.

6   Ibid., 69ff.

7   Ibid., 239.

8   Ibid., 316.

9   David A. Charters, *The British Army and Jewish Insurgency* (London: Macmillan, 1989), 46.

10 Ned Temko, *To Win or to Die: A Personal Portrait of Menachem Begin* (New York: William Morrow & Co., 1987), 95.

11 Sykes, 305.

12 Ibid., 307.

13 Alan Bullock, *Ernest Bevin: Foreign Secretary, 1945–51* (London: Heinemann, 1984).

14 David Charters, *British Army and Jewish Insurgency* (London: Macmillan Press, 1989), 26.

15 Bullock, 296.

16 Charters, 58–59.

17 Howard M. Sachar, *A History of Israel: From the Rise of Zionism to Our Time* (New York: Ferra Strauss Giroux, 1985), 347–53.

18 Benny Morris, "The Origins of the Palestinian Refugee Problem," in *New Perspectives of Israeli History*, ed. Laurence J. Silberstein (New York University Press, 1991), 42–56.

19 Howard M. Sachar, *The Course of Modern Jewish History* (New York: Vintage Press, 1990), 589–90.

Chapter Twelve

HOW CHRISTIANS
PORTRAY JEWS
IN THE CHRISTIAN STORY

*Presented at the Canadian Council of Christians and Jews board
meeting at the Calgary Jewish Academy on May 13th, 2004.*

I VERY MUCH APPRECIATE THIS OPPORTUNITY of addressing the board in
connection with my quest to have all New Testament texts with
possible anti-Jewish implications commented on during
church services in all Christian denominations as a matter of routine.

We are all grateful to Michael Duggan for his excellent introduction to the Pontifical Biblical Commission document *The Jewish
People and Their Sacred Scriptures in the Christian Bible*,[1] dated the
feast of the Ascension 2001, hereafter referred to as "the document."
As will be clear from the two-page table of contents reproduced in
the short version, the commission took considerable care to
explain the historical and theological background to the story of
Jesus. Great understanding and respect is shown to all aspects of
Judaism. The authors have their hearts and minds in the right
place. Thus, for example, they fully recognize the essential place of
the Hebrew Bible in the scriptural canon of the Christian Church.
That this could not always be taken for granted is clear from
repeated attempts to "de-Judaise" Christianity.

The care taken by the authors is reflected in the length of the full
document, which runs to seventy-two pages of text and sixteen
pages of notes, all in small type. In connection with the subject I
was given, the key part is the final section, beginning with para-

graph seventy, namely the sections entitled "Jews in the Gospels and the Acts of the Apostles" and "The Jews in the Pauline Letters and other New Testament Writings." The preceding historical section entitled "The Jews in the New Testament," beginning with paragraph sixty-six, is also useful.

The document carefully reviews the attitude to the Jews in each book of the Bible,[2] listing the number of references to the Jews, whether they were favourable or unfavourable, and whether they applied to particular groups, like the high priests, the Pharisees, "the crowd," and so forth. To put us on a firm foundation, I will quote brief excerpts just from the conclusions on each of the gospels.

On the Gospel according to Matthew (p. 59):

> More than the other Synoptic Gospels, St. Matthew's is the Gospel of fulfilment, Jesus has not come to abolish, but to fulfil, for it insists more on the continuity with the Old Testament, basic for the idea of fulfilment. It is this aspect that makes possible the establishment of fraternal bonds between Christians and Jews.

In the case of St. Mark (p. 60), any attempt is rejected to use his gospel to "pin responsibility for Jesus' death on the Jewish people":

> Such an interpretation, which has had disastrous consequences throughout history, does not correspond at all to the evangelist's perspective, which . . . repeatedly opposes the attitude of the people or the crowd to that of the authorities hostile to Jesus. Furthermore, it is forgotten that the disciples were part of the Jewish people. . . . Rather, it is well to recall that the passion of Jesus is part of God's mysterious plan.

On the Gospel according to St. Luke and the Acts of the Apostles (Ac.) (p.63):

In Luke's oeuvre . . . there is a profound respect for the Jewish reality insofar as it has a primary role in the divine plane of salvation. Nevertheless, in the course of the narrative, tensions become obvious. But he is unable, it seems, and does not wish, to hide the fact that Jesus suffered fierce opposition from the leaders of his people and that, as a result, the apostolic preaching finds itself in an analogous situation.

In the opinion of the commission, St. Luke's presentation does not amount to anti-Judaism:

The Gospel message, on the contrary, invites Christians to follow the example of Jesus. Lk. 6:27–28: "But I say to you who are listening: Love your enemies, bless those who curse you, pray for those who treat you badly." As to the outcome of Jesus' trial, Lk. 23:24,34: " Pilate gave sentence that it should be as they required". And at the crucifixion: " Jesus prayed, Father, forgive them; they do not know what they are doing." And in Ac. 7:60 you read about the first Christian martyr [Stephen]: "And he kneeled down, and cried out in a loud voice, Lord, do not hold this sin against them. And when he said this he died." This is one of the basic lessons of Luke's work. It is regrettable that in the course of the centuries following it has not been more faithfully followed.

Finally, on the Gospel according to John (p.65):

In the Johannine communities, there was an insistence on the close relationship between Son and Father and on the divinity of Jesus. This teaching provoked opposition from the synagogue leaders, followed by the whole Jewish community. Christians were expelled from the synagogues, John 16:2, and also and at the same time, Christians were exposed to harassment by the Roman authorities, since they no longer enjoyed the franchise granted to the Jews. Jesus foresaw this: "Indeed the time comes that whoever kills you thinks he does God's service."

The polemic escalated on both sides. The Jews accused Jesus of being a sinner, John 9:24: For the second time the Jews summoned the man who had been blind, and said: "Speak the truth before God." John 10:33. And further on: "We are not stoning you for doing good work but for blasphemy; you are only a man and you claim to be God." Those who believed in him were considered ignorant or accursed, John 7:49: " But this rabble knows nothing about the Law – [he] is damned." On the Christian side, Jews were accused of disobedience to God's word, John 5:38: "And you have not his word abiding in you: for whom he hath sent him you do not believe." See also, John 5:42: "But I know you, that you have not the love of God in you." And pursuing vainglory, John 5:44: "How can you believe, since you honour one another for approval and seek not the honour that cometh from God ."

Still on the Gospel according to St. John, as to any part played by Jews in the arrest and crucifixion of Jesus, the commission concludes (p. 65):

Historically, it can be said that only a minority of Jews contemporaneous with Jesus were hostile to him, that a smaller number were responsible for handing him over to the Roman authorities; and that fewer still wanted him killed, undoubtedly for religious reasons that seemed important to them. But these succeeded in provoking a general demonstration in favour of Barabbas and against Jesus.

I would now like to open up some questions not covered in the document. As a historian, I want to know to what extent the account in the Gospels and the Acts of the Apostles, for example, reflects the course of the actual happenings, apart from any matters purely of faith. Put at its simplest, were the evangelists accurate recorders of events, or were they putting forth a spiritual message? Or were their writings partly the one and partly the other, as I would argue. Thus we owe a large number of presumably genuine sayings of Jesus to the Gospels and an account of a great many developments in the nascent church to the Acts of the Apostles. At the same time, the evangelists were bound to see the story from the point of view of the promotion of their faith, being mindful of those who were hindering them or might help them. Therefore the telling of the story of Jesus is affected by historical constellations well after the crucifixion, depending on the date of writing. All this very much affects the place of the Jews in the story, and consequently the Christian ways of looking at the Jews.

One is struck very much by the treatment of the Pharisees in the gospels. I still remember Father Pat O'Byrne, with his close friend Rabbi Ginsburg, a leader of the interfaith movement, as the priest in Bragg Creek, Alberta, at the end of the 1970s, frequently raising the question to which he could not find an easy answer: "Why was Jesus so hard on the Pharisees?" Recent research, while it does not go so far as to claim that Jesus was actually a Pharisee, places him close to them in some ways, and in any case does not visualize him as their out-and-out enemy. As Géza Vermès points out in his book *Jesus the Jew: A Historian's Reading of the Gospel:* "There is no evidence . . . of an active and organized participation on the part of the Pharisees in the planning and achievement of Jesus' downfall."[3]

However we see Jesus, he was certainly in the tradition of the fiercely independent prophets who were liable to be disliked by the establishment, in his case by the High Priests and their party, the Sadducees. Jesus had his arguments with other religious thinkers, and some of his disagreements extended to individual Pharisees, but why are there so many accusations against the Pharisees in the text? Actually, it was the High Priest who was involved in the proceedings which led to the crucifixion. But by the time some of the gospels were written or finally redacted, the Pharisees, as the main force in Judaism after the destruction of the Temple in the year AD 70, had become the chief stumbling block to the new faith making progress among the Jews. Indeed, it was mainly the merit of the Pharisees that the Jewish faith not only survived political and religious catastrophe, but entered a phase of renewal. Thus the alleged outburst that Jesus made against the Pharisees in Matthew 23 may in fact target them as the main obstacle to the advance of Christianity among the Jews. There are accusations of hypocrisy (verse 13), that "everything they do is done for men to see" (verse 5), of an undue regard to place and honour in society (verse 6), as well as to the outward appearance rather than the spiritual and the sacred (verse 28). The Pharisees are coupled with the teachers of the law, who are accused of having neglected its important aspects, such as justice, mercy, and faithfulness (verse 23). It is sad that such a distorted impression has been left in the Christian world of a deeply spiritual movement in Judaism. This caricature of the Pharisees has, in fact, become part of the Western cultural heritage. The *Concise Oxford Dictionary*, after summarizing their religious significance, adds: "a self-righteous person; a hypocrite."

The Vatican document also puts into perspective the treatment of "The Law" in the Christian scriptures. In polemics, Christian theology has often voiced a negative and somewhat condescending attitude to the Law. The document (paragraphs 43–45) recognizes that Torah, translated (though not quite precisely) as "Law," is the "highest source of wisdom," occupying "a central place in the Jewish Scriptures and in their religious practice from biblical times to our own day." The document is sensitive in emphasizing the key importance of the Law also in connection with its integration with God's covenant with Israel, as set out in Exodus 19:24. According to Matthew (5:18–19), Jesus affirms the permanent validity of the Law, but in a new interpretation. Clearly, Paul was in a quandary over the issue of the Law. In his apostolate he could not enforce the marks of Jewish identity (circumcision, dietary regulations, and calendar) on non-Jews. However, as the Pontifical Commission states (p.37), he was "aware of the positive function of the Law." Overall, the commission regards Pauline theology of the Law as "imperfectly unified" (p.37) according St. Paul's letters. There are a "variety of positions relating to the Law expressed" in the Christian scriptures (p.38). The commission comes to the following conclusion (pp. 38–39):

> James does not announce in the Letter to the Hebrews, like Paul in his Letters, the end of the Law's reign; but he agrees with Matthew, Mark, Luke and Paul in underlining the priority not only of the Decalogue but also the precept of love of neigh-

bour (Leviticus 19:18) which leads to the perfect observance of the Decalogue and to do still better. The New Testament then depends on the Old. It is read in the light of Christ, who has confirmed the precept of love and has given it a new dimension: "Love one another as I have loved you" (John 13:34; 15:12), that is to sacrifice one's life. The Law is thereby more than fulfilled.

How did the, on the whole, comparatively restrained Christian criticism of Jews in the Bible as described by the Pontifical Commission gradually turn into a hostile attitude towards the Jews on the part of the Church? Soon the fronts hardened and, apart from a small minority of followers of Jesus who tried to remain within the Jewish fold, a choice had to be made. There was mutual recrimination. The church began to carry its mission to non-Jews, and as those who still remembered the situation in Jesus's time passed away, there was no longer the clear realization that Jesus and his followers during his lifetime had been Jews. Jesus began to be regarded as "the first Christian" and as "the founder of Christianity." The Jews were deeply divided in their attitude to Rome, and in AD 132, a further rising against the Empire took place. Most of the time they benefited from their privileged position of being exempt from worship to the emperor – a privilege the Jew who had become Christian no longer enjoyed. Indeed the Christian church underwent a severe persecution at the hands of the Roman authorities. In this conflict, Christians and Jews were on different sides. Actually for much of this early period in the Common Era, Jews and Christians competed with each other for proselytes. There were flourishing Jewish Diaspora communities in North Africa, Asia Minor, Greece, and Rome, as well as Babylonia. Perhaps this competitive atmosphere between the two religions helps to explain, if not to excuse, the abusive language used in controversy between them. In this context, one of the most pernicious developments was the formulation of the doctrine of deicide by Melito, bishop of Sardis, in the second century. It so happened that the church in Sardis, situated near the western coast of Asia Minor, was up against a synagogue that was much better supported, as archaeological evidence has revealed.[4] Bishop Melito preached: "God has been murdered, the King of Israel has been slain by an Israelite hand." Deicide, whatever the "murder of God" may mean, tragically proved to be one of the most durable concepts during the last two millennia.

In the fourth century, Emperor Constantine ended the persecution of the church, and Christianity gradually became the religion of the Empire.[5] During the age of the Church Fathers, strong attacks were made on the Jews, whom many Christian theologians regarded as obstinate for failing to see that salvation came through Christ. *Objectively*, the Pontifical Commission may be correct in relativizing anti-Jewish sentiments in the Christian Bible, but *subjectively*, many theologians of the patristic age focused on whatever appeared to be negative in Jewish attitudes towards Jesus during his lifetime. Jews, who continued to be regarded as deicides, were generally discriminated against for not converting to Christianity, treated with contempt, and subjected to demeaning laws. St. Augustine, who died in AD 430, argued that "the Jews, by their mere existence, their failure and humiliation symboliz[ed] the triumph of church over synagogue."[6] For these theological reasons, as they are still the chosen people, while being kept in subordinate conditions, they were not to be eliminated.[7] Even that did not save them from recurrent pogroms. Since Jews are part of God's design, since they were witnesses to the truth, Moses Mendelsohn commented ironically on Augustine: "Blessed be the ashes of that humane theologian who was the first to declare that God was preserving us as a visible proof of the Nazarene religion. But for this lovely brainwave, we would have been exterminated long ago."[8]

The story of Jewish suffering is well known and need not be repeated here. However, in this context there is one historical question of great importance: the connection, if any, between Christian anti-Judaism and modern anti-Semitism. There is not yet any agreement in academia on this question. Some Christian church historians see the two as entirely separate. My own view, for what it is worth, is that, at the very least, Christian anti-Judaism removed some of the barriers that might have impeded the development of modern anti-Semitism. But as George Jonas recalled in an article in the *National Post* on May 10th, 2004, one of the people to whom he and his Jewish family owed their survival in Hungary during 1944 was a government official who "had the traditional prejudices many gentiles have about Jews," but could not stand by idly while the killing of innocent people was going on.[9] There are also obvious differences. During Christian anti-Judaism, baptism normally led to reception into the general community, whereas under the Nazis, it did not save the so-called non-Aryan from the gas chambers.

After all the terrible events of our time, it is pleasing to report that the Christian churches in general have since the end of the Second World War adopted a positive attitude towards the Jews and have broken with nearly two millennia of anti-Jewish prejudice. If we just take the Roman Catholic Church, the declarations relating to the Jews during and after the Second Vatican Council, *Nostra Aetate* and *Religious Relations with the Jews*, have been spiritually healing for those who have been persecuted.[10] With the statements of Pope John Paul II, a strong supporter of the Jews hailing from a nation not known as particularly friendly to them in recent history, this has gone some way towards helping to alleviate the wounds left from the Nazi period. Dabru Emet's *A Jewish Statement on Christians and Christianity* issued by the National Jewish Scholars Project in the United States generously responded to the steps taken by Christian Churches.[11]

There has also been a heartening statement by the Christian Scholars Group in the United States entitled *A Sacred Obligation: Rethinking Christian Faith in Relation to Judaism and the Jewish People* issued in September 2002. This document arises from the following conviction I wholeheartedly support. The signatories state:

> We believe that revising Christian teaching about Judaism and the Jewish people is a central and indispensable obligation of theology in our time. It is essential that Christianity both understand and represent Judaism accurately, not only as a matter of justice for the Jewish people, but also for the integrity of Christian faith, which we cannot proclaim without reference to Judaism.[12]

The signatories make ten points:

1. God's covenant with the Jewish people endures forever.
2. Jesus of Nazareth lived and died as a faithful Jew.
3. Ancient rivalries must not define Christian–Jewish relations today.
4. Judaism is a living faith, enriched by many centuries of development.
5. The Bible both connects and separates Jews and Christians.
6. Affirming God's enduring covenant with the Jewish people has consequences for Christian understandings of salvation.
7. Christians should not target Jews for conversion.
8. Christian worship that teaches contempt for Judaism dishonours God.
9. We affirm the importance of the land of Israel for the life of the Jewish people.
10. Christians should work with Jews for the healing of the world.

One could not wish for more. Under point 8 it makes a practical suggestion of great importance: "We urge church leaders to examine scripture readings, prayers, the structure of the lectionaries, preaching and hymns to remove distorted images of Judaism." To my mind, this revision is long overdue. I ask for your support for this endeavour. In the meantime, there is the urgent task of regular commenting, as a matter of routine, on all readings containing critical remarks about Jews in all services of all denominations. A leaflet providing brief commentaries on all such readings is required as soon as possible. In my opinion, the Christian Scholars Group in the United States would be exceptionally well qualified for that task. It could also draw on the report of the Pontifical Biblical Commission. Here the reasoned interpretation of biblical texts by the commission could be one useful source for the commentaries.

The support of all favourably inclined Christian groups, as well as of the national and international organizations such as the Council of Christians and Jews, and the World Council of Churches, as well as of Jewish organizations such as the World Jewish

Congress and B'nai Brith, should be sought for a revision of lectionaries and the introduction of commentaries into church services.

Notes

1   The Pontifical Biblical Commission, *The Jewish people and their Sacred Scriptures in the Christian Bible*, dated on the day of the Ascension 2001 (24 May 2001), Vatican City.

2   Book, chapter, and verse are mentioned in the text. Several translations are used, including the King James and the Jerusalem Bible.

3   Géza Vermès, *Jesus the Jew: A Historian's Reading of the Gospels* (Philadelphia: Fortress Press, 1983), 36.

4   Marc Saperstein, *Moments of Crisis in Jewish-Christian Relations* (London: SCM Press, 1989), 5–6.

5   James Carroll, *Constantine's Sword* (New York: Houghton Mifflin Co., 2001).

6   Paul Johnson, *A History of the Jews* (New York: Ben Gurion, 1987), 165.

7   The Bamberg and Naumburg cathedrals, among others, have statues on their portals of young women symbolizing the Synagogue (blind-folded and with broken staff) and the Church (in a triumphant posture wearing a crown).

8   Paul Saperstein, *Moments of Crisis* (Tuscaloosa: University of Alabama Press, 1973), 212.

9   George Jonas, *Canadian National Post*, 10 May 2004, 12.

10 Second Vatican Council, *Nostra Aetate* of 28 October 1965; also "Guidelines on Religious Relations with the Jews," 01 December 1974.

11 Dabru Emet, "A Jewish Statement on Christians and Christianity," *New York Times* and *Baltimore Sun*, 30 September 2000.

12 Christian Scholars Group, *A Sacred Obligation: Rethinking Christian Faith in Relations to Judaism and the Jewish people* (http://www.bc.edu/dam/files/research_sites/cjl/sites/partners/csg/Sacred_Obligation.htm).

Chapter Thirteen

CBC INTERVIEW: MOUNTAINTOP CLASSICS

Interview of Frank Eyck conducted by Andrea Marantz on November 9th, 1996. Transcribed by Brandon Eyck and edited by Rosemarie Eyck.

ANDREA MARANTZ: The choice of my guest this afternoon on Mountain Top Classic is Frank Eyck, Professor Emeritus of the History Department at the University of Calgary.

This Monday is Remembrance Day, with that in mind we are going to listen to Frank Eyck who now lives in Bragg Creek. During the Second World War he was a member of the secret British Psychological Warfare Branch of the British Army.

Now take me back to the Berlin of your youth, prior to the Nazis, when your family was a prominent Jewish family. What are your memories of those early years?

FRANK EYCK: Well, they are memories of great happiness, of tremendous stimulation, of a feeling that my mother and father could look after me. They showed me very great warmth, and that all suddenly changed when the Nazis came to power.

ANDREA: Your father was a prominent and respected lawyer. He was an outspoken man, wasn't he?

FRANK: Yes, he spoke very strongly against the Nazi conception of the law, whatever that was.

ANDREA: Now, when Hitler came to power, did everything change instantly?

FRANK: In the way I remember it, yes, definitely. Because although technically you still had a coalition government, and the Nazis only had a certain limited number of ministries, you felt that there was change – that the streets were taken over by the Nazis. And I think from that time onwards I never felt safe the way I had felt before. I had the feeling my parents could not protect me anymore from what was going on.

ANDREA: Oh! And you were a teenager at this point?

FRANK: Yes, I was born in 1921, so I was 11 years and a few months old when the Nazis came into power, and I grew up very fast in certain respects – I mean politically not in other ways. I knew exactly what you could say and how careful you had to be. I had that advantage coming from a political household.

ANDREA: And your father's law practice was dismantled – destroyed.

FRANK: It dwindled to nothing within a short period of time. I mean who was going to employ a Jewish lawyer at that time?

ANDREA: And there was a clear example when – was it the last client that your father defended who was not found guilty and then arrested again immediately?

FRANK: It would have been one of the last, I am not sure the last but certainly towards the end of his act of practicing, that happened. The law had ceased, and it became completely arbitrary. There were certain tremendous disappointments in my father's life. One was that the law was no longer honoured – a law in which he believed, and I think the Jewish heritage was important. And the other worse thing was that so many Germans that he had known before jumped on the bandwagon, and of course we were cut off and ignored by a lot of people who just did not have anything to do with us anymore.

ANDREA: Very painful!

FRANK: This was a terrible time.

ANDREA: When you were at school you were occasionally asked to teach the class if the teacher was away. Now this is an interesting situation since many of your classmates would be Aryan children. How did this happen?

FRANK: Well, first of all we had a principal who was appointed after the Nazis came in and may or may not have had some affiliation with the party. He was a very fair-minded person and somehow he liked me. So he gave me all the jobs to do which were particularly important, at a time when one was so ignored and sidelined, it was good to have someone who had confidence in me. There was at the school a tremendous tolerant atmosphere kind of – well – these days you would say it was elitist. But what does this mean? There were a lot of boys who came from very well-educated families, and my school mates were good company, and even those who were quote "Aryan" accepted me in this position, and I even had the feeling that nobody would ever spoil it. I mean my greatest problem was to know what the homework would have been – which I had not always done.

ANDREA: So it was a fairly normal existence in an abnormal time.

FRANK: At school, yes, yet there was outside interference. One day there was issued a decree from on high that Jewish boys were not allowed to row any more.

ANDREA: You mean rowing on a team?

FRANK: Yes. We used to go out on excursions, rowing excursions, which for us were very beautiful on the lakes near Berlin. The principal got this modified so that those who were sons of Front Fighters in the First World War were not affected by this, but my father was not, so I was not acceptable.

ANDREA: Well – then I suppose the plan was to make it impossible for something so small could become ruled against.

FRANK: Yes, it was an attempt to place you on the sideline and forget you completely. And that was one of many examples. This was a comparatively harmless one.

ANDREA: Now you said your parents managed to get you out of Germany in 1937 to London where you went to St. Paul's school?

FRANK: Yes. It was quite legal because my father had some money in Switzerland that paid for some of their expenses and for my education, which came in handy.

ANDREA: So, it must have been difficult situation for a fifteen-year-old boy.

FRANK: I think it was difficult at that age, as you are attached to your friends, then suddenly to have to get out of the country and have to learn a completely different language I hardly knew. And the first time I had to fill in a form for the immigration officer where I had to put "yes or no," I spelled yes with a *j*.

ANDREA: Of course, perfectly sensible. Then your parents were able to follow you the following year?

FRANK: They came out the following year – that is right. I was moving backwards and forwards until the summer of 1937 when it became increasingly difficult. And I think by the end of 1937 it was time to get out and stay out. My parents also had that feeling, so they came out soon afterwards. My parents had considerable worries at that time since they had not officially immigrated. So all their books and furniture were confiscated until a certain tax was paid to release them – a flight-tax [*Reichsfluchsteuer*] assessed from his German capital. This had been introduced to prevent people from taking their capital out [to save taxation] and now it applied to Jews who were forced out. My parents were assessed for an earlier year but now did not have the money anymore until my uncle – still in Germany – helped them out. My father also lost his nerve when he saw the British immigration officer, he was so afraid of being sent back he said he was just coming for a visit, but that was sorted out fortunately. However, that was only one of many worries in the beginning. And what were we to live on? So, to begin with, my mother rented out rooms of our apartment then ran a guest house and eventually took it over, she really rallied at a time without money.

ANDREA: After the outbreak of the Second World War, many German refugees came under suspicion and they became known as enemy aliens. That had to be a painful time for people like yourself.

FRANK: Yes, it was a very difficult time, Andrea, and very soon the British government decided to put everybody in front of tribunals. I was cycling from where the school was being evacuated to Reading, which is close to London, and I remember being exempted and put into one of the best categories.

ANDREA: What sort of questions would they ask?

FRANK: Why I had come out of Germany, what my feelings were, and so on. It was straightforward, and they were very, very, friendly, and I felt this was a positive stance. So I became what was then called a friendly enemy alien.

ANDREA: And what did that mean? Did they still have certain restrictions for you?

FRANK: Yes. There still were certain restrictions, and they would not in a way honour us at all, but we could live quite happily. But then things became very serious, in the spring and summer the government changed its mind and started even interning friendly enemy aliens.

ANDREA: Was you entire family interned?

FRANK: My father was not. My mother produced some letters from all sorts of Liberal politicians.

ANDREA: Why you then? What did they think?

FRANK: I was teaching as a junior master at a school outside of London. We were sent to internment camps, but I was released in October 1940 and joined the British Army.

ANDREA: So you went to join the army? The resentment, I guess, did not run as deeply as your commitment against the Nazis.

FRANK: Well – you see I had written to *The London Times* and said I was ready to serve, and I wanted to be treated like any other young man, and I did not want special privileges. So I would say I joined the army in spite of the internment and that at last I was where I wanted to be: on the side that was fighting the Nazis.

ANDREA: Your first job was anything but glamorous.

FRANK: I don't know how much I contributed to the war effort with that loading and unloading of railway wagons and concreting roads and so on. It was a time that was not always pleasant and one felt frustrated. I think looking back I learned a tremendous lot. I really learned the pleasure of physical work, of exerting yourself physically, and I read with more pleasure during that period of time than I did in any other period of my life. My father sent me galleys of his books and I devoured these and also gave lectures myself. There was a Cambridge don and I who ran a whole series of modern British history, and we did alternate centuries. In the end, my kitbag was full of books and very few clothes which I, as somebody serving in the ranks, had to carry from one place to the other.

ANDREA: But eventually the British Army realized that this was not the best use to put very well educated and intelligent young men.

FRANK: Yes. That was a wonderful thing. Actually, some British civilians, particularly a widow of a Labour member of parliament, got interested in this, and I used to receive letters from her: Who is in your unit? What kind of people could be doing better things, and so on. So this pressure worked and I was an Army co-education instructor for fifteen months and lectured on what is called *The British Way and Purpose.*

ANDREA: This is a good way to break for the first choice of music.

FRANK: This is Remembrance Day, and I would like to play something in memory of all the people who died in the war and in the wars on both sides of the battles and also of all those civilians, including Jews, that were killed. Something based on a Psalm, Psalm 110 (authorized version 111) "Praise ye the Lord," sung by Emma Kirkby with the Parley of Instruments, directed by Roy Goodman and Peter Holman.

Music and commercial

ANDREA: Frank, how did you transfer into the British Publicity and Psychological Warfare Branch? What exactly did this branch of service do?

FRANK: Well, the name is a bit highfalutin and probably rather pretentious. I was on the so-called "Psychological Warfare" side and had to monitor French radio stations, particularly those on which the French radio traitor Jean-Hérold Paquis and people like that spoke. And if anything happened, we recorded it and made notes, and this information was sent to the Intelligence branch at headquarters. British Intelligence ran at a high level and in many ways used every source of information it could get and was very good at analyzing them. For instance, listening to these radio broadcasters and the intelligence people would then say: well, um, these French people think things are going well for the Nazis or they are not going well for the Nazis. You could detect certain fears or a great deal of hope or whatever. This was in 1944. I was only twenty-three years old. And then one day – that was still in Normandy – somebody came to me and said: "We want you to interrogate German prisoners of war. We want material for a phony German soldiers' radio station, which was really an Allied station called *Soldatensender Calais.* Now this was not Kelly as was once spelled in an article done about this but Calais the French port which was still in German hands at the time. So I found myself face to face with Germans, officially Germans again after having left seven years before and practically hounded out of the country, and these people of course were very surprised to talk to somebody in British uniform whose German was reasonably fluent, and I tried to find out discreditable information about what the German officers were doing, mistresses they had among the French and all this kind of thing. I don't know how successful I was.

ANDREA: How do you start these kinds of conversations? Are people very reluctant to talk? Do you have to warm them up?

FRANK: That is very good question because they were not reluctant at all.

ANDREA: Oh!

FRANK: I assumed they would be hostile, nothing in that line at all. They felt they had finished with the war, finished with the Nazi regime, and now things could go better again and it could all be put behind them now. It was not quite as easy at that! But from the point of my interview we talked quite normally, and I mean frankly. I do not want to claim any credit for this. It never occurred to me to treat them any different from just ordinary people with whom you just have a civilized conversation.

ANDREA: I guess there is something different about dealing with an idea of the Nazis and dealing with an individual young man same age as you would have been at the time.

FRANK: Yes.

ANDREA: I am interested in this radio station, the Calais Station: now what kind of thing would you say? You would be walking a fine line between showing your cards you know and thereby making it obvious that it was not legitimate and giving the false impression, how?

FRANK: Well, you know, they pretended to be good Germans, who wanted a German victory but that shall we say it was very unfortunate that Major so and so spent most of his time with a certain French woman called ABC.

ANDREA: I see. It sort of does a little bit of damage to their credibility and authority. Part of your job was also to monitor Goebbels's broadcasts.

FRANK: Yes.

ANDREA: What were your impressions of him?

FRANK: I was just amazed when I heard Goebbels because here was this man with a soft gentle voice who, according to his own declaration, was a God-fearing man who wanted all the best for his people. All the time he declared it was the poor Germans who were being persecuted by others, and if one had not known the story, if one went merely by the internal evidence, one would have said: oh, well this is an excellent man. He was devilishly clever and satanically so, in the way that the regime was satanic.

ANDREA: So you could understand why people listening to him believed him?

FRANK: If you live in a closed society and only heard what is fed to you, as happened in these fanatical nationalistic settings, then unless you are intelligent and make an effort to hear something else, you are going to be conditioned – you are brainwashed – and this happened for many years.

ANDREA: Well, let's pause for another choice of music.

FRANK: One of the instruments I particularly like, that I find very moving, is the organ, and perhaps we can play Peter Herford: the Organ Concerto No.4, in F major, by Georg Friedrich Handel, conducted by Joshua Rifkin, the second movement.

Music

Frank Eyck (1995, Bragg Creek, Alberta) looking at a picture of himself in Flensburg, 1945–46.

ANDREA: Now, going on. Following the war you were sent to Germany as part of the occupying army. And part of your job was to restore the German newspapers, away from that kind of propaganda reporting that they had learned so well to do and back to journalism.

FRANK: It was a tremendously interesting and very exciting task, and I wanted to get back into Germany. I wanted very much to go to Hamburg, a great port, because I had quite a few family connections with that branch of my family that had lived there and they fortunately all got out. So, moving back into Germany with the British Army of occupation was another strange experience. I was wondering how the Germans would take all this. We had reports, well more a speculation, that the Germans were arming for a last-ditch-resistance and so on.

ANDREA: You were quite disturbed by the destruction that you saw in Hamburg.

FRANK: Yes, I felt that this had been a very quick revenge of fate or God, whatever one believed. But one did not have any *Schadenfreude* or feel sort of happy about it because one could see that a lot of innocent people had also suffered this. But, what was interesting, once one reached a major city like Hamburg, was to produce a newspaper for the German civilian population and to start telling what we regarded as the truth after years when they had been fed a lot of lies. To give them a sense of democracy again, to voice what democracy and the rule of law could do. And in that situation we obviously had to use some Germans to help us to get the whole thing going. I mean not only the printing, but it was much easier for us if editorially we had some German journalists that we could work with.

ANDREA: So the point was not to produce a German language British newspaper but rather to reintroduce that kind of journalism to the German people.

FRANK: That is right. And to have a very clear separation between news and comment.

ANDREA: Yeah! Because that had been lost completely.

FRANK: It had been lost. But that was also something rather British, you know, perhaps the German press had not had it quite as

Hamburg, 9 May 1945.

People queuing for the first issue of the news sheet of the military government.

strongly. So, we had all sort of ideas as to what we wanted to do. I worked on these newspapers in Hamburg and Flensburg. They had a high [large] edition, very high circulation figures – some reached a million copies – and they were certainly eagerly read by the Germans.

ANDREA: People had an appetite for it?

FRANK: That is right; people had an appetite for this. They were distributed free, and I still have some pictures of people queuing to get them, practically taking these things out of each others' hands.

ANDREA: Was it difficult for them to accept what had happened, to now believe the stories that we were printing?

FRANK: This was a problem for some people, but for others it made a great deal of sense because they had either known of these things or suspected them. I mean, if you had kept your eyes open, you could see a number of things that were happening when a whole number of Jews suddenly disappeared. I mean, they were not sent to a holiday camp. But there was all this double talk at the time in the Nazi regime. So it was not made easy for people to put two and two together. I was just going to say that I suppose there is a real desire not to know during those times, that people could only live with themselves if they ignored it. So, while they might have suspected it, they would choose not to know.

ANDREA: In one sense, I think, it made it easier for them, you know, along the lines you suggested. Also, I would say that people were very busy with their known problems, being bombed out and all this kind of thing. I mean, the bombing raids were very, very heavy. You mentioned Hamburg, there had been fire bomb raids on Hamburg and there was more rubble than houses standing.

FRANK: So then there would be all those problems with hygiene, with getting food, and all those basic survival problems, and evacuating yourself from a city that was constantly bombarded, etc.

ANDREA: Oh, hum! Very difficult! At this point you were, you had joined the Church of England, or was it the Methodists?

FRANK: Methodists. The day after D-day I was baptized by the Methodist Church in England as I was mobilized for overseas service. This was done at a Synod of the church, because it had to be done quickly as I did not know if I would still be in the same place the next Sunday, and I felt at the time though of course in a sense it was awkward to change ones' religion due to the suffering of the Jews, my people; however, I felt I needed the spiritual support of a religious faith, because as with so many people, I did not know what was going to happen.

ANDREA: And you had been separated from Judaism for some time at that point?

FRANK: My father was a sort of liberal Jew who did not practice, but he had still gone through Jewish education; but I had really very little or nothing because I was normally exempt from the Jewish religious teaching we had at school.

ANDREA: So, at the time that you were in occupied Germany did you find yourself still identified with the Jewish community there, or had had you sort of separated from that part?

FRANK: What I try to do, and I have done ever since, was to say: I am a Jewish Christian. The early Christians were Jews and even Jesus lived on Earth as a Jew. So, I am happy to say that I have been accepted by Jewish communities and Jewish groups and still belong to some of their organizations that I can share, but I can also share in the Christian church. When it comes to Jewish groups in Germany, I have to say, the Jews were practically eliminated after all, they had been deported and there were just a few survivors, people who lived in hiding, but I did not necessarily see any of those at the time.

ANDREA: It is a heart breaking time. Did you come into contact with people that you knew before you left Germany, did you run across those?

FRANK: Yes. That was a tremendous experience. Perhaps the most striking one was when I visited Berlin in March 1946, basically to see my old friends. I traced one lady of my father's generation, somebody we had very much admired; she had always been anti-Nazi. When I traced her down she told me, and I am sure quite truthfully, that she had hidden one of the people who had been involved in the plot of July 20th, 1944.

ANDREA: Really!

FRANK: Yes. Until this man, who was a close friend, told her and her husband, and was a participant in the plot, surrendered himself to the police he just could not go on hiding and also, I am sure, he did not want to get his friends into difficulties. She visited him before his execution.

ANDREA: Would you be placing yourself at risk even to visit him?

FRANK: Yes, it shows tremendous courage. She was a Protestant German of very deep faith – you know, the best of Germans, somebody who made no compromises, who stuck to the truth and stuck to loyalties, a marvellous person.

Andrea: Now, you settled back in Britain following that experience but eventually actually came to Calgary. How did you end up here?

FRANK: There were two reasons for this. One was that I was not making the next grade professionally. At least it was not happening quickly enough because in Britain if you are a University Lecturer or Senior Lecturer, at some stage you want to get a chair. I was going in for things but the move was very, very slow. Also the situation with Britain was not good in the winter of 1967/68, the Pound Sterling was devalued, and Prime Minister Harold Wilson said "the Pound in your pocket was still the same." And this did not make sense to my wife and myself. So we thought, why not get some information on this as there was a coupon, an advertisement coupon in the newspaper saying if you want to immigrate to Canada, apply for information, so we sent the coupon. And at the same time, there was an offer from Calgary because one of the people I knew had heard about a job there. When I got in touch with the people in Calgary they offered me a post as a full professorship and I decided to accept it. We went through the immigration procedures; fortunately I had the forms and within a few weeks in the summer of 1968 we had all our papers and came to Calgary.

ANDREA: And you have been ever since.

FRANK: Yes, we have been here since.

ANDREA: Before we send you to your Mountain Top, you can choose one book to take with you. What is the book of your choice?

FRANK: James Boswell, *Life of Samuel Johnson*. I am interested in this, I suppose, to some extent as a biographer myself, and this is one of the great biographies that has ever been written because it has so much actual conversation with the hero, and I think it is something you can read again and again. If I had a while on the Mountain Top, I think it would come extremely handy.

ANDREA: And where would you go?

FRANK: It's the hill called Two-Pine in Bragg Creek, in the Elkana Estates, from which you have an absolutely marvellous view all around, and you can see the Rocky Mountains, all the friends from overseas that I have taken up there thought it was absolutely wonderful and quite unique.

ANDREA: And you are a great walker, so is this a place you walk to quite often?

FRANK: Yes, I do like walking. It is one way to keep fit, the other is swimming.

ANDREA: Well, you have also one final choice of music.

FRANK: I think I like Gertrud Kottermaier on the *Hammerflügel* [Hammer Piano] from the year 1785 playing Menuett and Trio, Koechel 1, by Wolfgang Amadeus Mozart which was performed in the Mozart House in Augsburg, Germany.

ANDREA: Thank you very much for coming in today. I have really enjoyed our conversation.

FRANK: Thank *you*, Andrea. [*Music*]